Radical Solidarity

Radical Solidarity

Ruth Reynolds, Political Allyship,
and the Battle for Puerto Rico's
Independence

• •

LISA G. MATERSON

The University of North Carolina Press Chapel Hill

Set in Charis by Westchester Publishing Services
Manufactured in the United States of America

Library of Congress Cataloging-in-Publication Data
Names: Materson, Lisa G., author.
Title: Radical solidarity : Ruth Reynolds, political allyship, and the battle for
   Puerto Rico's independence / Lisa G. Materson.
Description: Chapel Hill : The University of North Carolina Press, [2024] |
   Includes bibliographical references and index.
Identifiers: LCCN 2024029884 | ISBN 9781469679914 (cloth) |
   ISBN 9781469679921 (paperback) | ISBN 9781469679938 (epub) |
   ISBN 9781469682563 (pdf)
Subjects: LCSH: Reynolds, Ruth M., 1916-1989. | Women political activists—
   United States—Biography. | Political activists—United States—Biography. |
   Puerto Rico—History—Autonomy and independence movements. |
   BISAC: SOCIAL SCIENCE / Women's Studies | BIOGRAPHY &
   AUTOBIOGRAPHY / Political | LCGFT: Biographies.
Classification: LCC F1971 .M37 2024 | DDC 320.092 [B]—dc23/eng/20240801
LC record available at https://lccn.loc.gov/2024029884

Cover art: Ruth M. Reynolds (RMR_b37_f02_0002), People Lined Up Outside a
Building with Soldiers facing Them with Guns (RMRe_b39_f02_0005), Insular
Police (RMRe_b48_f04_0002). All in Ruth M. Reynolds Papers, Archives of the
Puerto Rican Diaspora, Center for Puerto Rican Studies, Hunter College, CUNY.

This book will be made open access within three years of publication thanks
to Path to Open, a program developed in partnership between JSTOR, the
American Council of Learned Societies (ACLS), the University of Michigan
Press, and the University of North Carolina Press to bring about equitable
access and impact for the entire scholarly community, including authors,
researchers, libraries, and university presses around the world. Learn more at
https://about.jstor.org/path-to-open/.

For Rosa María Navarro Sosa Materson

Contents

Maps and Figures

Abbreviations in the Text

ACLU	American Civil Liberties Union
ALPRI	American League for Puerto Rico's Independence
APRI	Americans for Puerto Rico's Independence
CFDC	Carlos Feliciano Defense Committee
CGT	General Confederation of Workers (Confederación general de trabajadores)
CIA	Central Intelligence Agency
CJPR	Committee for Justice to Puerto Ricans
COI	UN's Committee of Information
CORE	Congress of Racial Equality
CPI	Congreso Pro-Independencia (Pro-Independence Congress)
CPRD	Committee for Puerto Rican Decolonization
CPUSA	Communist Party USA
ELA	Estado Libre Asociado (Free Associated State, or Commonwealth of Puerto Rico)
FBI	Federal Bureau of Investigation
FOR	Fellowship of Reconciliation
FSUMC	First Spanish United Methodist Church
MIRA	Movimiento Independentista Revolucionario Armado (Independent Armed Revolutionary Movement)
MPI	Movimiento Pro-Independencia (Pro-Independence Movement)
NAACP	National Association for the Advancement of Colored People
OWA	One World Association
PIP	Partido Independentista Puertorriqueño (Puerto Rican Independence Party)

PPD	Partido Popular Democrático (Popular Democratic Party)
PRSA	Puerto Rican Statehood Association
PRSC	Puerto Rican Solidarity Committee
PRSU	Puerto Rican Student Union
PSP	Partido Socialista Puertorriqueño (Puerto Rican Socialist Party)
RRDC	Ruth Reynolds Defense Committee
UNCIO	United Nations Conference on International Organization
UPR	University of Puerto Rico at Río Piedras
USCFF	US Committee to Free the Five Puerto Rican Nationalists
WDL	Workers Defense League
YLP	Young Lords Party

A Note on Terminology

Given the complex history of Puerto Rico's political status, there are multiple terminologies for discussing the people and places that inhabit this book. None of them are perfect. The story that follows revolves around the solidarity that emerged among two groups of US citizens—those of Puerto Rican descent and non–Puerto Ricans. Acknowledging the contested nationhood and national identities discussed within, I regularly use "Puerto Rican" to identify the former and "North American" or "American" in reference to the latter, even though I recognize that each of these are fluid, overlapping, and contested categories. I likewise employ "Puerto Rico" and the "United States" to discuss the colonial relationship at the heart of the book, even though these geographical categories both overlap and diverge in multiple ways. Finally, Puerto Rico is an archipelago with three main inhabited islands—the large island of Puerto Rico and the two smaller islands of Vieques and Culebra—as well as several other small islands (see map F.1). This work refers to Puerto Rico as an archipelago.

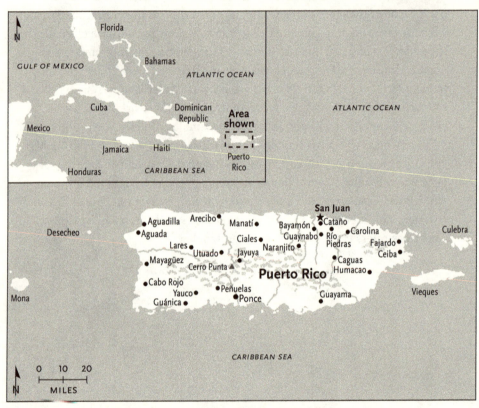

MAP F.1 The Archipelago of Puerto Rico. Source: Map created by
Brian Edward Balsley, GISP.

Radical Solidarity

Introduction

· ·

"Sleeping is seldom considered illegal, even in Puerto Rico," Ruth Reynolds wrote friends about the events surrounding her predawn arrest on November 2, 1950. At two in the morning, the sound of men yelling outside had startled her awake. Quickly throwing on some clothes, Reynolds opened her front door to find dozens of heavily armed policemen and National Guardsmen. With more machine guns pointed at her than she had ever before seen in one place, Reynolds demanded a search warrant. But, she recalled, "I did not resist when they entered anyway." Under the cover of early morning darkness, the men confiscated Reynolds's papers and other personal belongings and transported her to police headquarters in San Juan for interrogation.[1]

The thirty-four-year-old activist had been in Puerto Rico for over two years, investigating a government crackdown on student protesters at the archipelago's flagship university and its connection to the campaign to crush demands for Puerto Rico's independence from the United States. A full draft of Reynolds's manuscript was among the papers police confiscated.

Reynolds's arrest came on the heels of several heady days of protest, violence, and instability. Rising up against US dominion over their country, members of the Nationalist Party of Puerto Rico had just days before declared a new nation, the independent Republic of Puerto Rico. Two party members also attempted to assassinate US president Harry Truman in Washington, DC. The United States had invaded Puerto Rico in 1898 during the Spanish-American War and held the archipelago as its own territorial possession ever since. Since the 1920s, the Nationalist Party had been demanding independent sovereignty. Now, in 1950, the US government was working closely with Puerto Rico's most powerful politicians to assert a new governing formula that threatened the Nationalist Party's sovereignty demands. In the proposed recalibration of the existing US–Puerto Rico relationship, the Nationalist Party saw only enduring US control of Puerto Rico for many generations to come.

Reynolds had not been involved in either the Nationalist Party uprising or the presidential assassination attempt, but, like hundreds of Puerto

Ricans arrested before and after the 1950 uprising, Reynolds faced charges of violating the notorious Insular Law No. 53—or the Gag Law, as it was widely known—that had been passed specifically in response to the student protests she had been documenting at the time of her arrest. Insular Law 53 criminalized public demonstrations of support for Puerto Rico's independence. Awaiting trial in prison, Reynolds reassured shocked friends that she did not, in fact, endorse Nationalist Party violence. She also pointedly noted, however, that she likewise rejected state violence directed at Nationalist Party supporters. They were targeted "simply because they tell the truth about Puerto Rico's political and economic situation."[2] At her trial, she similarly directed the court's attention to the insurrection's causes. She testified, "The basic violence is the imperialism of the United States, and of the Insular authorities who help enforce it."[3] In 1951, the court sentenced her to two to six years in prison in Puerto Rico for conspiracy to overthrow the government there.

Yet Reynolds was different from most of the others who had been incarcerated in connection with the uprising—and not only because she was not herself a Nationalist Party member. Reynolds was a white North American with no family ties to the archipelago. She was what many in Puerto Rico referred to as a "continental"—a North American from the continental United States—and she was dedicated to helping the United States realize its professed commitments to liberty, representative government, and consent of the governed. She was also a radical pacifist who opposed violence as a political tool. She preferred to contest US colonialism by exposing her fellow "continentals" to the discrepancy between the United States' democratic ideals and its subjugation of Puerto Rico.

This book tells her story, and in doing so, tells the story of radical solidarity. Although Reynolds did not use the term "radical solidarity," this book introduces the concept in order to capture the significance of her thought and activism. What made Reynolds's solidarity activism "radical" was that it did not seek to soften the hard edges of the US colonial system by alleviating the symptoms of economic and cultural domination. Rather, it sought to dismantle that system altogether. Reynolds worked side by side with Puerto Rican Nationalists in pursuit of their stated agenda: independence. Her solidarity activism was radical because it amplified the work of colonial subjects resisting empire without neutralizing or eroding that resistance.

The movement for Puerto Rico's independence was one of the most determined liberation struggles for national sovereignty in the twentieth century. The United States tried to crush that struggle in the name of democracy, but it never extinguished the desire and drive for independence. The form of "radical solidarity" that Reynolds pioneered, which enabled her to create and sustain effective configurations of outsider allyship over four decades, facilitated the longevity of this struggle in the face of profound state opposition.

Reynolds led an extraordinary life. Like the history of Puerto Rico itself, however, the stories of women like her who challenged US colonial exploitation are largely unknown beyond those who had direct connections with them. Such erasure is a symptom of both the marginalization of Puerto Rico—both its politics and its status debates—in US history and the centering of men's experiences in the history of liberation politics. Telling Ruth Reynolds's life story not only shifts the gendered center of gravity in liberation politics; it offers a nuanced counternarrative of the American past that, forged in a complex history of colonialism and anticolonialism, does not align with a history written by the victors.

The History of US Colonialism in Puerto Rico

At the time that Reynolds began investigating the history of US control of Puerto Rico, "consensus" historians of the 1940s and 1950s characterized US conquest during the Spanish-American War as a temporary colonial aberration.[4] As Reynolds was to discover, the consensus historians were wrong. There was a long and enduring history of US colonial control of Puerto Rico and use of repression to maintain that control.

When the United States invaded Puerto Rico a few short months after declaring war on Spain in 1898, some Puerto Ricans hoped that the United States would champion democracy there. Instead, the United States reversed the limited autonomy that Spain had granted Puerto Rico in 1897. Spain's decision to approve an Autonomy Charter for Puerto Rico, which granted the right to self-government within the confines of the empire, emerged from the empire's failure to quell separatist sentiments in Puerto Rico and Cuba, its last two colonial possessions in the Americas. In Puerto Rico, this separatist sentiment had erupted most famously in the 1868 uprising that became known as the "Grito de Lares" ("Cry of Lares") after the mountain town where it was centered and where participants proclaimed the Republic of Puerto Rico. Though Spanish authorities crushed this uprising, the demand for independence endured. By the 1890s, a community of independence-minded Puerto Ricans had coalesced in New York and continued to work toward national sovereignty.[5]

The United States, however, had other plans. Strategists in Washington, DC, sought control of Puerto Rico as a strategic site for fueling navy ships and controlling a planned canal through Central America.[6] Between 1898 and 1901, the United States ruled its new possession by military government.[7] In 1901, it installed a colonial civilian government with a North American appointed governor. Unlike its previous territorial possessions on the continent, the US federal government did not set Puerto Rico—or its other wartime territorial gains of Guam and the Philippines—on the path to becoming a state.

Instead, the United States Supreme Court asserted the constitutionality of this arrangement with legal arguments similar to those previously used to oppress Indigenous people and African Americans. Justices in the nation's highest court employed a type of doublespeak much like that used to justify the constitutionality of Native Americans' disfranchisement as "domestic dependent nations" and uphold "separate but equal" Black/white racial segregation in public accommodations. The Supreme Court defied logic when it deemed Puerto Rico and other territorial possessions acquired in 1898 as "foreign to the United States in a domestic sense." In the "Insular Cases" between 1901 and 1922, the US Supreme Court embraced this oxymoron as part of its invention of the notion that Puerto Rico, along with Guam and the Philippines, comprised "unincorporated territories." The 1917 Jones Act made Puerto Ricans US citizens but did not extend constitutional protections or federal voting rights. Puerto Ricans woke up one day to learn that they were formal citizens of a nation that denied them substantive political representation and rights.

Then, during World War II, the United States committed itself to the idea of a new world order—one that was free of colonial relationships. The formation of the United Nations in the wake of the war was supposed to advance this better world. Even as global events inspired independence movements across the Americas, Asia, and Africa, the colonial powers attempted to hold onto their colonial possessions with governing formulas short of full independence. The French Union had its "overseas departments," for example, while Portugal had its "overseas provinces." It was not enough to quell the drive for full sovereignty. Between the mid-1940s and 1970s, colonized peoples across the globe struggled for national independence from the handful of powerful empires ruling the majority of the world's population. Amid brutal wars over decolonization, dozens of new African and Asian nations declared independence from the crumbling British, French, and Dutch empires.[8] The United States, however, held on to Puerto Rico.

As the tense wartime alliance between the United States and the Soviet Union quickly turned into an expansionist race for "spheres of influence" across the globe, the military bases that the United States had constructed on expropriated land during World War II to secure water and air routes and conduct war-game maneuvers only grew in strategic value.[9]

Yet in the era of the Cold War, the United States also sought to protect its reputation as a defender of liberty against totalitarian forces represented foremost by the Soviet Union. US officials advocated making Puerto Rico a showcase of US democracy and capitalism in the Caribbean and found a willing partner in the influential politician Luis Muñoz Marín, who after years of working for independence had concluded instead that Puerto Rico's economic growth required a governing relationship with the United States.[10] Together these powerful US and Puerto Rican authorities pushed for the transformation of the archipelago into a governing formula that, like the post-war experiments of European empires, offered local autonomy without actual independence. Together, they suppressed pro-independence voices to achieve that goal.

On July 25, 1952, almost two years after the failed Nationalist uprising and on the fifty-fourth anniversary of the US invasion of Puerto Rico, Governor Luis Muñoz Marín inaugurated the Commonwealth of Puerto Rico, or the Estado Libre Asociado de Puerto Rico, as it is called in Spanish (translated as the Free Associated State of Puerto Rico). This new commonwealth status gave Puerto Ricans more input in matters of local governance, but otherwise it did not fundamentally alter the existing unequal relationship between the two entities: the United States remained empowered to make unilateral decisions for a population denied formal representation and fundamental US constitutional rights. Still, President Harry Truman's administration hailed the commonwealth status as evidence of US "adherence to the principle of self-determination and to the ideals of freedom and democracy" and "a convincing answer to attacks by those who have charged the United States Government with imperialism and colonial exploitation."[11]

Reynolds became a social justice activist and eventually a powerful voice for Puerto Rico's independence amid all these profound domestic and global currents.

An Unlikely Champion for Puerto Rico's Independence

Reynolds was among the cadre of social justice activists in the United States that proliferated between the 1940s and 1980s. During these years, diverse activists from civil rights, peace, and labor union groups confronted systemic injustices in the United States and abroad.[12] Anticolonial and antiracist activists were largely members of colonized and racially minoritized communities materially affected by the hard edges of US global power and domestic inequality. Whether through empathy, outrage, or the sense of a shared commitment to anti-imperial democracy, outsiders who were drawn into this sphere of activism often came from very different backgrounds and perspectives than those with whom they allied themselves.

As Reynolds was an outsider, her advocacy for Puerto Rico's independence emerged within the limits and through the privileges of existing power structures. She strategically made the most of her privileged identity as a white citizen of the United States to confront its leading politicians and pundits about its colonial past and present. Her vision of solidarity activism and organizing required confrontation, patient suffering for justice and truth, and interrogation of state violence.

In her origins, however, Reynolds was an unlikely champion for Puerto Rico's independence, although she always demonstrated an independent streak. Reynolds was born in Terraville, South Dakota, in 1916, thousands of miles away from Puerto Rico. Her politically conservative parents expected their three daughters to "conform to what they believed and any step outside that was an error which should be corrected as soon as possible."[13] When Reynolds was a child, her family life revolved around a deep Methodist faith—a faith that catalyzed the circuitous route that eventually landed Reynolds in a Puerto Rican jail cell. Unlike her sisters, Reynolds never married or had children. In the 1930s, she attended a private Methodist college and took a teacher's job on a Lakota reservation for a year, her first exposure to the dynamics of dispossession and US imperialist violence. The following year, she taught in a predominantly white South Dakota ranching and farming community. After two years of teaching, Reynolds left her home state for graduate school at Northwestern University near Chicago to further her career in education.

Swept up in the student pacifist activism that she encountered on campus, Reynolds devoted herself to learning nonviolent theory and tactics. Toward this end, in 1941, she moved to New York to join a cooperative pacifist community protesting racism in the United States as well as British colonialism in India. Through this community, she also met Puerto Rican independence activists, including Nationalist Party of Puerto Rico president Pedro Albizu Campos, who taught her about US exploitations in Puerto Rico. Pro-independence forces were split between those willing to work with the

US government through Puerto Rico's electoral system and the Nationalist Party, which refused to cooperate with the US government and even advocated armed struggle against the US government as a political strategy. The Nationalist Party's top male leaders had been convicted for inciting violence against colonial officials and incarcerated in US prisons since the 1930s. By the 1940s several of them, including Albizu Campos, were out of prison and in New York.[14]

Apart from some colonial administrators and missionaries, few North Americans of any background knew about, much less cared about, Puerto Rico in the 1940s.[15] Reynolds herself had thought little about Puerto Rico before meeting Nationalists in New York. Intrigued by what they told her, Reynolds set out to learn more—and was disappointed. "What material has penetrated the popular press," Reynolds noted in 1946, "has either been written by government apologists or has urged 'reforms' within the existing framework."[16] To counter that material, she began to share the stories of US injustice that others had relayed to her. Reynolds was driven to communicate to justice-oriented Americans about the righteousness of demanding Puerto Rican independence. They would, Reynolds seemed to believe, care about the situation if only they knew Puerto Rico's history. But first, she had to research and map out that history that she first learned from Albizu Campos. New York served as the base from which Reynolds embarked on this work and then mobilized for Puerto Rico's independence for the remainder of her life.

In this role as solidarity leader, Reynolds worked with a handful of colleagues to fill a critical void in the US anticolonial Left. When Reynolds began her solidarity work during World War II, the Communist Left, the Black freedom struggle, and the pacifist movement were focused on liberation struggles in India, Africa, and the British Caribbean—not Puerto Rico. Black civil rights activists, for example, conceptualized their efforts as part of broader African diasporic struggles for national sovereignty.[17] Pacifists and civil rights activists further embraced Mahatma Gandhi's nonviolent resistance strategy and pursued ties with India's independence movement from Britain.[18] During the 1930s and 1940s, even the Communist Party USA (CPUSA)—which had vocally supported Puerto Rican independence as early as the 1920s—strategically muted its public advocacy of the Nationalist Party so as not to contradict the Communist International's Popular Front policy.[19] In the United States, the Popular Front translated into support for Franklin Roosevelt's New Deal coalition, which was led by the same politicians committed to preserving US control of Puerto Rico. Although CPUSA leaders continued to offer financial and legal support to incarcerated Nationalists during the 1930s and 1940s, they did so discretely.[20]

After entering this largely empty political space, Reynolds spent the next four decades challenging other North Americans to join her in advancing Puerto Rico's freedom and, at the same time, their own liberation from holding another nation in bondage.[21] The task of serving as a critical interpreter for North American audiences consumed her for decades. She testified before Congress and the United Nations, led pro-independence organizations, and worked for the release of political prisoners. She developed a unique voice among North American colleagues as one of those political prisoners whose body bore the visible and invisible scars of imperial injustice. She spoke to hundreds of Puerto Ricans to gather material for two books, although only one was ever published. By the time she died in 1989, she was a leading voice of the US solidarity movement for Puerto Rico's independence and a vital link across activist generations. In short, Reynolds pioneered the type of anticolonial history of the United States that entered mainstream US history only beginning in the 1980s and 1990s.[22]

Reynolds was also an unlikely champion for Puerto Rico's independence because she became a solidarity leader in an era when politicians and pundits celebrated white women as wives, mothers, and homemakers and elevated rosy images of them as consumers as evidence of US capitalism's superiority over Soviet communism. Conversely, politicians and media stigmatized nonconformity to such ideals as a threat to US democracy and, ultimately, the United States' ability to win the global Cold War with the Soviet Union.[23] As the most public face of solidarity politics for Puerto Rican sovereignty in the United States for many years, Reynolds repeatedly disrupted this US Cold War gender ideology of white womanhood to its core. Among critics, her activist focus on the gaping hole in US Cold War foreign policy—that the "leader of the free world" was a colonial power—resonated in distinctly gendered terms that intertwined the dangers of gender transgression with national security concerns.

Reynolds was among a diverse group of women whose organizing sustained social justice movements during some of the most politically repressive decades in US history. But she found that even movements demanding radical change—including the pacifist and Puerto Rican independence movements—often replicated hierarchical gender roles by assigning formal leadership positions to men and relying heavily on women for less visible informal leadership and organizing.[24] In building a solidarity movement that first required building critical consciousness where none existed,

Reynolds performed unglorified but critical labor that was often gendered female. Yet she also occupied formal leadership positions in organizations she helped to form.

In this and other ways, Reynolds and the women with whom she worked in the Puerto Rican independence movement—both North American and Puerto Rican—led lives that were thoroughly transgressive of the racialized gender conventions of their era. Reynolds did not explicitly link her activism to advancing a women's rights agenda as did Black and white contemporaries involved in, for instance, the Communist Party's Congress of American Women.[25] She did, however, defy the celebrated roles of wife and mother expected of middle-class white women.[26] She also approached empire differently than generations of white women settlers, missionaries, and reformers who asserted a shared "civilizing mission" with white men of conquered Indigenous populations in order to claim an equal role with them in the US polity.[27] For Reynolds, it was the opposite: contesting colonialism served as an avenue for asserting her intellectual and strategic parity with men whose roles in shaping policy and knowledge derived from their own socially prescribed privileges.

As she worked for Puerto Rican political rights, first in New York and then in Puerto Rico, Reynolds was subject to the surveillance that the FBI and Puerto Rico's insular police had authorized for decades against opponents of US rule.[28] And she experienced firsthand the colonial state repression of pro-independence voices that facilitated the commonwealth's creation. Government surveillance and repression made mobilizing a mass solidarity movement for Puerto Rico's independence in North America extremely difficult, as potential sympathizers kept their distance to avoid government attention. At the same time, pacifist colleagues openly condemned Reynolds's ties to the Nationalist Party. Reynolds was never able to reconcile how pacifist critics could "support the large violence" of US military and policing powers over Puerto Rico "and be so opposed to the small violence" of those who resisted such state-sanctioned bellicosity.[29]

Even though the constant threat of government reprisal often made her work feel solitary, she was always part of a community and enmeshed in networks. Reynolds experienced profound joy and humanity as well as shared suffering with those who made up the overlapping political and religious networks that stretched across the Americas: the Nationalist women with whom she was incarcerated during her darkest moments; the racially diverse group of pacifist colleagues who raised funds to pay for her legal defense; the civil rights lawyer who drew upon his experience challenging racial segregation to contest civil liberties violations in Puerto Rico's courts; the Nationalist Party exiles in Cuba with whom she corresponded; and the New Left youth activists with whom she collaborated for the release of political prisoners in Puerto Rico and around the world. She took risks, endured hardship, and emerged as a thought leader precisely because she belonged to and nourished communities—no matter how small—that likewise nourished her radical solidarity.

Radical Solidarity

This book includes information about Reynolds's life as it excavates her political thought and practice, radical solidarity. In Reynolds's case, the personal was truly political, and the political was also personal. Her private emotional life was animated primarily by the deep and loving bonds that she developed with the small community of pacifists and Nationalists in her world. Principal among these were Pedro Albizu Campos, Julio Pinto Gandía, Thelma Mielke, Conrad Lynn, Isabel Rosado Morales, and Laura Meneses de Albizu Campos. And there were others. Their relationships unfolded over the course of decades in person at the Harlem Ashram, in prison in Puerto Rico, and through detailed correspondence. These friendships were both the center of her social world and expressions of her solidarity politics. Her path of radical solidarity was sometimes lonely, but she was never alone.

The use of "solidarity" as a political concept is often traced to nineteenth-century European labor movements. Expressions and theories of solidarity, however, have had a life of their own well beyond such origins.[30] Fundamentally, political solidarity involves individuals and groups that have pursued alliance building to support those struggling against social injustice.[31] This book configures the sentiment of common cause against injustice as radical solidarity in its excavation of Reynolds's approach to supporting the goals of a community as an outsider.

In this work, the challenge that Reynolds faced was providing support without replicating hierarchical relationships between colonizer and colonized in rendering that support. Reynolds's understanding of allyship did not make support for colonized peoples contingent on conforming to the colonizing nation, including the political agenda of its most justice-oriented dissenters. Rather, she practiced a form of solidarity that recognized the experiences and positionality of Puerto Ricans as colonial subjects, as well as her own positionality as a colonizing citizen. Her view of Puerto Ricans as agents of their own national destiny—and likewise her focus on her *own* agency in shaping the United States' political destiny—made her unique vision of solidarity potentially transformative rather than hegemonic.

Reynolds's radical solidarity entailed three central components. First, rather than dwell on the contradictions of radical pacifist and Nationalist ideologies, Reynolds emphasized what they held in common: a critique of US colonialism and state violence. Second, she insisted that North American allies like herself could pick their protest tools against US colonialism, but they should not tell Puerto Ricans what tools to use in *their* struggle for national sovereignty. Nor should they tell them how to run an independent Puerto Rico. Third, Reynolds advocated for an independent Puerto Rico based on her identity as an American citizen and her fundamental beliefs about US democracy, thus leveraging her privilege within a colonizing nation through the lens of her firmly held beliefs in that nation's stated values.

To develop her radical solidarity, Reynolds melded her understanding of Puerto Rican nationalism, her radical pacifism, her Methodism, and her commitment to US democratic ideals. Her pacifism was grounded in Gandhi's strategy of nonviolent confrontation and patient suffering for justice and truth, as well as Christian theology emphasizing personal responsibility for social injustice. Likewise, the example of Jesus's crucifixion, or the "way of the cross," informed her belief that "voluntary acceptance of any necessary sacrifice or suffering in the service of Truth and Right—leads not to defeat but to victory."[32] Reynolds's admiration of the principles of liberty set forth in the US Constitution guided her insistence that Puerto Rico's independence from the United States was essential for any kind of justice in Puerto Rico and also for the integrity of the United States itself. These pillars formed the core of her single-minded dedication to Puerto Rico's independence.

Political solidarities take shape and endure in distinct historical contexts. For Reynolds, the shifting diasporic politics of US colonialism, migration, and repression were critical factors in the development and ultimately endurance of her radical solidarity. The book examines how the historically specific Puerto Rican communities that Reynolds interacted with in New York over the course of forty years shaped the development of her approach to allyship. Following the repression surrounding the commonwealth's establishment, for instance, the vibrant pro-independence voices in New York that had educated her on US colonialism became more muted. Their views became more difficult for outsiders to access, much less understand and develop a politics of solidarity around later.

Just as colonial migration and diasporic politics provided the circumstances that allowed her to meet Puerto Rican independence activists in New York, government repression ensured that Reynolds joined them in their suffering and made her an insider to a distinct community of political prisoners. Reynolds's own suffering and witness to the pain of others amid the United States' colonial reconsolidation at mid-century expanded what she held in common with those with whom she claimed allyship. The shared trauma of incarceration fueled her solidarity activism for many years to come.

Her committed support for the Nationalist Party attracted enormous criticism. To discredit Reynolds, contemporary critics focused on her relationship with Nationalist Party leader Pedro Albizu Campos and other Nationalists. Critics portrayed Reynolds's relationship with Albizu Campos as sexualized in nature. Never mind that Albizu Campos was a devoted and inspirational friend and colleague, not a sexual partner.[33] At the same time, critics dismissed her as being intellectually subservient and portrayed her as merely Albizu Campos's mouthpiece. Reynolds's thorough insight into Nationalist Party strategies and the political thought of Albizu Campos, however, was not a weakness. It formed the bedrock of her brilliance in crafting a unique and syncretic anticolonial strategy.

The distinct way that Reynolds's radical solidarity informed her support of Puerto Rican independence repudiated yet another set of criticisms, that she was an advocate of violence. As a pacifist, she never glorified or endorsed Nationalist violence. On the contrary, she found it counterproductive. To maintain her position, it may have helped that the Nationalist Party's militant actions in the 1950s were few and focused on political targets. Fundamentally, however, she could hold such tension because she saw her primary role as condemning the larger violence of US colonialism—what she referred to as the "basic violence" at trial—instead of telling Puerto Ricans what to do or condemning individual transgressions. This was a dilemma that other political coalitions had faced and stumbled over. As Reynolds explained to her family in letters she wrote from prison, "I have never presumed to tell any Puerto Rican in what manner he ought to work for the independence of his country. . . . My job," she insisted, "is to understand and interpret, not to condone or condemn."[34]

Reynolds's story has broad relevance beyond the long history of the Puerto Rican independence struggle in the second half of the twentieth century. Reynolds's approach to solidarity holds lessons for activists in the United States for how to act and be in solidarity with colonized peoples or, indeed, other groups resisting oppression. Her journey captures the complexities and possibilities of working across difference within the context of state-sanctioned violence and colonialisms. It forces a consideration of the boundaries of allyship and prompts justice-oriented individuals to think about not only the future of Puerto Rico for Puerto Ricans but also what it means to believe in US democracy and to take personal responsibility for US government–sanctioned injustice.

Radical Solidarity chronicles key moments in Reynolds's life history to illustrate her transformation from an observer of the Puerto Rican independence movement to a leading advocate for and actor in it. At each stage of her activist career—as a reporter, protester, political prisoner, historian—she both advanced her political agenda and offered critical commentary on her changing perception of the tactics the United States employed to maintain Puerto Rico as a colony. Taken together, these key moments elucidate a US history of solidarity activism shaped by gender dynamics and profound power differentials. They reveal the intersection of the long struggle for an independent Puerto Rico with revolutionary struggles for US democracy that preceded the more familiar radical protest movements of the 1960s and 1970s. They also point the way to an anticolonial history of the United States that places US colonial exploitations front and center.

· · · · · ·

This book is divided into three parts. Part I is set in the continental United States between the 1910s and 1940s. Over the course of three chapters, this section explores the cultural and political seeds of Reynolds's devotion to US democracy, as well as her critique of its implementation. It begins in the Midwest, from which Reynolds drew upon a spectrum of conservative and radical cultural experiences during these years in later crafting her radical vision of solidarity. The book then follows Reynolds to New York in the 1940s to examine the transnational networks of radical pacifists, civil rights workers, India independence activists, and Puerto Rican Nationalists alongside the migration circuits that intersected in Harlem. Through these networks, Reynolds began her decades-long political relationship with Albizu Campos. She also began working with several New York–based activists in expanding their anti-imperial agenda—beyond opposing British imperialism in India to denouncing US imperialism in Puerto Rico—to make a common cause with Puerto Rican independence activists who supported armed revolution.

The chapters that make up Part II shift geographically to Puerto Rico and the monumental years between 1945 and 1952, when US-based and Puerto

Rico–based architects of the commonwealth harnessed legislative, carceral, and surveillance powers to inaugurate this new status for Puerto Rico. They pursued a strategy for inaugurating a commonwealth that combined groundwork in the electoral arena with campaigns to silence opponents. This section traces the arc of Reynolds's transformation from a chronicler of such status-related events who was attempting to figure out their meaning for a North American audience, to a political prisoner, prosecuted and incarcerated because she was working to expose the government's persecution of its opponents. This section explores Reynolds's transition from an outside witness to a participant and government-identified subversive. Part II ends with an examination of her arrest during the 1950 uprising and her subsequent conviction and incarceration.

Part III analyzes the broad sweep of Reynolds's postincarceration solidarity work between the 1950s and 1980s. For many in the United States and the international community, the commonwealth's inauguration—along with the lengthy prison sentences of its most vocal opponents—"resolved" the case of Puerto Rico. The United Nations removed Puerto Rico from its list of colonies. The mainstream media dismissed convicted Nationalists as deranged fanatics and then forgot about them. Reynolds continued to lobby for the freedom of Puerto Rican political prisoners and for the United Nations to focus on decolonizing Puerto Rico. By the 1970s, however, she had a lot more company in this work. The solidarity movement for Puerto Rico's independence emerged as an essential building block of the "Third World" US politics that blossomed during this era of global decolonization. As a direct witness to the United States' repression of the Nationalist Party and as a leading voice demanding the release of Nationalist Party supporters who remained incarcerated, Reynolds offered new generations of independence activists links to that earlier era.

"Tyranny," Reynolds insisted, "can be responded to only by submission or by resistance, and submission negates one's birthright as a human being."[35] Reynolds asserted this birthright. In the process, she crafted a powerful vision of radical solidarity and globally engaged justice activism.

Part I
....

1 Black Hills

It would be hard to imagine a more unlikely advocate and ally for Puerto Rico's independence than Ruth Mary Reynolds.

She was born in South Dakota, over 2,600 miles away from the Caribbean archipelago, on February 29, 1916—right in the middle of World War I. Her family was made up of politically conservative Anglo-Americans who had settled there after the United States wrenched the territory away from the Sioux during the Black Hills War of the late nineteenth century.

Reynolds was born into a social world that valued Christianity for its patriarchal character. Church, family, and school prepared her to be a wife and mother who would propagate like-minded family and community among future generations. Despite the fact that Reynolds had a college education, one of the only career options available to her as a woman in the 1930s was teaching.

Reynolds may have been set on a trajectory to replicate this social world; instead, she bucked it. She deviated from the expectations for a woman in her community and set a new path for herself—one that would bring her into contact with marginalized communities and unfamiliar worldviews that would shape her in unexpected ways.

However, even as she left much of her conservative upbringing behind, many facets of her early life continued to inform her life's work. This same religiously conservative community and legacy of conquest also fueled Reynolds's commitment to social justice and the first inklings of her understanding of allyship. As a faithful Methodist, she was drawn to the social gospel movement and its call to apply the teachings of Jesus toward achieving racial and economic justice. In South Dakota, her first teaching post was at the Rosebud Reservation. These experiences, and the contradictory messages she received throughout her young life regarding democracy, freedom, and equality, contributed to Reynolds's incipient critique of US empire long before she knew anything about an archipelago colonized by the United States in 1898, nearly eighteen years before she was born.

Settler Colonial Origins

Reynolds hailed from a region known as the Black Hills; she was born in the small South Dakota mining town of Terraville, about four miles away from the notorious gold rush city of Deadwood. The Black Hills mountain range was sacred to the Lakota Sioux's world order, towering several thousand feet above the northern Great Plains.[1]

The archeological record indicates that Indigenous peoples had occupied the Black Hills mountain range for millennia. Lakota contact with the Black Hills precedes the historical record. Accounts by European traders and explorers suggest, however, that the mobile Lakota people had lived within a four-hundred-mile range of the mountains since at least the 1600s. During the 1700s and early 1800s, a combination of epidemics, intertribal conflict, and hunts for trading pelts led the Lakota to migrate the center of their territorial range toward the Missouri River, the northern Great Plains, and the Black Hills. This period saw a complex history of conflict, alliances, trade, and intermarriage unfold among Indigenous groups, including the Lakota, who spent time in the Black Hills. It resulted in Lakota dominance of the mountain range.[2]

Between the mid-eighteenth and early nineteenth centuries, small numbers of European and US traders and explorers, including Lewis and Clark, passed through the Black Hills.[3] Then, between the 1840s and 1860s, thousands of Americans made the overland journey through Lakota territory in the northern Great Plains on their way to Oregon, Utah, California, Colorado, and Montana in search of farmland, gold, and, in the case of Mormon migrants, a place to establish a religious kingdom on earth. Even after the US government negotiated two treaties with the Lakotas, in 1851 and then again in 1868, recognizing Lakota title to the Black Hills, Americans continued to breach Lakota territory.[4]

Reynolds's upbringing in the Black Hills was the culmination of several generations of settler colonialism, a system of conquest and erasure as settlers claimed Indigenous land as their own and eliminated the Indigenous presence there. Colonial settler countries like the United States, Australia, and South Africa have relied on a combination of violence, removal, forced assimilation, mythmaking, and asserting sovereign powers to replace original inhabitants.[5] In the 1630s and 1640s, and possibly the 1620s, Reynolds's ancestors were among the first waves of English settlers in the Massachusetts Bay and Connecticut colonies who sought to make the region their own.[6] During the nineteenth century, subsequent generations settled in

Kentucky, Illinois, and New York. They also followed the US expansion westward to Nebraska territory, Wyoming territory, and Dakota territory.[7]

Classic settler colonialist structures preceded the arrival of Reynolds's ancestors to Dakota territory by several years: "Wild West" frontiers and capitalist enterprise, calls for the defense of settlers and private property against "savages," military and state legal intervention, and forced Indigenous resettlement. The gradual trickle of illegal miners prospecting for gold into the Black Hills during the 1860s and early 1870s transformed into a full-fledged gold rush after 1873. That summer, US Army lieutenant colonel George Armstrong Custer led a large expedition force to explore the region, officially to identify a location for a US Army fort but unofficially to determine the extent of Black Hills gold deposits. Despite limited evidence of gold, the expedition did not disappoint. After newspapers across the nation published Custer's dispatches announcing the "discovery" of gold, thousands of prospectors illegally entered Lakota territory during the next two years in order to strike it rich.[8]

Initially, the US government adhered to the 1868 Fort Laramie Treaty that recognized the Black Hills as permanent Lakota territory and ordered the army to evict illegal prospectors. By 1875, however, government officials were intent on confiscating the Blacks Hills for the United States. Believing that skirmishes between prospectors and Native Americans would justify US intervention, the federal government turned a blind eye to American incursions into the region that might precipitate conflict. Unable to convince Native Americans to sell or lease their land to the United States, the federal government shifted strategy, ordering "Lakotas living outside the permanent reservation to report to their agencies" and sending three columns of US troops to the region to enforce the directive. Among these troops was Custer's Seventh Cavalry. Under the leadership of Lakota warriors Sitting Bull and Crazy Horse, Lakota and Cheyenne bands gathered at the Little Big Horn River to the west of the Black Hills famously destroyed Custer's entire cavalry in June 1876 as the US troops pursued the defiant Native American bands.[9]

The federal government's response to the Battle of Little Big Horn decisively paved the way for the arrival of Reynolds's family. Congress used Custer's defeat as the excuse it had sought to confiscate the Black Hills, promptly passing legislation in 1876 demanding millions of acres of Lakota land and threatening to withhold promised rations—and preparing to take the land by force if the Lakota refused. Facing dwindling bison herds and the threat of war, the Lakota—with the notable exception of Sitting

Bull—conceded. Congress ratified the "agreement" in February 1877.[10] The Black Hills were officially open for US mining and settlement.

If family oral history is correct, Reynolds's grandfather, Walter Scott Wilmarth, arrived in 1877, the very same year that Congress ratified the "agreement" confiscating the Black Hills. Wilmarth was a widower. His first wife had died while giving birth to their son, who remained in the care of family in Illinois for several years. Reynolds learned from her mother that this grandfather (whom she never met) "was very proud that he had waited until it was legal to be there." Reflecting on this point over one hundred years later in a 1985 interview, Reynolds pierced the logic of such law-abiding respectability cherished by settlers like her grandfather—those who had waited until the government legally sanctioned their presence in the region: "Now, what is the understanding of legal?" Reynolds asked in the course of the interview. "Depends [on] a point of view. Whether US law was appropriate in that area at that time is a big question, and whether a treaty forced upon Indians at gunpoint, we know it was not just. Now, when is it legal and when isn't it? These are questions."[11]

It was in the small mining town of Terraville that Wilmarth met Reynolds's maternal grandmother, Mary Stewart.[12] Hailing from western Kentucky, Mary Stewart and her twin sister traveled over 1,500 miles by train and stagecoach to Dakota territory in 1882. The sisters helped their aunt and uncle run a boarding house occupied largely by unmarried miners streaming into the region.[13] The twins met their future husbands at the boarding house, where both men rented rooms. Unmarried women who were not sex workers were a minority in many Dakota mining towns in the 1880s, making both women desirable marriage partners for prospectors seeking respectable marriage and family. Mary Stewart married Walter Wilmarth in 1886, and gave birth to Reynolds's mother, Margaret Edna Wilmarth, the following year. Margaret Edna was the first of four daughters. The son from Walter Wilmarth's first marriage eventually joined them as well.[14] Reynolds's mother remained in the Terraville region her entire life, attending both elementary and high school there and working briefly as a teacher before marrying Reynolds's father, Harry Bryant Reynolds.[15]

Reynolds's father, like Wilmarth, had relocated to South Dakota to enter the mining industry. Originally from Nebraska, Harry Bryant Reynolds was born in 1876, just days before Nebraska became the nation's thirty-seventh state. One of ten children, he completed the eighth grade and began a string of odd jobs that took him from Nebraska to Wyoming territory and eventually to South Dakota territory.[16] There, he began a lifetime of work as an employee of the Homestake Mining Company.

When Harry Reynolds arrived in the Black Hills region, the Homestake Mining Company was expanding rapidly. Homestake was a small mining company when it was founded in 1878 at the height of the Black Hills gold rush; its adoption of the cyanide process of treating iron ore in 1893 cut production costs and quickly transformed Homestake into the nation's largest gold mine.[17] Harry Reynolds found work in Homestake's cyanide plant—first helping to build the company's cyanide processing plant and then working in it to treat gold ore.[18]

By the time that Harry Reynolds and Margaret Wilmarth married in 1909, the presence of white women and children in Christian sanctioned families had advanced the settler colonial project in the region. Church and family replaced the sexual and political economy that had revolved around single male miners in the 1870s, when Walter Wilmarth had first relocated to Dakota territory. The stability associated with Christian-oriented small-town life had replaced the "Wild West" volatility associated with Deadwood and some of its famous residents, from Wild Bill Hickok to Calamity Jane.[19]

In the early twentieth century, Harry and Margaret Reynolds and their three daughters—Helen, Ruth, and Jean—were among the families who made up this Black Hills small-town life. Anglo-Americans with few opportunities had long propelled settler colonialism by grabbing at the possibility of upward mobility it offered them. While financial constraints continued to mark family life, Harry and Margaret Reynolds fulfilled this promise when they harnessed his working-class salary to purchase a modest house. The whole of Terraville was visible from their house: to the north, the Homestake cyanide plant; to the south, the tunnel that burrowed through the mountainside and connected Terraville to the hospital, businesses, and regional high school that operated in the larger neighboring town of Lead. The church was also close by, where the family practiced a strict Methodist faith, extolling traditional gender roles and prohibitions against alcohol, smoking, and public dancing.[20]

Cracks in the Mold

The same community that inspired Reynolds's love for this dramatic landscape initially instilled in her an uncritical belief in US democracy. In her final years of life, Reynolds described these early lessons in American democracy: "You grow up loving the area and everything in it," she noted in an interview. "You go to school and you are taught that your country stands for the right of all people, that we believe all men are created equal." As Reynolds recalled, "The view that all men are created equal, we didn't begin to think about—we were not taught in school to think about—that some people were not treated as though they had been created equal."[21]

In 1927, a brief meeting with Lakota chief Yellow Robe sparked her interest in the Indigenous connection to her own community. Reynolds was eleven years old. She met the aging Lakota leader in the mythmaking environment of Deadwood's Days of '76 festival. In 1924, local business leaders created the Days of '76 with the aim of harnessing Deadwood's Wild West reputation at the time of its 1876 founding toward making the town a tourist destination every summer.[22] The annual Days of '76 celebration was a variety of the popular "Wild West" amusement shows that had been drawing large audiences in the United States and Europe since the 1880s. Even as the Wild West shows that had initiated such performances were in decline by the 1920s, rodeos, films, and community festivals like Deadwood's Days of '76 continued to celebrate the centrality of frontier violence and Native American dispossession to the creation of modern US identity.[23]

The festival was especially exciting to attendees in 1927 because President Calvin Coolidge was the guest of honor. The ceremonies and performances weaved together a seamless history of defeat, triumph, and reconciliation that glossed over the legacy of US western expansion evident in reservation poverty. In 1924, Coolidge had signed the Indian Citizenship Act, making Native Americans born in the United States US citizens. Three years later, the Lakota extended membership in their nation to him. Together, it was an advanced stage of erasure and replacement. Coolidge and his wife spent the summer of 1927 in the Black Hills, traveling to various local sites, punctuated by the induction ceremony.[24] The national press reported on the event—the president awkwardly wearing a full headdress, listening to the "melodious language of the Chief of the Sioux," and surrounded by hundreds of Lakota, several of whom had participated in the Battle of Little Big Horn.[25]

That day, Days of '76 revelers watched frontier reenactments at the festival and a dramatic parade of 300 Sioux.[26] Yet, had revelers traveled over 100 miles to the southeast to the Pine Ridge Reservation that the 300 Sioux called home, the legacy of conquest would have laid bare the illusion of reconciliation between former enemies.

It was Yellow Robe—one of the Lakota who had led Coolidge's induction ceremony that day—and not the US president who left the lasting impression on the young Reynolds. Born during the last decade of Lakota control of the Black Hills, Yellow Robe was the son of a Lakota chief and the great nephew of Sitting Bull.[27] Yellow Robe was part of a generation of Native Americans who experienced the hardening of the reservation system and the ascendancy of assimilationist schools. He attended the most prominent of these institutions during the 1880s and 1890s, the Carlisle Indian Industrial School, a boarding school in Pennsylvania.[28] As an adult, he served as a "cultural broker" between the Anglo- and Native American communities he moved between, marrying a white woman and raising three biracial daughters, and teaching in several Indian schools. He had also denounced the Wild West shows for their depictions of Native Americans as "the lowest degree of humanity" and a threat to "accomplishing the ideas of citizenship."[29]

When Reynolds met Yellow Robe in person during the Days of '76, it was her father who made the introduction at the Sioux temporary encampment in Deadwood. Harry Reynolds stopped there with his daughter to speak with a fellow Mason.[30] In the late nineteenth and early twentieth centuries, Native American leaders and cultural brokers like Yellow Robe found in Freemasonry's secretive rituals and emphasis on a mythic past an avenue "to perpetuate versions of oral tradition, to perpetuate ritual and secrecy, and to maintain tribal ideas about hierarchy."[31] As the scholar Joy Porter argues, Freemasonry "provided a context for Indian individuals to assimilate into the dominant culture without sacrificing their individual claims to essential difference." The fraught cross-nation idea of fraternity might have shaped Harry Reynolds's perspective on Native American dispossession, despite his reluctance to answer his young daughter's probing questions about the genealogy of family land. "Yes, every part of the US at one time belonged to the Indians," Reynolds remembered her father explaining hesitantly, "but this was the part that was taken from them most recently."[32] "Then this place where we live by right should belong to the Indians," she remembered querying further. After evading the question, her father eventually confirmed that they were indeed living on stolen land that rightfully belonged to the Sioux with a simple "yes" to her query. "So, that was the first time I consciously understood that there was great injustice in this country," Reynolds proclaimed in describing the long-ago conversation.[33]

Reynolds's encounter with Yellow Robe as an eleven-year-old was formative in the development of her ideas about injustice. In a 1980s interview,

Reynolds's reference to the experience was what the historian Jennifer Ritterhouse coins a "drama of social inequality" in her analysis of how children learned race in the early twentieth-century US South. Ritterhouse shows that Southern white civil rights activists frequently detail participating in or witnessing white racism against African Americans—as well as the emotions of guilt, shame, confusion, or power that they felt—in their oral history and autobiographical accounts of childhood. For Reynolds, who was socialized in a world created by US settler colonialism just as these Southern white activists were socialized in the Jim Crow South, such identity-shaping moments contributed to their eventual rebellion against the social worlds of their origins.[34]

Where her encounter with Yellow Robe catalyzed her awareness of the injustices of US territorial expansion, it dovetailed with her belief that Christian faith was best demonstrated by working through social justice—a belief she could trace back to the minister who led her youth group. Like many clergy after World War I, the minister included Social Gospel and pacifism in his ministry.[35] The violence and injustices of the war had led many Protestant leaders to take on social justice teachings that previously had been limited to historic peace churches like the Quakers and Mennonites.[36] According to Reynolds, this minister introduced her to the faith-based activities of others "who were doing things quite outside the traditional church as we knew it." He introduced, for instance, the medical missionary work of Alsatian-German physician Albert Schweitzer in Africa. He discussed the Presbyterian-inspired pacifism and voluntary poverty of Japanese labor leader and reformer Kagawa Toyohiko, whom the US press often identified as "Japan's Gandhi."[37]

Within those church walls, small-town life became highly cosmopolitan. The reach of Social Gospel Methodist ideas to her youth group introduced Reynolds to the international impulses of interwar pacifism, despite the physical remoteness of her small Black Hills mining town. "I started to question in high school everything under the sun," she recalled. Of particular interest was the question of why the mainline churches were not more committed to the "application of the principles of the faith on the social level."[38] As her high school years came to a close, she would continue to ask questions and seek answers in the unexpected new directions her life would take her.

A Future on the Line

In the fall of 1933, Reynolds moved over 300 miles eastward to attend Dakota Wesleyan University in Mitchell, South Dakota. Higher education for women at the time was expanding, but it was still remarkably rare. Reynolds was among the roughly 10 to 12 percent of young women in the United States who attended university during the 1930s.

Her move into higher education coincided with the Great Depression. In South Dakota, the global economic downturn was exacerbated by a severe drought that made the state part of the Great Plains "dust bowl." South Dakotans experienced farm foreclosures, unemployment, and bank failures. By 1934, 39 percent of the population was receiving public assistance, compared with about 13 percent nationwide.[39]

In the midst of such widespread economic instability, her father's steady employment at Homestake made a university education financially possible. Reynolds's "work-study" assistant position in the English Department also helped. The National Youth Administration, the New Deal agency devoted to helping young Americans find work and pursue an education, enabled thousands like Reynolds to afford college through such work-study jobs.[40]

At Dakota Wesleyan, Reynolds studied English literature, but her biggest education came from the experience of challenging authority in the name of justice. It was, Reynolds later explained, "the first occasion in my life when I realized that there are times when you have to put your life on the line, your future on the line because of things that are wrong."[41] In 1937, Dakota Wesleyan's newly appointed president fired three popular professors—one for criticizing his reinstatement of the school's dancing prohibition, and the other two for protesting their colleague's dismissal. Responding to the injustice, Reynolds headed a group of students whose successful demand for an investigation into the dismissals led to a bitter dispute among ministers over liberalizing campus rules and contributed to the eventual resignation of the college's new president. At the time, Reynolds was president of the Women's Self-Government Association and a member of the Student Senate.[42]

Dakota Wesleyan University was still a small private religious college when Reynolds entered in 1933.[43] Dakota Wesleyan's formal relationship with the Methodist Episcopal Church governed compulsory chapel attendance as well as prohibitions against smoking, card playing, drinking, and until 1933, dancing.[44] As with universities across the nation, sex-segregated dormitories and nightly curfews also regulated student sexuality primarily by controlling women's behavior. In loco parentis rules granting educators legal responsibilities over students "in place of parents" fell heaviest on women students.[45]

The reprisals that followed after the president's resignation were instructive. His allies on the Board of Trustees unsuccessfully attempted to block

FIGURE 1.1 A 1937 portrait of Reynolds at the time of her graduation from Dakota Wesleyan University. Source: Ruth M. Reynolds Papers. Ruth M. Reynolds Portrait: RMRe_b37_f01_0001. Archives of the Puerto Rican Diaspora, Center for Puerto Rican Studies, Hunter College, CUNY.

Reynolds's graduation (see figure 1.1). Worse, as a sympathetic board member shared with her, the former president also wrote the superintendent of a school district where she sought employment warning against hiring an agitator.[46]

The action exacerbated a job market already wretched for unemployed women like Reynolds, even in feminized professions like teaching. And even when jobs could be found, women were typically paid less than men. In large measure, this inequity stemmed from the false assumptions of the "family wage"—the idea that a man earned enough to support a wife and children, and that women depended on the financial stability of a male breadwinner. Except in the case of wealthy white women, this model largely did not work—either because a woman was unmarried or estranged from a husband, or because a man did not, in fact, earn a sufficient wage to support a family much less himself. In practice, the idea of the family wage contributed to female poverty and unemployment.[47] In the midst of the nation's worst economic crisis, it facilitated framing the government-sanctioned hiring of men over women as an antipoverty strategy. Under these circumstances, the number of male teachers increased by 5 percent, while the number of women teachers declined by 10 percent during the Depression.[48]

The entire experience proved difficult but powerful for Reynolds's sense of her individual agency. "I learned about the need for doing what you can to right injustice, though it may cost you something," she later reflected. "That's what I really learned at Dakota Wesleyan University. I got a lot of other things in my head there. I got a good education, but those are the most important things that I learned."[49] Ironically, the retaliation she experienced accelerated her movement away from the social world of her origins by causing her to grapple further with settler colonialism. After applying and being rejected from dozens of jobs and with just weeks before the start of the new school year, she finally landed a position teaching high school on the Rosebud Reservation.[50]

The Rosebud Reservation

During the 1930s, the discovery of more Black Hills ore led to elevated gold prices, and the Gold Reserve Act created more jobs at the Homestake Company. It was a boom time set against the Great Depression. In Terraville, Harry Reynolds served as foreman of the construction of new ore-processing facilities.[51]

Meanwhile, the Rosebud Reservation, located 200 miles from Terraville in south central South Dakota, was a world away economically. During these years, the fragile economy of the Rosebud Reservation plunged deeper into crisis. While the US confiscation of Lakota territory in the 1870s helped William Wilmarth and his descendants make a modest living in the Black Hills, it destroyed Lakota subsistence patterns and left many Lakota reliant on government rations that were institutionalized on reservations like Rosebud. By the 1930s, the reservation system was an articulation of the land dispossession that resulted from decades of white settler colonialism.

The land that became the Rosebud Reservation was originally part of the significantly larger Great Sioux Reservation that covered half of the contemporary state of South Dakota.[52] Established in 1868, the Great Sioux Reservation became the home of nearly all of the Lakota by 1877, when the federal government forced the majority of Lakota to accept an "agreement" requiring that they relinquish millions of acres of territory to the United States.[53] This 31 million–acre reservation was short-lived. In 1889, the federal government forced the breakup of the Great Sioux Reservation and again transferred vast tracks of Indian territory to the United States. When they divided the land, the worst parts went to Native Americans. The so-called Great Sioux Agreement of 1889 demarcated six smaller reservations and designated "eleven million acres outside the separate reservations to the public domain for non-Indian homesteading."[54] Rosebud, established as a reservation for the Sicangu Lakota, was one of these six reservations.[55]

Along with the slaughter of the bison, the reservation system disrupted a way of life based on being able to move across the plains in relationship to seasonal migrations and changes in the land. As a result, native peoples began to rely on food rations from the US government. However, Native American use of rations had begun even before the Great Sioux Agreement of 1889. The 1868 treaty that created the Great Sioux Reservation had promised annuities and rations, and the US threat of withholding future rations was a key reason that the federal government was able to force Lakota leaders to sign the 1876–77 "agreement" that handed over millions of acres of Lakota land to the United States. The majority of Lakota leaders concluded that the decline of the buffalo on the Great Plains—and their inability to chase it—left them little choice but to accept US support.[56]

By the 1930s, the reliance among many Rosebud residents on rations had been further cemented through the land allotment system that the US government established on Rosebud and other reservations at the end of the nineteenth century. Beginning in 1893, the federal government began distributing plots of land to Native Americans of the Rosebud Reservation as part of a federal effort to engineer Native assimilation into the United States. This process of designating plots of land to families and individuals was a manifestation of the 1887 General Allotment Act (Dawes Severalty Act). This allotment process was repeated on reservations throughout the United States in the late nineteenth and early twentieth centuries. By allotting individual tracts of land to Native Americans and simultaneously putting an end to communal tribal lands, US policymakers disrupted communal traditions that endured on reservations by theoretically promoting self-supporting farmers with "modern habits" and "discipline."[57]

While the vision of the US allotment policy was one of self-sustaining Native farmers, the reality was quite different. On the Rosebud Reservation, as elsewhere, it was nearly impossible to survive off of an allotment. Many allottees raised subsistence gardens and even sold produce from these gardens. But these gardens typically did not yield enough to serve as a sole source of support. Allottees lacked access to the capital and the amount of land necessary to support commercial farming, or the better regionally suited cattle.[58] Many leased out their land to white tenant farmers and ranchers. In 1935, non-Native farmers cultivated over 146,000 acres of reservation land compared with 32,000 acres by Lakota.[59] With such limited options, the Lakota of Rosebud turned to rations supplied by the federal government to make ends meet. Between 1880 and 1900, every family on the Rosebud Reservation received government rations. These numbers wavered in subsequent years, but in the years just before Reynolds's 1937 arrival on Rosebud, the combination of drought and depression drove these numbers back up.[60]

Reynolds taught at a county school for the children of white tenant farmers, cattle ranchers, and merchants who lived on the reservation. White tenants were hardly the independent farmers as envisioned in the Dawes Act. Economically, many were barely better off than the Lakota from whom they rented. The federal government only provided schooling for Lakota children on the reservation. But Reynolds speculated that even if white residents had been eligible to send their children to the federally funded school, "they wouldn't have gone anyway" because of their racism. "Our school was a tar paper shack," she recalled. "We had seventeen students, two rooms heated by wood stoves or coal, whatever you wanted to put in them. Mr. Poost taught ancient history, mathematics, and science. I taught American history, speech, and English."[61]

In 1937, at the end of her first year, Reynolds decided not to go back. Though eager to leave behind the isolation of her life there, Reynolds's brief time at Rosebud stayed with her, contributing to her disillusionment with the nation she had inherited. As she recalled, "It was a valuable experience in that I could see with my own eyes, observe though not intimately, what the living conditions for the Indians were like. I didn't get close enough to them, but what I could see on the surface was enough. The attitude of the white people toward them was abominable."[62] Reynolds's ability to transform her opposition to racism into sustained acts of solidarity with those who directly shouldered its burdens began to take form in a new student community of her choosing.

Committing to Pacifism

After Rosebud, Reynolds taught at another high school located in the South Dakota ranching and farming community of Newall. She did not stay long. In 1938, she enrolled at Northwestern University in Evanston, Illinois, to pursue a master's degree in English literature.[63] During her time in Evanston between 1938 and 1941, Reynolds completed the master's degree, looked for a teaching position, and "fell in with a group" of young pacifists who "were particularly taken with the methodology" of nonviolent resistance "that Gandhi was using in India for the liberation of his people and studied that in great detail."[64] The pacifism she explored in this group offered a faith-based activist language and network that nurtured her approach to allyship for decades.

During the 1930s, Evanston and neighboring Chicago were the sites of robust student movements that claimed secular and religious peace components. Disillusioned by World War I and the ongoing economic crisis, Northwestern students were among the tens of thousands of college students who renounced military service and participated in peace strikes and assemblies.[65] Over 1,000 of them, for instance, joined the 1935 National Student Strike Against War that saw a walkout of about 175,000 students nationwide.[66] The motivations and political leanings of the interwar student peace movement Reynolds encountered varied significantly. A great many of the student protestors were not pacifists. The Communist and Socialist youth activists who led these national walkouts opposed militarism but also advocated class struggle and accepted anti-imperial wars.[67] Isolationist students, by contrast, grounded their opposition to US militarism abroad in a nativist ideology that celebrated US provincialism and exceptionalism.

Reynolds's commitment to pacifism was an expression of faith and was energized within Northwestern University's distinct religiously inspired activist community and its cross-generational student-clergy networks. This was the first activist community that nourished her politics, but it was not the last. Within this community, Ernest Freemont Tittle, her pastor at the First Methodist Church of Evanston, and A. J. Muste, a regular visiting speaker based in New York, were particularly influential to Reynolds's political trajectory.[68] Both Tittle and Muste were leading figures in Methodist pacifism who lectured and published widely on Christian-inspired nonviolence. Reynolds was one of 150 to 175 Protestant, Catholic, and Jewish students in Tittle's pacifist youth group at First Methodist and a student of both men's pacifist theories.[69] Tittle taught the group that enduring and just peace required *active* nonviolence against state violence, not mere passive nonresistance and withdrawal.[70] Both leaders' interest in integrating Gandhian ideas of nonviolence into Christian theology appealed to the younger generation. The students, Reynolds recalled, explored Gandhi's liberation methodology "in great detail, feeling that there was a demonstrable alternative. . . . We felt that he was giving an example to the world of the way in which social evils could be corrected without this war system."[71]

Reynolds's faith-based activist community also introduced her to the Fellowship of Reconciliation (FOR), an international Christian pacifist organization founded during World War I.[72] Tittle was the chairman of its Midwest office, and Muste became the FOR's new executive director in 1940. Reynolds joined the FOR at this pivotal moment—that is, when in his new role, Muste worked to make nonviolence training central to the organization's mission. For some time, FOR leaders had rejected strikes and boycotts as inimical to a freely chosen repentance at the heart of Christian reconciliation. Muste, a longtime critic of this approach, also sought to make the organization a pioneer in the advancement of Gandhian ideas in United States.[73]

Reynolds's deepening pacifism took place against the backdrop of US preparations for war. In September 1940, Congress enacted the nation's first peacetime draft. Shortly after, President Franklin Roosevelt won a third term by promising to keep the United States out of the war in Europe. Yet by March 1941, the president had escalated US involvement through the Lend-Lease program to lend war supplies to the Allied forces. In August 1941, Congress lowered the draft age from twenty-one to eighteen and extended conscription terms of duty. Public opinion polling that summer showed that a sizable portion of Americans believed in the inevitability of US entry into the war as a belligerent.[74]

In the summer of 1941, Reynolds took a hard turn off her path toward a teaching career—and more generally off the beaten path taken by young, college-educated white women of her generation. Reynolds was still searching for a teaching position and supporting herself through a restaurant job when she learned that the Fellowship of Reconciliation was offering a training course on "total pacifism" in New York.[75] She headed to New York to learn more about nonviolent resistance and to join an interracial pacifist cooperative located in Harlem.

2　Harlem

On January 26, 1944, some twenty women and men gathered in the living room of the Harlem Ashram for a protest "poster walk." Equipped with leaflets and signs exclaiming, "This Is India's Independence Day," "It's 1776 for India and Puerto Rico," and "4 Freedoms for India and Puerto Rico," they made the long trek from upper Manhattan to the British consulate in Brooklyn.[1] The Harlem Ashram was one of several cooperatives that pacifists established in the early 1940s with the goal of centering nonviolence in American protest politics, and it offered training in radical pacifism.[2] By 1944, Reynolds had been living at the Ashram for nearly three years and had become its assistant director. That January day, she warned demonstrators of police threats of arrest. Reviewing local protest ordinances, Reynolds insisted to her audience, "We're going to have the prettiest, most legal march that ever occurred in this city." She later recalled that her knees trembled as she spoke.[3]

Her prediction proved accurate: nine protesters, five women and four men (Reynolds among them), were arrested and detained that day for disorderly conduct before being released on bail in the early hours of January 27.[4] It was Reynolds's first arrest.

For several years, members of the Harlem Ashram had directed their training in pacifism toward denouncing white racism against African Americans in the United States and protesting British colonialism in India. Their shift in interest to the Caribbean, however, was more recent. Reynolds suspected that it was this new focus on Puerto Rico that had drawn police attention. Authorities had not issued threats of arrest before previous peaceful Ashram demonstrations; Reynolds may have been correct in her assumption.[5] While none of the protesters were Puerto Rican, the impetus behind their more expansive agenda was their Puerto Rican neighbors.

The local was truly global in 1940s Harlem. The global migration circuits and political networks that intersected in Harlem made it the ideal laboratory for the emergence of protest against US colonialism in the Caribbean. North American leftists did not need to travel to Puerto Rico to learn about US imperialism there. Vocal proponents of Puerto Rican independence dwelled in upper Manhattan or temporarily passed through its expanding Puerto Rican community. White and Black leftist activists who made their way to Harlem from cities throughout the United States met them there, coming face-to-face with evidence of the hardships of life in Puerto Rico under US rule.

It was no coincidence that white and Black civil rights and Free India activists from across North America and independence proponents from Puerto Rico met in Harlem in the 1940s. Interracial and leftist politics flourished there as they did in no other American neighborhood during the period. There, political activists from around the world crossed paths and exchanged ideas in the streets, at protests, and in each other's homes. Chance encounters created enduring political collaborations. In this environment, Reynolds helped to craft the transfer of anti-imperial agendas from one colonial context to another to consider common cause with Puerto Rican independence fighters who supported violent revolution.

At the Harlem Ashram, Reynolds also rebelled against 1940s gender conventions, although she often played a supportive role to male leaders, just as many other pacifist women had. Still, living in a mixed-sex communal home, especially an interracial one, was an unconventional choice for a young, white, middle-class woman from the Midwest. She shared center stage with male colleagues in protest actions, and her arrest and brief imprisonment disrupted incarceration as primarily a male form of resistance against state power during World War II. Indeed, Reynolds's 1944 arrest for picketing the British consulate was a key link in the unlikely chain of events that deepened the Ashram's ties to the Puerto Rican independence movement.

The Harlem Ashram

Reynolds arrived at the Harlem Ashram in the spring of 1941 in order to deepen her knowledge of nonviolence as a pacifist strategy. She had been intrigued by the teachings of Indian nationalist leader Mahatma Gandhi on nonviolence that she encountered while a graduate student at Northwestern University. So, unable to find a job in Chicago in 1941, she applied to a Fellowship of Reconciliation (FOR) workshop exploring "total pacifism" being offered at the Harlem Ashram.[6]

Reynolds's political development in New York was nurtured within this community. Though they remained small—with usually no more than a dozen permanent residents—pacifist cooperatives such as the Harlem Ashram, the Newark Ashram in New Jersey, and the Ahimsa Farm outside

Cleveland shaped the landscape of mid-twentieth-century American political culture by serving as incubators for emerging leaders of the American liberal Left.[7] Jay Holmes Smith, an American missionary and pacifist, founded the Harlem Ashram in 1940 as an interracial pacifist community committed to using Christianity to inspire nonviolent protest against war and racial injustice. Reynolds was part of a cadre of young white and Black pacifists that included civil rights leaders James Farmer and Bayard Rustin who participated in this interracial "cell" community.[8]

Key ideas about nonviolent civil disobedience that Reynolds encountered at the Harlem Ashram and eventually redirected toward the struggle for Puerto Rico's independence initially took shape in India, where Smith and fellow missionary Ralph Templin crafted a form of Christian pacifist activism during their several years of Methodist missionary work there.[9] Smith's and Templin's time in India was part of American Protestantism's long tradition of transnational activism and proselytizing, and the years they spent there coincided with the India independence movement's intensification of its nonviolent civil disobedience campaign. The two men were among a group of American missionaries who had spent time with independence leaders Mahatma Gandhi and Jawaharlal Nehru, and they became supporters of the Indian independence movement.[10] While in India, Smith also lived as part of the Sat Tal Ashram that Methodist missionary E. Stanley Jones created in 1930 after experiencing Gandhi's own Ashram. The Sat Tal Ashram helped to launch the Christian Ashram movement in India and beyond.[11]

Smith and Templin absorbed Gandhi's vision of satyagraha, "meaning civil insistence on or tenacity in the pursuit of truth."[12] Instead of using violence as a tool for social change, practitioners of satyagraha believed that "suffering love" was the key to challenging injustice. Satyagrahi engaged in peaceful civil disobedience and protest, and they patiently suffered arrest and violence for their principled position. They also pursued transformative dialogue with adversaries.[13]

Smith and Templin's journey transferring satyagraha and *kristagraha*— its Christianized version—from India to Harlem began in 1940. That year the British expelled them and two other US missionaries from India for denouncing the British government's decision to declare India a combatant in World War II without the consent of the Indian National Congress.[14] This Christianized version asserted individual personal responsibility for social injustice and atonement for it through sacrifice. Reynolds and other Ashram members explored the work of A. J. Muste and embraced his assertion that, like Jesus's suffering on the cross, disciplined, self-sacrificing, and faith-based nonviolent resistance could revolutionize human relations.[15] Under Smith's leadership, Harlem Ashram residents practiced "voluntary poverty" and engaged in daily prayer and Gandhian meditation. Through hours of study, Ashram members absorbed Gandhian and Christian-based understandings of nonviolence as a strategy for social change.[16]

In the early 1940s, Ashram participants funneled their intensive study of nonviolent resistance toward the causes of India's independence and Black civil rights. Smith ran the FOR's Free India Committee out of the Ashram, and in 1943, Ashram members—Reynolds among them—picketed the British Embassy in New York while Smith and Templin undertook an eight-day "sympathy fast" in Washington, DC, demanding Britain's release of Mahatma Gandhi.[17]

The Ashram's focus on racial justice was part of a larger effort among radical pacifists to make theirs a mass movement by connecting pacifism with the expanding civil rights movement.[18] Reynolds was like many young white radical pacifists in her readiness to embrace racial justice as her primary political cause. It was an intention she pledged to mother-turned-activist Annie Waller, who had stayed at the Ashram during a national tour funded by the Workers Defense League (WDL) and the National Association for the Advancement of Colored People (NAACP). At the time, Waller and WDL leader Pauli Murray were publicizing and fundraising for the case of Odell Waller, the nephew Annie Waller had raised as her own. Waller was a Black sharecropper from Virginia facing execution for the shooting death of his white landlord. Despite international pressure to commute the sentence, the state executed him in 1942.[19] Shortly after, Reynolds wrote Annie Waller a letter: "I am going to spend my life building friendships between negroes and white people. I am going to tell white people exactly what I think of them—why I am sometimes ashamed to be white. I am going to help them get some sense in their heads—or get the sense knocked out of mine in trying."[20]

Between 1941 and 1944, Reynolds joined other Ashram community participants in numerous civil rights actions, including an interracial walk from New York to Washington, DC, to protest poll taxes and a picketing campaign against New York City's segregated YMCAs.[21] At the Ashram itself, Reynolds was one of several young pacifists involved in the Congress of Racial Equality (CORE), one of the leading civil rights organizations of the twentieth century. Founded in 1942 by several young FOR members with the goal of developing Gandhian nonviolent direct action as a foundational tool for undermining racial discrimination in America, the CORE supported a New York branch that held Friday meetings at the Ashram.[22]

During this time, Reynolds remained resolute in the unconventional path that she was forging, despite parental disapproval. Reynolds recalled her mother warning against bringing any new acquaintances who were Black home to South Dakota. Reynolds responded with her characteristic direct-ness. "If my friends, of whatever hue, cannot come with me, I won't come myself," she recalled telling her mother. "And that was the end of that," meaning presumably that her mother dropped the issue. "On pacifism, they never understood it," Reynolds explained about her family members, but within a few years, her parents eventually "came to accept that [she] was an adult not cut in a pattern, and image of them."[23] She wrote Ashram colleagues during a visit home in 1943, "My folks still don't like the Ashram, and wish I would teach school, but are resigned to their fate." Still, she continued, "I think they're slightly proud of me, but they'd never say so."[24] The networks that Reynolds encountered through the Ashram, however, would send her in directions that would profoundly defy a life guided by the social conformity that her parents intended for her.

Reynolds's trajectory also diverged from some Ashram members. The global political and migration circuits of 1940s Harlem brought this community together within the walls of the Ashram, then sent them in different directions. Several emerged as leading civil rights activists. One-time Ashram resident and CORE founder James Farmer, for instance, organized numerous civil rights protests between the 1940s and 1960s, most prominently the 1961 Freedom Rides to desegregate interstate bus travel. James Peck, who frequented CORE meetings at the Ashram, also would gain national attention during the Freedom Rides, when a white mob in Alabama severely beat him for traveling on a racially integrated bus.[25] Others who spent time at the Ashram, however, increasingly focused on Puerto Rican independence. And it was Reynolds who took this interest the furthest. By 1944, she pivoted away from her civil rights and Free India activism and made the struggle for Puerto Rico's independence her life's work.

Shifting Focus to Puerto Rico

The Ashram's shift in attention to Puerto Rico was inspired by multiple contacts with Puerto Ricans in New York. By the 1940s, nearly 85 percent of all Puerto Ricans residing in North America lived in New York. While Puerto Rican migrants established communities throughout New York City, the neighborhood that stretched across several blocks in East and South Central Harlem—where the Ashram was located—was the city's largest Puerto Rican neighborhood. Residents called it *el barrio* (the neighborhood) and *la colonia hispana* (the Spanish colony).[26]

The roots of New York's Puerto Rican population stretched back to the nineteenth century. Puerto Ricans had migrated there in search of work and free political expression since before the 1898 US invasion. The majority, however, migrated to New York after 1898, and especially after Puerto Ricans became US citizens in 1917, with larger numbers arriving in the 1920s. With the inclusion of Puerto Rico in the US tariff system, US businesses profited by purchasing large swaths of farmland for sugarcane crops and turning Puerto Rico into a sugar monoculture. The disruption of local industry and land usage practices under US rule fueled under- and unemployment. Thousands sought work, first leaving the countryside for Puerto Rico's urban center and then leaving the archipelago altogether. Restrictions on European immigration during World War I created openings in manufacturing and service jobs in the United States, as did a robust economy during the 1920s. All of these factors led to substantial migration from Puerto Rico to New York. Even as high unemployment during the Depression resulted in reverse migration back to the archipelago in the 1930s, New York's Puerto Rican community continued to expand to over 61,000 by 1940.[27]

Reynolds and others were introduced to Puerto Rican independence politics through the Ashram's contact with two key individuals connected to New York's Puerto Rican community: Reverend Hipólito Cotto Reyes and Pedro Albizu Campos. Cotto Reyes was part of the ebb and flow that was active in *el barrio* associational life—the kind of leadership that occurred through institutional community-building. Cotto Reyes led a Spanish-speaking Baptist congregation located just blocks away from the 113th Street branch of the Harlem Ashram (see map 2.1).[28] As someone who had personally experienced the establishment of US rule over Puerto Rico, Cotto Reyes was an excellent messenger for relaying the hardships and humiliations that Puerto Ricans had experienced as a result of US control.

Born in 1890, when Puerto Rico was still a colony of Spain, Cotto Reyes was among the first generation of children who attended the public schools that the US government began organizing in 1899 as part of a larger project of consolidating US authority over the archipelago. US officials attempted to use these schools to mold students like Cotto Reyes into colonial subjects who welcomed the United States as a benevolent presence.[29] But, as a Baptist minister between the 1910s and 1930s, he witnessed the economic

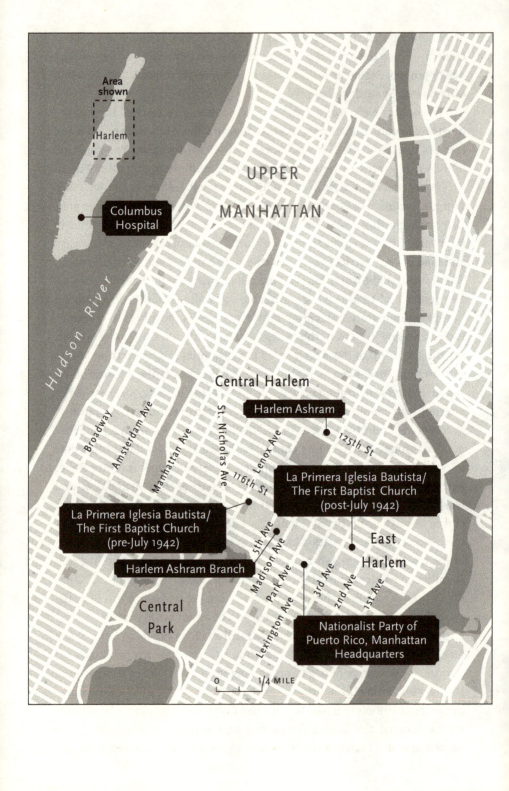

Area
shown

Harlem

Columbus
Hospital

Hudson River

UPPER

MANHATTAN

Central Harlem

Harlem Ashram

125th St

Broadway

Amsterdam Ave

Manhattan Ave

St. Nicholas Ave

Lenox Ave

116th St

La Primera Iglesia Bautista/
The First Baptist Church
(post-July 1942)

La Primera Iglesia Bautista/
The First Baptist Church
(pre-July 1942)

East
Harlem

Harlem Ashram Branch

5th Ave

Madison Ave

Park Ave

Lexington Ave

3rd Ave

2nd Ave

1st Ave

Central
Park

Nationalist Party of
Puerto Rico, Manhattan
Headquarters

0   1/4 MILE

hardships and political repression of Puerto Ricans across the archipelago.[30] The years that he served as a minister in Ponce, Yauco, and Carolina between 1922 and 1937 were especially difficult. The 1930s saw rising unemployment, widespread labor unrest, and increased tensions between the US colonial government and Puerto Rican nationalists.[31] Meanwhile, the Baptist Church, which had always struggled in the predominantly Catholic archipelago, witnessed a drastic reduction of financial support from members during the economic downturn of the 1930s. While the precipitous decline in jobs in New York led many Puerto Rican migrants to return to the archipelago in the 1930s, a job offer in New York provided a solution to Cotto Reyes's unstable financial situation.[32] In 1938, he relocated his family to upper Manhattan and began nearly a quarter-century as minister of New York's first Spanish-speaking Baptist congregation.[33]

In New York, Cotto Reyes added his pro-independence voice to a community already awash in such sentiment. Support for a sovereign Puerto Rico was long-standing among New York's Puerto Rican migrant population.[34] During the 1930s, however, calls for Puerto Rico's independence swelled across the community. The continued marginalization of Puerto Ricans in the United States—despite the extension of citizenship in 1917—and a wave of government violence against the pro-independence Nationalist Party in Puerto Rico precipitated this moment.[35] One of the most important chroniclers of the period, Bernardo Vega, who first migrated to New York in 1916, noticed a change in the political air after he returned to the city in 1939 after an extended time away. The longtime labor activist observed upon his return that "those who had belonged to radical groups had become staunch advocates of national independence." In this sense, Cotto Reyes was politically at home in *el barrio*, where support for the Nationalist Party agenda was widespread even among those who were not party members.[36]

MAP 2.1 (*opposite*) Location of the Harlem Ashram and the Harlem Ashram Branch in relation to Reverend Hipólito Cotto Reyes's congregation, the headquarters for the Nationalist Party in Manhattan, and Columbus Hospital. Source: Map created by Molly Roy. The locations of the Primera Iglesia Bautista/First Baptist Church and Nationalist Party headquarters in Manhattan are based on information from S. Soto Fontánez, *Misión a la Puerta: Una historia del trabajo Bautista hispano en Nueva York*. Santo Domingo: Editora Educativa Dominicana, 1982; Centro de Investigaciones Históricas, Colección Material Audiovisual: CDs / DVDs, Federal Bureau of Investigation, Carpetas de Organizaciones e Individuos Independentistas, serie: Partido Nacionalista de Puerto Rico (PNPR), subserie: 1–52, caja 1, número 19-A, subseries 5.

Reynolds and other Ashram members first met Cotto Reyes around the fall of 1941 or 1942, when the minister encountered them in the street and inquired about Ashram activities. Moving their conversation from the street to the Ashram apartment, where pro-India independence posters lay strewn about ready for future actions, Cotto Reyes channeled his encounters with US imperialism in Puerto Rico into a simple but powerful question to Ashram members: Why was the group protesting British imperialism instead of US imperialism? Reynolds later recalled that Cotto Reyes expressed surprise about their focus on England and India, given the fact that they were living in a Puerto Rican community.[37]

Emphasizing the transformative power of this initial meeting, Reynolds remembered, "It hit us between the eyes because we didn't have the slightest knowledge about what our government was doing in Puerto Rico. . . . We felt that a blow had been delivered to our thinking and we had to respond to it."[38] A series of meetings between Ashram members and Cotto Reyes ensued; the minister gave them a rudimentary education on the history of Puerto Rico and US involvement there, and these initial conversations became the first steps toward Ashram members' reevaluation of their anticolonial activism.[39]

For Reynolds, meeting Cotto Reyes was also the first step toward crafting her authority to speak for Puerto Rico's independence—as a patriotic but pacifist American defending US democracy. Reynolds recalled the strategic differences between independence activists and pacifists: "We couldn't look at this as pure abstraction, that we as pacifists support [only] independence movements that are pacifist in nature. . . . We had to say, 'we as pacifist[s] oppose all imperialism and especially, that of our own government wherever it is.'" It was a crucial moment in the development of Reynolds's ideas about allyship when she and her colleagues chose to collaborate across ideological divides. At this juncture, Ashram members who expressed solidarity with the cause of Puerto Rican independence highlighted their Americanness when concluding that they could not "take a position of liberty for other peoples half way around the world, without taking a position of liberty for those whom our own government is oppressing."[40]

By the winter of 1944, Ashram members had officially expanded their anti-imperial agenda to include Puerto Rico's independence as part of their demands. The January 26 New York poster walk that serves as the opening vignette to this chapter was, in fact, a key moment in Ashram members' protest efforts against US imperialism in Puerto Rico.[41] Twenty-one protesters from seven organizations—including the New York FOR, the Free India Committee of the FOR, the New York chapter of the March on Washington Movement, CORE, the Modern Trend Progressive Youth Group, the Socialist Party of New York, and the Young People's Socialist League—traveled on foot from the Ashram, through Harlem's Puerto Rican community, and then by subway to Brooklyn, in order to picket the British consulate located there.[42]

Reynolds and her fellow protesters strategically took advantage of US postwar promises of a world free of colonial relationships to point out the hypocrisy of continued US control of Puerto Rico. In a statement issued to the press, the activist groups involved in the protest made explicit their assertion that US control of Puerto Rico was part of a worldwide system of imperial relations that included British colonialism in India. They lambasted the hypocrisy of the US and Britain's World War II aims of promoting self-determination while remaining imperial powers themselves. "Do people need to be *saved* from democracy?" protesters asked in their issued statement. "It does not make sense!" Yet, as the statement declared, "that is exactly what the United States is doing in Puerto Rico and England in India" by maintaining these colonial systems. It roared, "SAVING MILLIONS FROM THE 'MENACE' OF FREEDOM *is hardly in harmony with the Atlantic Charter*"—the agreement that established the agenda for the postwar world based on political and economic freedoms.[43]

With generous capitalization and underlining throughout, the statement further denounced leading members of the United Nations, "*whose cause is made a mockery as long as empire, in any form, is allowed to endure.*" The statement's authors also invoked President Franklin Roosevelt's 1941 State of the Union speech, which called for "a world founded upon four essential human freedoms," when they urged "all true patriots who care for the four freedoms, or any freedom to speak and act against the sabotage of the aims of this war."[44] The Allies could not have it both ways, protesters insisted: "Either this war *is* for freedom, or it is *not*." And if World War II was, indeed, a war for freedom, then the United States had to end its imperial rule in Puerto Rico. According to protesters, "nothing can sabotage [the United States'] moral front more than repression against any genuine liberty movement." From the protesters' perspective, what was at stake was nothing less than the meaning of America and American democracy. They insisted, "IT SHOULD BE MADE CLEAR THAT AMERICA MEANS THE END OF ALL EMPIRE, and that *unless the war is to end empire it is not America's war.*"[45]

Protesters not only pointed to the hypocrisy of the World War II Allies' war aims; they compared Puerto Rico and India's demands for independence to America's own struggles for independence. They argued that India and Puerto Rico's freedom fighters were no different from America's own founding fathers. "In both Puerto Rico and India great liberators, like our own George Washington, Thomas Jefferson, and the other fathers of our American democracy," they asserted in the issued statement, "languish in prisons not better than those of Nazi tyranny . . . for no reason except that THEY WANT LIBERTY, just as our fathers wanted it, ENOUGH TO STRUGGLE FOR IT."[46]

Protesters further asserted that President Abraham Lincoln's decision to issue the Emancipation Proclamation declaring the end of slavery in the midst of the Civil War showed "every war for a righteous end has a moral front more important than all the military fronts." The Allies, they asserted, had lost that "moral front" by maintaining colonial holdings. Loosely paraphrasing Lincoln's famous "House Divided" speech—"THE WORLD CAN NOT LONGER REMAIN HALF SLAVE AND HALF FREE"—protesters argued that American empire preserved such an "incompatible" divide of a "free world and an imperialist world." Emphasizing their commitment to ending war, they asserted that war would never cease "unless this basic aggression, imperialism, is ended."[47] It was their belief that the United States and the United Kingdom should lead the way.

After her arrest, watching from the back of a police paddy wagon as a crowd of spectators, police, and press gathered around her and the other arrestees, Reynolds leaned forward and looked directly into photographer Wilbert Blanche's camera. She smiled as he snapped a picture, perhaps with an expression of pride, and justifiably so. Reynolds had rejected social conventions that discouraged women's public protest. She had demonstrated her willingness to risk arrest and incarceration—a role more commonly played by male colleagues who could claim pacifist movement authority through draft resistance.

When Blanche's photograph appeared in the New York paper *PM* the next day, it caught the attention of Pedro Albizu Campos, the charismatic leader of the Puerto Rican Nationalist Party. He read the protest coverage from his Columbus Hospital room in midtown Manhattan. Albizu Campos, who at the time was receiving treatment for a heart condition, was curious. He asked Julio Pinto Gandía, his right-hand man and key contact with the world outside his hospital room, about why he had not yet met Reynolds.[48]

Meeting Don Pedro

Born in 1891 when Puerto Rico was still under Spanish rule, Albizu Campos grew up on the outskirts of Ponce. His mother, Juliana Campos, was an unmarried domestic worker of African descent. His father, Alejandro Albizu Romero, was an already married scion of a white-criollo Basque-Venezuelan family. Until his wife's death many years later, Albizu Romero did not extend the name Albizu to his son born out of wedlock. The Campos surname derived from Adolfo Campos, a hacienda owner who enslaved Albizu Campos's maternal grandparents and, until the end of legalized slavery in 1873, likely his mother as well. Albizu Campos's mother died when he was only four years old. His maternal aunt raised him and his siblings thereafter.[49]

An excellent pupil, Albizu Campos attended the University of Vermont in 1912 with a scholarship funded by the Masonic Lodge of Ponce, part of the Freemason fraternal order that professed a belief in a supreme being but rejected religious doctrine.[50] In 1914, he transferred to Harvard University, where he earned a bachelor's degree in 1916 and his law degree in 1923, becoming the first Afro-Latino graduate of Harvard Law School. In the midst of his studies, Albizu Campos delayed the completion of his law degree to serve in the army during World War I.[51] In 1922, Albizu Campos married Laura Meneses del Carpio, a Radcliffe student from Peru he met in Boston.[52] That same year, Union Party dissidents established the Nationalist Party of Puerto Rico after the United States successfully pressured Union Party leadership to remove independence from its platform.[53] In 1924, Albizu Campos joined the newly formed Nationalist Party. As a Nationalist Party member, he embarked on multiple trips across Latin America in order to foster mutual support toward a shared struggle against US imperialism in the region.[54]

Between entering college in 1912 and joining the Nationalist Party in 1924, Albizu Campos cultivated global anticolonial networks and innovated a syncretic vision of national liberation that drew on Catholic, Irish, and Indian independence ideologies.[55] Anthony Stevens-Arroyo argues that Albizu Campos's introduction to the Irish Catholic nationalism of Boston clergy and his membership in the Irish-Catholic Knights of Cambridge fueled his evolution away from Masonic free-thinking to a nationalist Catholicism that intertwined faith with independence politics.[56]

Through his leadership of the student-run Cosmopolitan Club and other Harvard networks, Albizu Campos encountered anticolonial leaders from India and Ireland, and he studied their diverse approaches to challenging

British colonial rule—from civil disobedience, to nonviolent resistance, to armed rebellion.[57] Albizu Campos was particularly inspired by the political thought of James Connolly, the Irish nationalist executed for leading the 1916 Irish rebellion. This included Connolly's creation of an Irish Citizen Army to serve as a military unit of the Irish independence struggle and his embrace of a just war theory rooted in the teachings of Catholic philosopher Thomas Aquinas.[58]

After he became president of the Nationalist Party in 1930, Albizu Campos focused his syncretic political ideas and legal acumen on transforming the Nationalist Party into a bold resistance movement. He energized the aspirations of anticolonialists who referred to him as "El Maestro." He also drew the ire of powerful opponents. Then when the party ran a slate of candidates in the 1932 election under Albizu Campos's leadership, it was with limited results. However, Albizu Campos also led several labor actions in the early 1930s, including the 1934 cane workers strike. Under his leadership, striking cane workers shut down sugar production across Puerto Rico. Their strike also tossed out the unfavorable contract that their union leadership—a subsidiary of the US-based American Federation of Labor—had negotiated with sugar plantation owners.[59]

Then, in 1935, Albizu Campos publicly announced armed resistance as a tool of the movement. He did so following the police killing of four Nationalists in an episode known as the Río Piedras Massacre, as well as in the wake of a smear campaign and rumored assassination plot against him. He denounced the insular police, the National Guard of Puerto Rico, and the US military as combatants. He also declared a state of war against the government of the United States.[60] The party did not engage in or support indiscriminate violence.

Albizu Campos grounded his views on armed struggle in international law and his belief that sovereign nations had a moral and legal right to defend their population from abuse. Puerto Rico had been a sovereign nation since 1897, he maintained, when Spain issued the Autonomy Charter acknowledging its colony's right to self-government. Albizu Campos thus denounced the 1899 Treaty of Paris as invalid with regard to Puerto Rico. Under international law, the Harvard-trained legal scholar insisted, Spain did not have the right to give the sovereign nation of Puerto Rico to the United States in the treaty that ended the Spanish-American War; Puerto Rico had neither participated in the treaty's writing nor approved it.

Alongside militarizing the Nationalist Party, Albizu Campos advanced a strategy of *retraimiento*, that is, withdrawal from and refusal to participate in US institutions.[61] The Nationalist Party repudiated cooperation with a government it considered illegitimate—either the US federal or local colonial government. Likewise, Nationalist Party supporters refused US military conscription and subsequent participation in elections under US rule.[62] By the close of the 1930s, however, the Nationalist Party's top male leadership, including Albizu Campos, was serving sentences at the federal penitentiary in Atlanta. In 1936, a federal court in Puerto Rico had found him and other top Nationalist Party leaders guilty of inciting rebellion.

Albizu Campos's conviction was the culmination of ongoing government efforts to silence him. The local colonial government perceived a threat in his growing popularity, as evident in the archipelago-wide demonstrations he inspired and the momentum behind his plan for a constitutional assembly that would draft a constitution for a free Puerto Rico—without US involvement or approval. The 1936 assassination of Colonel Francis Riggs, the head of the insular police, to avenge the 1935 Río Piedras Massacre accelerated US efforts to crush the Nationalist Party. But as Marisa Rosado points out, government plans to arrest Nationalist Party leadership were already in the works well before the dramatic Riggs assassination and police execution of the two suspects under custody. Thus, in 1937, after a failed appeal, the federal government transported Albizu Campos from Puerto Rico to the Atlanta Federal Penitentiary to complete the ten-year sentence.[63]

By the mid-1940s, several leaders were out of prison but still in New York. Meanwhile, in the summer of 1943, Albizu Campos was transferred to Columbus Hospital in Manhattan because of a serious heart condition—though he was still completing his sentence.[64] He remained at Columbus Hospital until the fall of 1945.[65] While just as far away from his beloved homeland as he had been for the preceding seven years spent in Atlanta, he was only several blocks away from the largest Puerto Rican community outside the archipelago: *el barrio* in Harlem.

In New York, Pinto Gandía was Albizu Campos's right-hand man. A lifelong Nationalist whose "life within the Party," as Reynolds recalled, "rose and fell over the years," Pinto Gandía had become active in the struggle for Puerto Rican independence in his twenties.[66] He had been one of several lawyers who defended Albizu Campos and other Nationalist Party leaders during their first trial in 1935.[67] Twenty years younger than Albizu Campos, in 1937, he assumed control of the party after the imprisonment of Albizu Campos and the party's other upper leadership.[68] In 1938, he was among eight Nationalist Party leaders who were convicted of attempting to assassinate the judge who had handed down Albizu Campos's conviction. Pinto

Gandía was sentenced to five years in prison at federal penitentiaries in the US South.[69] When he completed his sentence in 1943, he went to New York City. He immediately resumed his work with the Nationalist Party through daily meetings with Albizu Campos in his Columbus Hospital room.

Pinto Gandía's path to the Harlem Ashram came by way of the time he spent in federal prison and the ties that he established there with conscientious objectors. During World War II, the US federal penitentiary system operated as its own type of global political laboratory, bringing together men whose cities of origin and politics would otherwise have made their meeting unlikely. Men like Pinto Gandía, who accepted armed rebellion as a political strategy, encountered radical pacifists who rejected violence as a tool of resistance. While many peace activists concluded that the Nazi threat required their support of the US war effort, the radical pacifist men Pinto Gandía met had chosen incarceration over either draft registration or detention at a Civil Public Service camp for conscientious objectors. They insisted that even the camp bolstered the militaristic power of the state.

Through these encounters, radical pacifist and Nationalist Party men crafted political bonds grounded in male forms of resistance to state power and mainstream ideas about masculinity. In particular, the Nationalist Party's draft resistance pointed to agendas that this unlikely political pairing might develop beyond prison. In 1939, as part of the larger strategy of *retraimiento*, Albizu Campos had urged supporters to organize against compulsory service in order to escalate the party's insurgency.[70] He decried a US imperial government that denied Puerto Rico equal status, yet expected Puerto Ricans to make their sons "cannon fodder," as he put it, for the US war machine.[71] By the early 1940s, the US government increased arrests of Nationalist Party members who opposed the draft. Pinto Gandía had served time for an assassination attempt, but he also represented a political organization that, like radical pacifists, refused to participate in US wars.

Notably, pacifist men could rebuff charges of effeminacy by cultivating ties with Nationalist Party men, whose support of armed revolt more closely aligned with martial masculinity. In a culture that typecast men who rejected military service as effeminate, pacifist men asserted a defensive masculinity that characterized their imprisonment as the ultimate expression of masculine courage.[72] While incarcerated, they also sought ties with fellow prisoners who fit a recognizable stereotype of virile masculinity resting on aggressive physicality.[73]

In 1943, Pinto Gandía was invited to the Ashram for a meal by Alfred Winslow, a draft resister who had met Pinto Gandía while both were incarcerated in Petersburg, Virginia, and who had found a temporary home at the Harlem Ashram following release. Additional meals with Pinto Gandía and other Nationalist Party members at the Ashram followed; the guests helped their hosts deepen the lessons in Puerto Rican history that Cotto Reyes had begun. It was as a result of these varied conversations that Harlem Ashram members developed their belief that Puerto Rico should be an independent, sovereign nation and decided to mobilize on behalf of Puerto Rican independence.[74]

Thus, when Albizu Campos saw Reynolds's photo in the paper and asked Pinto Gandía why he had not yet met her, it was a good question. After all, Pinto Gandía had put him in touch with other Harlem Ashram members prior to the protest that led to Reynolds's arrest. It had been around the same time that Cotto Reyes—an admirer of Albizu Campos—was providing those early informal lessons on Puerto Rican history.[75] Despite her enthusiasm for what she had learned about Puerto Rico's status politics from Cotto Reyes and then Pinto Gandía and other Nationalists, it took Albizu Campos's direct request to meet her for Reynolds to finally connect with the party's top leader.

The gendered politics of the Ashram, where Reynolds played a supporting role to Smith's leadership style, contributed to this delay. As Reynolds described, "I didn't go see him for months, partly because by that time I was the assistant director of the Ashram and Jay [Smith] was spending all his time down there in that hospital room." Smith was among a string of leftist activists, including literary figure Pearl Buck, who made multiple visits to the ailing leader.[76] As Reynolds recalled, "Pinto would say, 'When are you coming to see Don Pedro?' and I'd say, 'Look Pinto, one person there is enough. How are we going to run this establishment?'"[77]

While Reynolds was not a part of these initial meetings in Albizu Campos's hospital room, she felt their immediate effect as a result of the enormous influence Albizu Campos had on Smith. Alongside the conversations with Cotto Reyes, it was Smith's discussions with Albizu Campos that inspired the Ashram's decision to include Puerto Rico in the "poster walk"— the demonstration that led to Reynolds's first arrest. Several days before the protest, Smith had written a letter as chairman of the Free India Committee announcing a simultaneous demonstration in Washington, DC, and calling for other local actions demanding the independence of India and Puerto Rico. Smith urged fellow activists, "We must come to life on the Puerto Rico issue." He bolstered his call to action by pointing to an illustrious group of pacifists and civil rights activists who also sought to initiate a campaign denouncing US imperialism in Puerto Rico: "A. J. [Muste], Pearl Buck, Norman Thomas, A. Philip Randolph, Bayard Rustin and many others," he explained, "have shown a keen interest in an exposé campaign for which there is an abundance of really amazing material."[78]

Indeed, Smith attributed his conversion to the cause of Puerto Rican independence to his "many visits to 'the Puerto Rican Gandhi' Dr. Pedro Albizu Campos, who has been recuperating from six years' poor treatment in [an] Atlanta prison." It was a significant moment—a group of pacifist activists aligning in purpose with a party leader who had openly embraced armed resistance as a political tactic. Smith elaborated in a 1944 article titled "The Gandhi of Puerto Rico" that while Albizu Campos had not "taken an outright pacifist" position, he held many similarities to the Indian nationalists—from their experiences serving in imperial armies, to noncooperation with the imperial government, to demands for the imperialist government's immediate withdrawal.[79] In a letter to supporters, Smith concluded, "Surely the idea of doing our best to make atonement for the sins of our country against our Puerto Rican neighbors will motivate us."[80]

For Reynolds, her eventual meeting with Albizu Campos was as important for the development of her political thinking as Smith's interactions with the Nationalist Party leader had been on his. Years later, Reynolds described it as a personal political turning point. She also described Albizu Campos's charisma in some detail: "This was a man of extreme intelligence and charm. He knew how to examine, to talk to a person on a first visit, ask questions in a way that felt [like] he was giving undivided attention. And . . . after he had asked questions, gotten answers for a period of say, half an hour, he knew that person completely. That was my experience with him and what I saw on other occasions with other people."[81] She said she "was immediately enchanted with his personality, goodness, intelligence, his absolute dedication to the independence of Puerto Rico."[82]

The meeting between her and Albizu Campos in February 1944 would begin an enduring political affiliation.[83] They shared a mutual deep affection, but the relationship was neither romantic nor sexual in nature. Their relationship was a "dissident friendship" grounded in commitment to a free Puerto Rico. Their conversations took place primarily in English. Albizu Campos was fluent in multiple languages, and Reynolds did not yet speak Spanish. It was nurtured through "hospitality in the midst of divisive political structures"—for instance, meals at the Ashram (in the case of Pinto Gandía) and conversations at the hospital.[84] It was Reynolds's impression that after a month or two, Albizu Campos "felt that he knew me well enough so that he could trust me in several ways with confidential information" about his background.[85] Trust and mutual respect remained a hallmark of their friendship in ways that enabled the depth of Reynolds's insight into US colonialism in Puerto Rico that few outsiders had at the time.

The racial and gender prohibitions of the era should have made it difficult for Albizu Campos, the married, mixed-race leader of the Nationalist Party, and Reynolds, a single, white woman with limited activist experience, to forge a lasting political relationship. Yet the cosmopolitanism of 1940s Harlem—the product of colonial migration, repression, and resistance—made this unlikely political alliance possible.

Decades later, Reynolds recalled fondly how much she learned from Albizu Campos. They spoke frankly with each other about many subjects— family, diplomacy, sexuality and politics, and the art of public speaking. Albizu Campos shared, for example, why he thought adopting a diplomatic tone was so important: it boxed in the colonizer. Reynolds recalled the following conversation:

> I asked him once about his courtesy to his enemies. He said, "You never went to Harvard, did you?" I said, "I was there one day."
> He said, "You don't know what the purpose of the rules of polite conduct are. You don't need all these rules to deal with your friends. You need them to deal with your enemies because otherwise there can be no conversation at all and there has to be conversation and negotiation, discussion with people of the opposing camp. The only way these conversations can be conducted is through a regimen on both sides of polite regulation. . . . You talk about diplomatic relationships and they are polite, though people are cutting each other's throats."[86]

Courtesy in conversations, moreover, protected the colonized. "The [Puerto Ricans] who are doing the dirty work for the United States government don't like it," Albizu Campos shared. As he continued, "I do berate them publicly, but not as individuals, as a class but if I happen to see them somewhere and have to talk to them, if I let down my guard of good manners, they have a further excuse to behave worse."[87]

Reynolds also remembered Albizu Campos's broad vision. He recognized every Puerto Rican as a potential nationalist. Just as important were members of the Harlem Ashram, as he believed that North Americans had a role to play in advancing Puerto Rican independence. Reynolds recalled that Albizu Campos "would give us any help that he knew how."[88]

Indeed, Reynolds learned public speaking from Albizu Campos during that period, as did her Ashram roommate Jean Wiley, and another US activist named Thelma Mielke. Albizu Campos had a reputation as a tremendous orator; he drew crowds in the thousands to hear him speak. Each week, Reynolds, Wiley, and Mielke met individually with Albizu Campos for an hour to work on public speaking. Reynolds described her lessons: "We were supposed to prepare a brief speech, 15, 20 minutes on some subject. He didn't care what subject, then we'd make our speech and he would criticize it." As much as she enjoyed the lessons, she concluded, "I think he enjoyed" them as well.[89]

Reynolds's ideas about solidarity with Puerto Rico initially took root in a very specific historical moment—that is, when public support for independence was a vibrant part of *el barrio*'s political culture. Migrants like Cotto Reyes and Nationalist Party leaders like Pinto Gandía and Albizu Campos reached out across the different life experiences that separated them from residents of the Harlem Ashram. The opportunity to discuss the implications of US colonialism in Puerto Rico with her Ashram colleagues, Nationalist supporters, and especially Albizu Campos helped Reynolds to craft her ideas about why and how to support the cause of independence.

Reynolds's conversion to the cause of Puerto Rican independence, which began with informal conversations with Cotto Reyes, deepened during 1944 with regular visits with Albizu Campos. "Within a month or so of knowing Don Pedro," she recalled, "I really felt that I had to commit myself to the struggle for the independence of Puerto Rico, and that it had to be primarily with North Americans, who like myself, felt it to be . . . the holding of Puerto Rico, to be an outrage to any principles we have." She explained, "Though I was in almost daily contact with Don Pedro, . . . the first thing we did actually was to start the formation of a group of North Americans to work for the independence of Puerto Rico."[90] Inspired by her conversations with Albizu Campos, Reynolds helped to found the American League for Puerto Rico's Independence (ALPRI) in 1944, and through it, Reynolds transformed herself from a supporter and helpmate in pacifist circles into a leading voice in the Puerto Rican independence movement.

3 Washington, DC

On April 26, 1945, Ruth Reynolds stood in front of a panel of US senators preparing to vote on a congressional bill outlining a pathway to Puerto Rico's independence. World War II had just ended, the conference that would establish the United Nations was just weeks away, and the world seemed to be on the brink of massive decolonization. Reynolds was determined that the United States be on the right side of history. "It is necessary for American citizens in each generation," she told the panel of senators before her, "to endeavor to rectify the mistakes of their fathers and to guide our nation according to the principles of liberty for all mankind that have been the core of American philosophy from the days of Thomas Jefferson until now." She insisted, "It is our sacred and patriotic duty in this period of history to see to it that our government withdraws from Puerto Rico, so that that nation may take its place as a sovereign American republic, and so that our nation may stand before the world free from any suggestion of imperialist ambition."[1]

Reynolds was an unconventional figure to serve as a champion of Puerto Rico's independence in Congress. She was a white, North American woman who had never even traveled to Puerto Rico. In fact, she had only recently learned about Puerto Rico's long struggle for independence from the United States. Since 1944, she had acquired much of this new knowledge during hospital visits with Pedro Albizu Campos, the bold leader of the pro-independence Nationalist Party of Puerto Rico, who was receiving medical treatment in New York. Clearly a quick and dedicated learner, here she was, just a year later, addressing the most powerful legislative body in the United States as a spokesperson for Puerto Rico's independence.

Though new to the struggle for Puerto Rico's national sovereignty, Reynolds made the journey from informal conversations with Albizu Campos to the hallowed halls of Congress by helping to establish the American League for Puerto Rico's Independence (ALPRI). Contact with Nationalist Party members in New York inspired Reynolds to shift her activist focus from the Black civil rights and Indian independence movements—which she had concentrated on as a member of the Harlem Ashram—to the cause of Puerto Rico's independence. Through the ALPRI, Reynolds was instrumental in bringing together activists who were not of Puerto Rican descent but who championed anticolonialism.

In her role as an ALPRI representative, Reynolds advanced her emerging ideas about allyship by strategically employing what set her apart from the Nationalist Party as well as what she held in common with US senators: patriotism toward the United States. By contrast, Nationalist Party members did not recognize the United States as their government and thus rejected participation in the Senate hearings. While Reynolds also objected to US governance of Puerto Rico, she recognized Congress as her *own* government. As such, she was perfectly positioned to address the members of Congress on the topic of Puerto Rican independence not as a spokesperson for the Nationalist Party but as an ally to its cause.

Significantly, Reynolds rejected membership in the Nationalist Party, or any Puerto Rican political group. This was a stance that she would maintain for the rest of her life. For her, such a distinction in membership was tied to the difference between lobbying for Puerto Rico's independence and lobbying for "what Puerto Rico should or should not do with independence." Both were the work of Puerto Rican political organizations. Non–Puerto Ricans like herself, Reynolds maintained, should only do the former, because doing the latter was merely "another form of imperialism."[2] This conviction was a critical facet of her solidarity that recognized the experiences and positionality of Puerto Ricans as colonial subjects, as well as her own positionality as a colonizing citizen.

Indeed, her overarching approach to solidarity activism in the wake of World War II was to work within the limits and through the privileges of existing power structures to advocate for an independent Puerto Rico. Reynolds made the most of her privileged identity as a white citizen of the United States—a colonizing nation—to confront its leading politicians and pundits. At the same time, she carefully navigated the gender politics that privileged male leadership in the activist community from which the ALPRI drew members. On the ground, this meant uniting with other founding ALPRI women members and using their collective voice to ensure the new organization's uncompromising focus on ending US rule in Puerto Rico.

Establishing the American League for Puerto Rico's Independence

In the fall of 1944, as her North American activist circles learned about Puerto Rico's status as a US colony and debated an appropriate response,

Reynolds was working tirelessly behind the scenes to ensure that an un-compromising approach to Puerto Rican independence prevailed as the guiding impulse among her American compatriots. An uncompromising approach meant working for immediate and full independence for Puerto Rico, and nothing else—no continuing US military presence, no economic privileges, and no alternative governing status for the archipelago. Meeting with Albizu Campos in his hospital room and connecting with other mostly female activists, she gathered support and momentum for the creation of a new and unprecedented leftist initiative—an organization of non–Puerto Rican Americans who would mobilize in the United States for immediate and total independence.

Through early outreach, Reynolds and a handful of activist colleagues sought to expand the involvement of New York–based activists of the liberal Left—not only pacifists—by emphasizing the urgency of the moment. As a recruiting letter explained, the emerging organization aimed to fulfill a "moral obligation to inform and enlist our fellow Americans to press for the earliest possible resolving of the Puerto Rican issue" and to prevent a "new era of imperialism." The letter continued, "All signs point to this as the strategic time to tackle this strategic issue."[3]

This sense of urgency likely stemmed from contradictory political developments. There were signs that Congress could be moved toward legislating Puerto Rico's freedom, though not without significant intervention to make it a just and authentic freedom. In 1943, the Puerto Rican legislature unanimously called on the US government to end "the colonial system of government" and allow the people of Puerto Rico to determine their own political status through free and democratic elections.[4] An independence bill followed with several of those glaring caveats that Reynolds, in alliance with her Nationalist Party contacts, opposed. However, the bill ultimately died by the end of 1944, before Reynolds was positioned to lobby against such caveats in alliance with like-minded North Americans in her new organization.[5]

At the same time, it appeared that an even more robust lobbying intervention was needed—and quickly—at the international level. There were many indications that the United States was backing away from its 1941 Atlantic Charter commitment of working toward a postwar world order based on national self-determination. Already, the Allied powers had moved to exclude colonial voices from any future United Nations at the heart of this new world order. At the 1944 Dumbarton Oaks Conference in Washington, DC, a wartime planning session for a United Nations organization was underway at the very same time that Reynolds was organizing the ALPRI along with several activist colleagues, including Jay Holmes Smith and Thelma Mielke. The Dumbarton Oaks Conference included the "Big Three"— the United States, the Soviet Union, and Great Britain. And it was clear that they were actively and strategically limiting their own exposure to criticism from colonial subjects under their rule by limiting membership in the United Nations to only nation-states.[6]

Amid these developments, Reynolds and her colleagues initially pursued a strategy for building a broad-based coalition opposed to Puerto Rico's colonial status. They did this by inviting leaders from diverse liberal-Left groups to join their new organization. In attendance at the first meeting, for instance, were such activist luminaries as American Civil Liberties Union (ACLU) executive director Roger Baldwin; the National Council of Jewish Women's Elsie Elfenbein; civil rights activist George Schuyler; Brotherhood of Sleeping Car Porters leaders A. Philip Randolph and Ashley Totten; founding NAACP and American Anti-Imperialist League member Oswald Garrison Villard; and publisher Richard J. Walsh, who along with Pearl Buck had led a World War II campaign to repeal Chinese exclusion from the United States.[7]

At these early meetings, however, it seemed that what Puerto Rican self-determination actually meant was up for debate, as was what the new organization's purpose should be in supporting it. The stakes were high. The results of these debates would ultimately influence whether this new organization would replicate hierarchical relationships between colonizer and colonized in its formulation of allyship. The decisions made in those early meetings would also determine the degree to which New Deal alliances and anticommunism would blunt membership and policy.

Some early participants agreed with Reynolds that only full and immediate independence was worth seeking. Others favored a referendum where Puerto Ricans would choose among different status options. Still others questioned whether they should even tackle Puerto Rico's status politics at all, arguing that the group should focus on uncontroversial charitable work like fundraising to provide milk to impoverished children there. Those in the latter camp believed that status debates should be left to Puerto Ricans.

Initially, participants called their new organization the National Committee for Puerto Rico, but Reynolds and a handful of like-minded colleagues navigated liberal political agendas and conflicting ideas about allyship until their agenda prevailed. Thus, the final name signified the group's commitment to Puerto Rico's status as a fully independent nation. They became the American League for Puerto Rico's Independence.

It was not an easy journey. Notably, for example, Reynolds's unyielding focus on independence made her wary of liberal leaders willing to temporarily put aside their own protest agendas during wartime. Roger Baldwin's insistence that the organization they were creating focus on charitable activities in Puerto Rico rather than the politics of status, Reynolds believed, reflected the ACLU's priorities to maintain close ties with President Roosevelt, whom the ACLU's leadership valued as a liberal ally.[8] The organization's reluctance to handle sedition cases or forcefully contest Japanese American incarceration reflected an ACLU understanding with the administration to limit actions that would embarrass Roosevelt.[9] In this context, Reynolds quite reasonably suspected that Baldwin's opposition to an independence league was part of a larger pattern of suspending wartime challenges of the administration. Clearly, an organization of non–Puerto Rican Americans challenging US control of the territory and the fact that the United States was maintaining a colony in the Caribbean would highlight the hypocrisy of US wartime rhetoric promoting national self-determination. However, despite her distrust of Baldwin's seemingly uncritical faith in Roosevelt as a defender of liberal democracy, Reynolds still initially welcomed ACLU involvement because its influence on the US liberal Left at the time was critical for building any kind of mass movement.

By contrast, Reynolds was unwilling to yield to redbaiting. Such a stance mattered both because of the significance of pro-independence communist voices and because many liberal organizations in the United States had ejected communist members in order to limit their exposure to redbaiting. But the Communist Party USA had lent its support to the Nationalist Party since the 1920s, and a CPUSA attorney (sent by Congressman Vito Marcantonio and the CPUSA's secretary general Earl Browder) was among those who accompanied Albizu Campos in his transfer from the Atlanta Federal Penitentiary to Columbus Hospital in 1943.[10]

That refusal to bow to redbaiting cost Reynolds some ACLU support. Baldwin's longtime ACLU colleague Norman Thomas attended some early meetings but withdrew after he learned that US representative Vito Marcantonio was also scheduled to speak at a sponsored event. Marcantonio had been the most vocal congressional proponent of Puerto Rican rights since the 1930s, and he had served as co-counsel for Albizu Campos's second trial in Puerto Rico.[11] Though not a Communist, Marcantonio had ties with the American Communist Party.[12] Thomas, a staunch anticommunist who had helped to expel Communist director Elizabeth Gurley Flynn from the ACLU, thus refused to participate in the ALPRI's formation.[13]

As Reynolds later recalled, Thomas's withdrawal was a significant pivot point in the development of her ideas about coalition-building. It was "the end of whatever honeymoon we had with that [liberal] tradition on the issue of Puerto Rico's independence," she said. Given Thomas's considerable influence on ACLU direction, his opposition, she explained, was fatal to mobilizing American liberals.[14] Indeed, it was a critical moment in her stance of radical solidarity. She saw with clarity that there was a cost to a stubborn focus on independence above all. Still, some ACLU leadership, including its president John Haynes Holmes, continued to lend nominal support, presumably giving permission for his name to appear in official letters.[15]

Tensions brewed within the fragile coalition in other ways. Jay Holmes Smith, for example, was willing to negotiate goals and purpose, calling for compromise and the inclusion of diverse views on the status question—something Reynolds and other female colleagues like Thelma Mielke and Pearl Buck rejected.[16] Nearly Reynolds's same age, Mielke was a white activist from Rochester, New York, who like Reynolds became interested in the Nationalist Party through her acquaintance with Albizu Campos in New York.[17] Buck, the Pulitzer Prize–winning author of *The Good Earth* and other best-selling novels, had also met Albizu Campos during his time in New York. Her mobilization against US control of Puerto Rico, as well as for India's independence through the India League of America, supplemented her central focus on running the East and West Association—an organization she had founded to educate Americans about Asia.[18] Collectively, these women insisted that the sole purpose of this inchoate organization was to lobby fellow Americans to support an independent Puerto Rico. In fact, it was the tenacity with which they clung to this vision that illuminates how radical their approach to allyship really was. It was no easy task to convince left-wing organizations to support their mission when they made few concessions to those much-bigger organizations' views on how things should be done.

Indeed, it was in community with this small group of women that Reynolds navigated conflicts associated with launching a solidarity organization in the midst of the postwar geopolitical and ideological changes sweeping the nation and the world. As Reynolds stubbornly asserted, "We are organizing to get Americans to do what they should in regard to Puerto Rico." Mielke similarly insisted that the organization had to frame its approach to the status debate "as Americans interested in liberty." Buck argued for ejecting participants uninterested in independence.[19] She found support in pacifist Jean Wiley, Reynolds's roommate at the Ashram, and Yolanda Moreno, Albizu Campos's former nurse at Columbus Hospital.

When disagreements over purpose and messaging emerged, this group of women favored fewer allies committed to an uncompromising support of independence over more allies who were not as committed. Such clarity of purpose came at the expense of building the broad coalition leadership initially envisioned for the new organization, and it led to conflict with influential men within their own activist circles. However, this clarity also ensured a strong base of support—despite the group's smaller size—to endure through the profound challenges of demanding that the United States leave Puerto Rico. It helped them weather surveillance, harassment, and dismissal without wavering in their collective commitment.

Still, while Reynolds rejected compromise on the issue of independence, she was uncertain of how to protect this agenda that she, Mielke, Wiley, Moreno, and Buck so strongly favored. As she recalled years later, Smith and his yielding ways on the question of independence had made her and her allies "simply furious." She noted that she and Mielke, Wiley, and Moreno "were four women . . . and while we ha[d] some kinds of brains, we had no prestige. At all. And the man whom we had been working with, whom we thought could lead this organization, [Smith] ha[d] shown weakness that we did not expect." In search of solutions, this stalwart group of women consulted Albizu Campos, who, by Reynolds's account, offered an analysis of gender inequity in leftist politics as well as a strategy. Given that the US Left often dismissed women's opinions and offered them limited leadership opportunities of the sort that seemed to accrue to male authority and offer political prestige, he encouraged the four women to maintain steady behind-the-scenes pressure, stay the course in pushing for a league for independence, and use Jay Holmes Smith for what he could offer them. "You women," he told her, "have the brains. . . . You have what it takes."[20]

Indeed, though Smith had been an Albizu Campos ally at the Harlem Ashram, Albizu Campos concluded that Smith was weak. Reynolds recalled Albizu Campos calling him "a good man" but saying that he was too eager to compromise and that the four women had to lead instead. Nevertheless, Albizu Campos advised placing Smith at the helm to get the organization up and running. Male leadership would confer legitimacy, he believed, and because Reynolds was a woman and young, too, she was unlikely to be seen as an effective head of the organization. Instead, he noted, she must be the "center." By surrounding Smith with strong people, Albizu Campos suggested, Reynolds could prevent him from faltering. "You have to know that you have to see it through," he told her. "You have to take positions and force them through. Otherwise your League is not going to happen."[21]

Notably, as Reynolds was figuring out what her vision of solidarity was and how to practice it, critics had already begun to dismiss her as merely a mouthpiece for Albizu Campos. By the summer of 1944, FBI agents who surveilled Albizu Campos at his Columbus hospital room—through wiretaps, informants, and agents—were documenting the interactions of Harlem Ashram members' meetings with Albizu Campos and their Puerto Rico–related actions more generally.[22] In December 1944, "Confidential Informant T-1" reported to the FBI that the Nationalist Party leader claimed to have personally planned and directed the ALPRI's formation.[23] Such comments minimized the creativity of Reynolds's unique approach to outsider allyship and politics.

After sleepless nights worrying about the prospect of publicly contesting Smith, Reynolds opted for radical solidarity.[24] From then on, her messaging about Puerto Rico's independence in her emerging solidarity activism was crystal clear. An uncompromising approach was not up for negotiation, even if that meant losing the involvement of influential North American figures. She was still putting together, in her own way, the diverse strands of religious and political thought she had encountered thus far toward practicing allyship—Methodism, radical pacifism, democratic ideals, and Puerto Rican nationalism—and the decision to not cede ground on the issue of independence was part of the process. It was a decision made in community—in consultation with Albizu Campos and a group of women who would remain some of her closest confidants and friends for years to come. Collectively, Mielke, Wiley, and Moreno shared a commitment to supporting each other in working for Puerto Rico's independence.

By the beginning of 1945, Reynolds and her close circle of women supporters had prevailed. They lost some powerful supporters but continued to lend their names in support of an independence league composed of those with no family ties to Puerto Rico. African American activists such as National Council of Negro Women president Mary McLeod Bethune and Brotherhood of Sleeping Car Porters president A. Philip Randolph, who were themselves focused on decolonization efforts in Africa and who had begun to perceive African Americans as an internally colonized people within the United States, remained committed to the ALPRI.[25] Going forward, the core of active ALPRI membership consisted mostly of those with ties to the Harlem Ashram, which also served as the ALPRI's physical headquarters.

Bethune and Randolph—ostensibly figureheads—lent their political capital to the organization when they permitted the ALPRI to include their names in its official correspondence and by serving on its board of directors.[26]

Thus, in its founding year, the American League for Puerto Rico's Independence maintained a two-tiered structure that Reynolds and Albizu Campos had privately strategized in the hopes of mitigating further conflict over gendered authority and avoiding the alienation of potential supporters. Smith fronted the ALPRI, and women formed its organizational backbone. Just as Reynolds was second in command at the Ashram, she served as second in command of the ALPRI. Smith was the ALPRI's chairman; Reynolds served as secretary.

At this formative moment in her emerging solidarity activism, Reynolds encountered some of the many challenges of advancing an organization that was unwavering in its commitment to an independent Puerto Rico. Among the US liberal Left, such a position whittled the number of potential influential allies, but it also set her up to go before Congress in Washington, DC, with a clear agenda: she would demand the end of US control of Puerto Rico and nothing less. She may have initially stayed behind the scenes in order to advance the ALPRI's singularity of purpose, but she did not remain behind the scenes for long.

Confronting Congress

In March 1945, shortly after the ALPRI's founding, Reynolds and Smith traveled to Washington, DC, to participate in the US Senate Committee on Territories and Insular Affairs hearings for the Puerto Rico Independence Bill (S.227). The bill was more commonly known as the Tydings Bill, in reference to Maryland's Democratic senator Millard Tydings, who introduced the bill and chaired the hearings. The Tydings Bill permitted voters in Puerto Rico to support or reject a constitution—drafted by a constitutional convention in Puerto Rico and approved by the president of the United States—for an independent republic. In other words, independence was on the table, but only as an "up or down" vote once the constitution was prepared. Puerto Rican politicians in power would have a voice in the process of developing a constitution, but the constitution had to pass muster with the US government, which was still thoroughly invested in maintaining its colonial interests in Puerto Rico.

Reynolds was thus engaged in her first lobbying effort on behalf of the ALPRI at a moment when the US and Puerto Rican governments pivoted toward enacting a new framework for their geopolitical relationship. Navigating the Tydings Bill's complexities while participating in discussions in the seat of US power was a crucial part of Reynolds's development as an activist and an ally. Reynolds's involvement in the hearings broadened her introduction to the independence movement beyond the Nationalist Party members she had met in New York. Unbeknownst to her, however, it also made her a witness to the very early stages of a monumental effort to make Puerto Rico a permanent colony of the United States in the name of democracy.

Unaware of this alternative battle brewing, Reynolds and Smith were focused on the bill before them. The Tydings Bill had several troubling caveats and contingencies that illuminated its tenuous role as a meaningful step toward independence and that were also concerning for radical pacifists opposed to US militarism. For example, the bill allowed the United States to keep its military, coaling, and naval stations, all of which the United States had expanded significantly during World War II by expropriating land for navy use, building large military installations, and, in essence, using Puerto Rico as a military fortress for US interests in the Caribbean.[27]

Further, if Puerto Rico's voters rejected a specific constitution, then the constitutional drafting process would be repeated until voters eventually approved a constitution that would then go forward to the US president for certification. If the president determined that the constitution did not conform to S.227, then the constitutional drafting process would start all over again. As such, the Tydings Bill hardly met the Nationalist Party's call for immediate and total US withdrawal from Puerto Rico. Nor did it meet the demands of either the electoral wing of the independence movement in Puerto Rico or the ALPRI's vision for a speedy and unconditional end to US control. Along with the explicit language granting the United States control of strategic locations, the protracted process was weighted toward protecting US military priorities.

The dubious motivations of US policymakers in introducing this specific bill were evident from the start. Tydings had been in the business of introducing legislation to liberate US colonies for several years. He had sponsored the successful Philippine Independence Act in 1934; the 1945 Puerto Rico Independence Bill was his third since 1936.[28] Tydings's motivations included curbing Filipino and Puerto Rican migration to the United States, seeking vengeance for the Nationalist Party's assassination of Colonel Francis Riggs in Puerto Rico, and protecting US economic interests.[29] His independence formulas preserved US military and economic control over both colonies.[30]

The Philippine Independence Act, for example, required a transitional ten-year commonwealth that permitted continued US military presence. His plans for Puerto Rico involved harsh economic terms.[31]

Fully anticipating Puerto Rican resistance to such terms for independence, director of the Puerto Rico Reconstruction Administration Ernest Gruening described the 1936 bill as a tool to undermine criticism of US colonialism. If Puerto Ricans had been offered independence but voted against it (regardless if they did so because of its harsh conditions), the United States could claim that it was not holding Puerto Rico as a colony and was therefore exceptional among imperial powers.[32] The terms of Tydings's 1943 and 1945 bills were less harsh than the previous efforts but still codified US military and economic privileges in Puerto Rico.[33]

Reynolds and other pro-independence advocates recognized the racist and retaliatory agenda of actors like Tydings, but they hoped to use the legislative door that Tydings had opened to negotiate for meaningful sovereignty. In other words, they supported the bill in principle, but they saw their presence as a means of "cleaning up" the bill or serving as a catalyst for a better one altogether. They wanted to rid it of the various compromises and contingencies that would leave Puerto Rico a colony by any other name. The Nationalist Party, however, was not in attendance at the Senate hearings. Its leaders refused to participate in the legislative proceedings of a nation whose rule over Puerto Rico they considered to be a violation of international treaty and law. Thus, the ALPRI played an important role for cause of independence in this space.

US representative Vito Marcantonio—a stalwart champion of Albizu Campos and Puerto Rico's independence—had likely played a key role in the ALPRI's invitation to participate in the hearing. Smith testified with Reynolds by his side.[34] He said that the ALPRI supported the ultimate goal of the Tydings Bill—independence—but objected to the unilateral power that the bill gave the United States in determining the conditions for independence as well as to its drawn-out implementation schedule. Instead, he urged the senators to pass a resolution supporting immediate recognition of Puerto Rico's independence, amnesty for Puerto Rico's political prisoners, and a treaty of "mutual economic benefit and military aid" between the two nations. The matter of statehood, he argued, would further aggravate US relations with Latin America—whose governments and organizations had repeatedly petitioned the United States for Puerto Rico's independence.[35]

Though Reynolds's involvement was muted because Smith took the lead in testifying, she may have collaborated with Smith in crafting his statement. She had, after all, written many of the ALPRI's communiques. She also may have had a hand in writing the incisive "Factual Background on American Rule in Puerto Rico," which the ALPRI simultaneously submitted into the Congressional Record. The document detailed US cultural impositions on Puerto Rico and the multifaceted struggle for independence by the Nationalist Party and other groups, and US suppression of that struggle.[36]

Though the Nationalist Party was not in attendance, the ALPRI was not alone in making the case for independence. The Congreso Pro-Independencia (Pro-Independence Congress; CPI), the electoral wing of the independence movement, sent a large delegation as well. Four CPI representatives, among them Congreso founder Gilberto Concepción de Gracia, addressed the committee in early March. *Independentistas*, mostly members of the Partido Popular Democrático (Popular Democratic Party; PPD), or *populares*, created the CPI in 1943 as a nonpartisan lobbying group to advocate for immediate independence.[37] In its legislative approach and willingness to work with the federal government, the CPI was distinct from the Nationalist Party, which refused to recognize US authority over Puerto Rico and openly advocated warfare as a tool of resistance. Still, the ties between the Nationalist Party and the CPI ran deep. Many CPI members admired or at some point had been members of the Nationalist Party. Concepción de Gracia, for example, had served as Albizu Campos's attorney in the 1930s. For Reynolds, the hearings were an opportunity to meet these independentistas whose strategy deviated from the National Party's own.

At the hearings regarding the Tydings Bill, Smith and Concepción de Gracia emphasized the high stakes of the issue—especially due to its timing. The United Nations Conference on International Organization (UNCIO) was commencing in San Francisco in just a few weeks. Representatives from Allied nations were thus gathering at the conference to write the charter outlining the purpose, structure, and procedures for a United Nations. The hearings represented an opportunity for the US Senate to demonstrate its support for the principle of national self-determination. Such an initiative would send a message to US delegates at the UNCIO to place the United States on the right side of history when drafting the UN charter's treatment of decolonization. As Concepción de Gracia told the senators, "The time is ripe."[38] Smith, who was planning to travel to San Francisco for the UN conference, urged Congress to consider how it would look for the United States to position itself as the leader of the free world at the UNCIO while simultaneously retaining a colony. Puerto Rico's presence at the United Nations as an independent nation, he argued, "will make it unnecessary for us to sermonize on democracy or international justice or freedom for all peoples."[39] Ramkrishna Shahu Modak, Reynolds's and Smith's colleague from the New York–based One World Association (OWA), similarly insisted that "freedom for such countries as Puerto Rico, India, Indonesia, Korea" was paramount "for the simple reason that these countries appear to be the test cases for the sincerity of the United Nations."[40]

Reynolds and her colleagues would have to wait, however, to learn about the fate of whether Congress was going to move forward with this independence bill and in what form. In keeping with the United States' unilateral power over its colony, the hearings had actually begun in March 1945, when Puerto Rican representatives themselves were largely unable to attend because their legislative assembly was still in session. The hearings were then delayed when Tydings granted Puerto Rican Senate president Luis Muñoz Marín's request to extend the hearings so that assembly members, including himself, could testify. Thus, despite the sense that the clock was ticking on the high-stakes international stage, Tydings called a temporary recess in the hearings for several weeks, until late April.[41] As a result, the hearings would be underway again at the same time—rather than concluding before—the UNCIO in San Francisco.

The ALPRI began operating on two coasts simultaneously. The ALPRI mobilized in Washington, DC, and in San Francisco to generate international pressure on Congress to act toward giving up its colonial holdings.

Leveraging Patriotism in the New World Order

Both the San Francisco–based UN conference and the Tydings hearings in Washington, DC, underscored the significance of the colonial question in postwar geopolitics. The future of whether and how a UN charter would advance a world order based on national self-determination was very much in the air. All involved understood the potential of this new international organization to shape how Congress and other sites of imperial governance around the world would respond to independence claims.

The world seemed to be on the precipice of a new world order defined by the end of colonies. Between the mid-1940s and 1970s, colonized peoples across the globe struggled for national independence. The profound breadth and scope of the geopolitical changes that took place during these years were achieved through peaceful diplomatic measures and brutal wars of liberation alike. By the 1970s, dozens of new African and Asian nations had declared independence from Britain, France, and Denmark.[42] But in 1945, it was only the beginning of this protracted process, when long-standing powerful empires were working very hard to hang onto their colonies.

At the same time, Latin America was looking to see if the United States was, in fact, going to be a "good neighbor." Over a decade before in 1933, President Franklin Delano Roosevelt had announced his Good Neighbor Policy, promising noninterference in the region after years of US military intervention in Latin America. Latin American countries, with the exception of Argentina, had also lined up in support of the US war effort. Now many in Latin America viewed independence for Puerto Rico as a bellwether of the sincerity of this promise—evidenced by the plethora of national and Pan-American petitions from the region demanding as much.[43]

Reynolds approached this moment with a set of ideas about internationalism shaped from different strains of political thought. One year into her conversations with Albizu Campos, she was well acquainted with his ideas about international law. Under Albizu Campos, the Nationalist Party practiced noncooperation with an occupying US government and repudiated US government laws as illegitimate. After all, Albizu Campos was a Harvard-trained lawyer with a deep respect for and understanding of jurisprudence. He recognized international law as the authority for adjudicating US withdrawal. For her part, Reynolds was committed to making her government fulfill its World War II promises to create a postwar world order based on self-determination as encapsulated in the Atlantic Charter.

Yet, despite this strong international grounding in her thinking, Reynolds did not travel to San Francisco to attend the UNCIO. With the UNCIO taking place at the same time as the recommencement of the Tydings hearings, Reynolds and Smith divided their tasks and attentions. Reynolds waited on the East Coast to represent the ALPRI at the congressional hearings once they resumed, while Smith left for the West Coast to participate in the UNCIO. Also in attendance in San Francisco were Thelma Mielke, Julio Pinto Gandía, and Ramkrishna Shahu Modak. Their goal was to demand that a newly created UN charter call for the end of colonies worldwide.[44] They joined hundreds of representatives of nongovernmental organizations gathered in San Francisco.[45]

Although Reynolds remained on the East Coast as the ALPRI's spokesperson on the domestic bill, she remained involved in the preparations for making sure that the UNCIO included the voices of colonized peoples. Indeed, the presence of colonized peoples at the United Nations' founding meeting was hard won after Dumbarton Oaks, where the delegates had planned for a UNCIO that limited participation to nation-states. NAACP leader W. E. B. Du Bois insightfully observed that for colonial peoples around the world, this formula meant that "the only way to human equality is through the philanthropy of masters."[46]

After weeks of lobbying by a diverse group of organizations and individuals, however, the United Nations eventually agreed to permit delegates from nonsovereign nations to attend the UNCIO.[47] Representing the newly created World Council of Dominated Nations, Modak and Pinto Gandía were not permitted to sit in formal sessions, but like other groups and observers in attendance, they lobbied their cause.[48] As a nongovernmental organization, the Nationalist Party applied for and received permission to send Thelma Mielke as its representative. With both Mielke (albeit in a different capacity) and Smith there, the ALPRI's core leaders had worked hard to strategically maneuver themselves into key UN forums to demand UN support for Puerto Rico's decolonization.

Though she did not travel to San Francisco after working so hard in preparation for it, Reynolds's understanding of the international moment was not wasted back in Washington, DC. Reynolds worked in concert with her colleagues on both coasts to bring the weight of the prestige of the UNCIO underway to bear on Congress's deliberations about whether to free Puerto Rico, and by just how much.

When the Tydings hearings did resume in April, Reynolds encountered a wider cast of characters than she had the previous month. With the end of Puerto Rico's legislative session, members and their delegations were freed up to travel to DC. Individuals representing several economic and cultural interests also made the journey—from newspaper editors to sugar barons and banking representatives. It was a milieu that Reynolds had little access to back home in New York, and the exposure played a key role in her evolving understanding of the archipelago and its politics.

With the exception of supporters of the statehood movement, many there had long advocated for Puerto Rico's independence. Reynolds did not know that was about to change among one powerful group. At the time, she was more concerned about the specter of statehood—one of the competing options that had support at the hearings. When Reynolds spoke at the Tydings hearings, she framed her testimony from the perspective of a loyal American speaking in defense of American interests. She argued that Puerto Rico's independence—not statehood—was in the United States' best interest because it demonstrated commitment to disentangling itself from imperial power.

Reynolds focused on explaining why statehood for Puerto Rico was a bad idea from the perspective of US interests. As she explained to the senators, the ALPRI opposed a plebiscite formula that included a choice between statehood and independence. Reynolds's testimony expanded on Smith's line of argumentation that the United States owed Puerto Rico its independence rather than statehood, because the United States had never had the right to determine Puerto Rico's status. "Statehood for Puerto Rico," she argued, "in the eyes of the world as well as of Latin America, would only give permanent sanction to an episode in our history of which we are ashamed and for which we now wish to atone."[49] Using the language of the Christian pacifism that she had studied, Reynolds drew powerfully on the idea of personal responsibility and atonement for the actions of one's own nation. While some senators like Marcantonio opposed statehood for this reason, others in Congress were opposed to the entrance of the predominantly Black and Brown population as a state.

She emphasized the implications of the international arena for US interests. Invoking Franklin Roosevelt's Good Neighbor Policy, she argued, "Our retention of Puerto Rico, despite the pleas of governmental bodies, international conferences, and prominent citizens of Latin America, is a continual denial of our protestations of good neighborliness." She insisted, "No step is more important for insuring hemispheric solidarity than the recognition of Puerto Rico's independence by our Government."[50]

With the unfolding UNCIO meetings in San Francisco exerting more international pressure on the self-determination issue at the domestic level, Reynolds entered the halls of Congress with the intent of similarly shaping congressional resolve against colonialism. Statehood was not in the interest of liberty, she argued, but rather signaled a US expansionist imperial agenda. Reynolds stated that the future of postwar Western solidarity hinged on the United States' ability to demonstrate its sincere commitment to its Good Neighbor Policy toward Latin America by granting Puerto Rico independence. "To incorporate Puerto Rico as a permanent part of our Nation," she told senators, "would imply that we ought also to incorporate those republics that lie in between" the United States and Puerto Rico.[51] In other words, it signaled imperialist intent toward hundreds of miles in the Caribbean, encompassing Cuba, Haiti, and the Dominican Republic. It would require "the type of aggression we condemn in other nations."[52] Making Puerto Rico a state, Reynolds asserted, would "let our imperialist venture there succeed" and in so doing, "undermine Latin American confidence in our sincerity" and US commitment to the Atlantic Charter.[53]

However, in a political space where every participant—senators and witnesses—was a US citizen, definitions of patriotism proved malleable.

Reynolds was not alone in wrapping herself in patriotism to make her case. Tydings, for instance, asserted his national loyalty when he suggested that Puerto Rico's independence was in the best interest of the United States because Puerto Ricans were too alien to assimilate. Moreover, during the hearings, Reynolds was also exposed to an invocation of patriotism from a new demographic: Puerto Ricans who advocated making the Caribbean territory the forty-ninth US state. Without shaking her own conviction, this experience opened new avenues of inquiry for Reynolds that she would eventually investigate further in Puerto Rico itself.

Indeed, the statehood movement that Reynolds encountered in 1945 was a conservative opposition movement with limited popular support. It had started out in 1899 primarily as a propertied and middle-class party with ties to the sugar industry and had forged a fragile electoral coalition with laborers at times. By 1945, all but the most conservative elements of the statehood party had abandoned it, as the party became home to those who opposed socioeconomic reform.[54] Independence threatened their economic holdings. The status quo or statehood better protected them.

The statehood advocates whom Reynolds encountered in Washington, DC, forecast dire economic and political consequences if Puerto Rico were to achieve independence. Puerto Rican Statehood Association (PRSA) president Reece B. Bothwell predicted that the twenty-year tariff schedule of the Tydings Bill, for example, would lead to the "total destruction of [Puerto Rico's] economy."[55] The unprecedented act of granting independence to a territory with a majority population of US citizens, PRSA delegates warned, would create novel dilemmas over how to recognize and protect their citizenship rights.[56] Ejected from US democracy, an independent Puerto Rico just might confront antidemocratic forces, as had its Caribbean neighbors. Obliquely referencing the ascendance of Trujillo in the Dominican Republic, Batista in Cuba, and Somoza in Nicaragua, Jorge Bird-Arias, who ran a large sugar corporation along with US investors, asserted, "I prefer liberty without independence to independence without liberty."[57]

While pointing to such consequences, these conservative voices swathed their appeals in patriotism, specifically military service and pride in US citizenship, while demonstrating their skills as cultural mediators. As they insisted, the Tydings Bill's plebiscite permitting Puerto Ricans to vote only for or against independence, without the option of statehood, was no choice at all.[58] Pointing out that he was the father of US soldiers serving abroad and the grandfather of a soldier who had fallen during the Allies' invasion of France, Bird-Arias questioned why the senators should reward Puerto

Rican Nationalists—who had assassinated US officials and hinted at the use of violence against President Roosevelt—with independence and not loyal American citizens (such as himself) with statehood.[59]

A Puerto Rican Women's Statehood Association representative further highlighted the benefit of bilingual and multicultural US citizens. Puerto Ricans' knowledge of "the idiosyncrasies of the Latin peoples," she argued, allowed them to access "both cultures equally at hand." Who better to facilitate the United States' Good Neighbor Policy toward Latin America?[60]

However, from the start, the deck was stacked against the idea of statehood. The committee's invitation to the PRSA and other pro-statehood organizations to testify was a mere formality. "I am offering a reward of $1,000 to anybody who will find 20 United States Senators that think statehood would be possible for Puerto Rico," Tydings condescendingly told PRSA representatives, to emphasize the lack of support for Puerto Rican statehood in Congress.[61] Statehood was not an option. He did not hide his underlying racist motivations, viewing Puerto Rico as too foreign and unassimilable for Congress to admit it as a state.

For Reynolds, the conservativism among both the Puerto Rican statehood proponents and the American legislators proved a complex space to navigate. Despite her antiracist agenda, Reynolds did not rebut or address the racism that framed Tydings's blunt rejection of Puerto Rican statehood before or after her testimony. Instead, she focused on challenging the statehood option itself. She did not yet realize that the real challenge to the Tydings Bill's plebiscite formula (voting for or against independence) was actually a formula that also included a "third way" option that would be championed by Luis Muñoz Marín and the Popular Democratic Party.

Indeed, Reynolds had encountered Muñoz Marín for the first time during the resumed hearings in April. By the time of their meeting, Muñoz Marín was already Puerto Rico's most powerful politician. His father, Luis Muñoz Rivera, had previously occupied this role in the waning years of Spanish rule and the early US colonial administration. Born in 1898 in San Juan, Muñoz Marín had also lived in the United States for several years during the 1910s and 1920s and moved comfortably among both Puerto Rican and US political elites. In 1932, he was elected to the Puerto Rican Senate representing the Liberal Party that his father had founded in 1902 (then called the Union Party).

As a leader in the Liberal Party, Muñoz Marín worked closely with the Roosevelt administration to introduce New Deal programs in Puerto Rico while also maintaining support for independence from the United States.

But in 1937, his Liberal Party colleagues expelled him and his followers from the party amid electoral losses and internal disagreement on the party's sovereignty status position.[62] In 1938, Muñoz Marín and his supporters founded the Partido Popular Democrático (PPD) under the slogan of "Bread, Land, and Freedom" ("Pan, Tierra, y Libertad"), and it became the home of the electoral wing of the independence movement.[63] The PPD narrowly won the 1940 elections and embarked on an agenda that included agricultural reform and industrial development.[64] Four years later, Muñoz Marín and the PPD won by a landslide, gaining control of the legislature.[65]

As Muñoz Marín's power grew, he prevented ruptures within his own party and among voters across Puerto Rico with what he called the "People's Catechism," which prohibited PPD candidates from campaigning on the political status issue.[66] He did so because even though he had once favored independence, he had privately been moving toward support for some kind of "dominion" or "commonwealth" option since at least 1940, increasingly convinced that Puerto Rico's economic development and health required a governing relationship with the United States.[67] Muñoz Marín's deliberate ambiguity about status, however, spurred a growing revolt among independentistas in the PPD, made visible when PPD members created the nonpartisan CPI in 1943. PPD independentistas, nevertheless, largely remained loyal to their party under Muñoz Marín's People's Catechism during the 1944 elections in Puerto Rico.[68]

As Muñoz Marín's involvement in the Tydings hearings proved, the patriotism Reynolds had leaned on so heavily was not the ideology at play in the hearings. Indeed, Muñoz Marín skirted rhetoric about US patriotism altogether. He had traveled to DC as head of a joint legislative commission calling for a referendum that would include, on the one hand, status options that Congress favored and, on the other hand, status options with some measure of support in Puerto Rico. Among Puerto Ricans, the commission statement explained, this list included "independence, statehood, and a form of dominion government based on full and final political rights." Any permanent solution, the commission submitted, required "certain minimum economic conditions" not addressed in the Tydings Bill that would ensure a degree of economic stability necessary for political stability.[69]

Thus, as Reynolds continued to wrestle with pro-statehood arguments, Muñoz Marín shifted the political landscape altogether by introducing other status solutions—dominion status and statehood—into the mix of testimony. Elaborating on the commission statement in his testimony, Muñoz Marín employed a strategy much like the "People's Catechism" of 1944 and avoided advocacy on any particular status resolution during the hearings. For instance, when asked about his views on independence and statehood, he said that either was "workable" as long as it met the "minimum economic conditions" for "a very modest civilized life" and political stability.[70]

He wrapped his testimony in assertions that a measure of autonomy in Puerto Rico was dependent on a level of economic stability not addressed in the Tydings Bill. "Puerto Rico was made poor by nature and is not to blame for that," he told senators. "It is for this reason," he continued, "and because of the fact that the economy has developed there under the legislation of the United States fundamentally for the last half century almost, that we believe the granting to it of these minimum economic conditions, under any political status, is fully warranted and justified." As he argued, "after you have given the conditions for maintaining life and civilization, then you have your political status. If you die you only have a graveyard status, whatever they may be." By the end of his testimony, the committee invited him to submit written amendments to the Tydings Bill for their consideration.[71]

After hearing Muñoz Marín's testimony, Reynolds queried Resident Commissioner Jesús Piñero about whether "he really agreed with Muñoz that Puerto Rico must forever be dependent on the charity of some other nation." She recalled Piñero replying, "Yes, but I think you should discuss the matter with him." Piñero quickly arranged a meeting. The next morning Piñero led her through a line of guards to the room at Washington's acclaimed Mayflower Hotel, where presidents and world dignitaries had stayed and socialized for years.

This experience contrasted sharply with her highly favorable first meeting with Albizu Campos in a New York hospital room the year before.[72] Muñoz Marín had a reputation for pursuing extramarital relationships and drinking.[73] Whether Reynolds was aware of it at that time is not clear. As Reynolds recalled, Muñoz Marín "received me en negligee [in pajamas and robe]" among empty bottles and glasses strewn about his Mayflower Hotel room from the previous night.[74] Also present were several "bleary-eyed" high-ranking PPD politicians, as well as Muñoz Marín's adult daughter from his first marriage to Pan-American feminist Muna Lee.[75]

Reynolds queried Muñoz Marín about his testimony that—as she characterized it—"Puerto Rico would starve if she were independent." Knowing that, as she told him, "in the 1930s, he had stated that Puerto Rico needed to be independent in order to survive economically," she wanted to know why he had changed his mind. "If you industrialize under the United States[s'] domination," Reynolds continued, "will it not be American businessmen who will profit more than the Puerto Rican people and they will have low-paying jobs?" To which he said, "We have to start that way, there is no other way and we can better it as time goes on."[76] Reynolds left the meeting without a clear answer from him.

The hearings ended with the expectation that Muñoz Marín would submit suggested revisions to the Tydings Bill. Reynolds was therefore shocked when she learned that Muñoz Marín and his commission had drafted a *new* bill altogether, and that Senator Tydings had introduced it into the Senate as the Puerto Rico Plebiscite Bill (S.1002), also called the Tydings-Piñero Bill, on May 16. Unlike the plebiscite formula of the Tydings Bill, which called for an up-down vote on independence, the replacement Tydings-Piñero Bill outlined a referendum asking voters to choose among three status solutions: independence, statehood, or an intermediate status that Muñoz Marín and his commission had proposed—that is, "dominion" status.[77] Regardless of the outcome of the vote, any change in status was subject to congressional approval. Moreover, the United States would retain property rights in Puerto Rico, including military bases, in all three scenarios.[78]

The proposal of the new bill suggested a sea change among the governing powers in Puerto Rico and Washington, DC, which took Reynolds by surprise. Privately, she was still trying to makes sense of Muñoz Marín's actions. Publicly, Reynolds projected confidence when she and Smith shot off a statement on behalf of the ALPRI denouncing the new Tydings-Piñero Bill as "a thoroughly unworthy and dangerous proposal."[79]

By then, Reynolds and Smith were back in New York, where they were facing multiple disappointments on the domestic and international fronts of their ALPRI efforts. In DC, the possibility of using legislative channels to achieve independence dimmed significantly. In place of independence, the outlines of a new status that would permanently subordinate Puerto Rico as a "dominion" of the United States gained traction in the halls of Congress. In San Francisco, the United Nations that emerged from the UNCIO preserved the wartime planning intergovernmental structure that extended membership only to nation-states and not to colonized peoples. The world's colonizing powers succeeded in establishing a United Nations that tolerated various colonial relationships and that designated imperial governments as the representatives of the very people they subjected. Such a structure left little room for the voices of colonized peoples at the United Nations. But where she could find room, Reynolds intended to harness it in her solidarity activism.

· · · · · ·

In September 1945, the ALPRI tried one more time to revive the original Tydings Bill, which, while still flawed, contained the much-desired "up or down vote" on independence. World War II was over. FDR had died, and the United States had a new president in Harry Truman. In a desperate bid, the ALPRI appealed directly to Truman, but to no avail.[80] In this round, Muñoz Marín was not a winner, either. The Tydings-Piñero Bill he backed with the dominion option did not make it out of the Senate committee.[81] Nevertheless, tensions between Muñoz Marín and PPD independentistas boiled over when Concepción de Gracia publicly denounced Muñoz Marín for sabotaging the independence movement in DC.[82]

It had been a long year. Reynolds had spent the year asking what she could do as a white US citizen and pacifist, with her thinking informed and influenced by the Nationalist Party's critique of US colonialism in Puerto Rico. She explored how to put together what she had learned since first meeting Albizu Campos in 1944 about the struggle for independence with the ideas about the social gospel she carried with her to New York from her studies at Northwestern. She took stock of how to put her new insights gleaned from meetings with Albizu Campos and other Nationalist figures in New York with the radical pacifism she was studying at the Harlem Ashram, alongside the postwar moment in which world leaders were creating an intergovernmental organization that championed self-determination.

In the process, Reynolds had gotten some clarity on the contours of radical solidarity under some challenging circumstances. Reynolds and a handful of women colleagues had maneuvered the gender politics of leftist leadership to create an organization of non–Puerto Rican Americans committed to mobilizing for Puerto Rico's independence. She learned that the number of solidarity activists could be compromised in the service of a clear and consistent objective. Throughout all this, she had learned to navigate the inherently fraught nature of her role as an "outsider" by insisting that allies like herself should not compromise the ultimate goal of independence for those whom they supported.

With that unequivocal stance on independence, Reynolds helped this new organization articulate why independence mattered, and why statehood and dominion status were not viable options. The experience had broadened her developing practice of allyship. She entered Congress as a silent partner to

Smith, and left as the voice of the ALPRI, with clear messaging of why Puerto Rico's independence benefited the United States and why loyal Americans should support Puerto Rico's independence. Her network of contacts with independentistas extended beyond the small number of Nationalist Party activists she had befriended in New York to include leading figures in the electoral wing.

Back in New York where she still lived at the Ashram, she was ready to grapple further with her evolving understanding of what was going on in Puerto Rico. As she recalled, "When I came back from these hearings, I felt I had a much better grasp on sentiment as it existed in Puerto Rico but that I had to get a much better understanding, a broader understanding."[83] With her grasp of Puerto Rican politics still largely dependent on her Nationalist Party contacts in New York, it was a critical moment in which she was still gathering and building her ideas about Puerto Rico. And so, rather than giving up in the face of defeat, Reynolds built on her expanding network and understanding to look for new strategies and locations to carry forward the ALPRI agenda.

She looked to Puerto Rico, and ALPRI supporters undertook a fundraising campaign to send her there. Introducing Reynolds to potential donors, the organization sent out a letter describing her as having a "mastery of the field . . . unmatched by any non–Puerto Rican in this country." The letter continued, "In order that she may speak and write with greater authority it is felt that Miss Reynolds should go to Puerto Rico for the purpose of making a thorough survey of the situation, interviewing all of the key people and returning in time to make the weight of her contribution count through the winter months."[84] But fundraising only went so far. Reynolds thus also took up two temporary jobs to cover the cost of a trip—answering phones in a physician's office and coding the questionnaires of European Jewish refugees for a Yale professor studying the group.[85] These two jobs were typical of the string of positions that Reynolds held for the rest of her life. Her goal was not to forge a career, but rather to pay the bills so that she could pursue her activism.

By October 1945, Reynolds had sufficient funds to travel for the first time to the nation that was so dear to friends and mentors.[86] When Reynolds arrived in Puerto Rico, it appeared to be at a critical crossroads with the Tydings-Piñero plebiscite bill, which was still pending in Congress. And so, for the first time, she shifted from listening to just the Nationalist Party and Puerto Ricans in New York to listening to Puerto Ricans in Puerto Rico.

Part II

4 Puerto Rico

· ·

On the first day of November 1945, just six months after the Tydings hearings where Ruth Reynolds advocated for Puerto Rico's independence at the US Senate, Reynolds arrived at the Capitol Building in Old San Juan. She later described the day as "one of those perfect tropical nights unduplicated in more temperate climates." But she was not there for a vacation.[1] She was there to meet with Senate president Luis Muñoz Marín, the man whose testimony at the Tydings hearings had dealt a severe blow to the cause of independence. His arguments undermined the independence bill that had been under consideration in Congress and, in its place, gave momentum to the idea of an alternative "dominion" status for Puerto Rico under continued US rule.

Muñoz Marín's office was in the majestic building whose construction began under the oversight of Muñoz Marín's own father, Luis Muñoz Rivera. The highly influential Muñoz Rivera had headed Puerto Rico's short-lived autonomous government in 1898 prior the US invasion and then led the dominant Union Party from 1904 until his death in 1916.[2] As Reynolds climbed the marble steps, she harbored suspicions that Muñoz Marín was no longer working for Puerto Rico's independent sovereignty. Reynolds had already interviewed Muñoz Marín in DC during the Tydings hearings. The conversation, which Puerto Rico's resident commissioner had suggested and quickly set up, was a pointed one that put Reynolds and Muñoz Marín at odds. This time, Reynolds was only able to obtain a sitting with him with great difficulty.[3] It was perhaps a sign that the leader no longer viewed Reynolds as someone who could be converted to his political agenda, and more likely as a threat to that agenda. Nevertheless, Reynolds pursued the meeting, focused on her goal of better understanding the political landscape in Puerto Rico.

Inside the grand building, as Muñoz Marín lit one cigarette after another, Reynolds and Muñoz Marín talked for four hours about Puerto Rico's economic and political future. Their conversation was respectful, intense, and sometimes argumentative. They debated his position that Puerto Rico's survival depended on "development wholly within the American economic framework."[4] He dodged her queries about what this meant for his long-standing support for independence. The man was, in many ways, a cypher. A chameleon. An incredibly astute politician who was beloved or reviled, depending on whom one asked. Reynolds departed just before midnight. She would later say that she was "firmly convinced" that the governor "was working through diverse channels to defeat genuine independence for his people."[5] If independence efforts failed, she predicted, he would be "more responsible than any other [person] for preventing the recognition of Puerto Rico's independence in 1946."[6] But while he was surely the most prestigious, Muñoz Marín was only one of the many Puerto Ricans whom Reynolds interviewed during her first three-month trip to Puerto Rico.

Reynolds made the trip on behalf of the American League for Puerto Rico's Independence (ALPRI). Describing her motivations for the trip, Reynolds wrote, "I had learned almost all I could from reading the available literature and from talking with hundreds of Puerto Ricans, those who have made New York their permanent home and those who have come for a brief time on political and business missions. But I wanted to see that land for myself, to talk with its leaders and with its common people, so that I might know what strength the ideals preached by various men might have, so that I might judge which of several conflicting viewpoints was correct."[7] In the wake of being blindsided during the Tydings debates earlier that spring, she realized that there might be gaps in the views she had been exposed to among activist communities in New York. So, representing the ALPRI, she set off for Puerto Rico, where she quickly developed a fieldwork methodology based on asking people about their views on independence and about their fears and hopes for Puerto Rico's future.

When Reynolds first left for San Juan in November 1945, she was already equipped with cogent critiques of US colonialism in Puerto Rico that, unfortunately, put her at odds with US federal authorities. By the time she returned to New York in the final days of the year, Reynolds was more convinced than ever that being an ally to Puerto Rico's opponents of US imperialism meant working for the archipelago's independence. In Puerto Rico, she had found great respect for Pedro Albizu Campos and the Nationalist Party—a respect that had not been crushed in his absence. She also discovered a wealth of independence sentiment well beyond Nationalist Party supporters. This sentiment extended to members of Muñoz Marín's own party, many of whom assumed that Muñoz Marín was still working for independence. Indeed, by the time of her return, she well understood that her ideas about solidarity for Puerto Rican independence put her at political odds with the popular and powerful Muñoz Marín, who emerged as the main obstacle to the cause within Puerto Rico.

Solidarity Methodology

Reynolds was a self-made and self-taught interviewer and investigator. Had she been born a few generations later, Reynolds might have developed her interviewing skills by attending graduate school in anthropology, sociology, or journalism and then pursued a career as an investigative reporter or a humanities researcher. The white men who dominated these professions, however, largely excluded the women of her generation, and she did not attempt to edge her way into one of these gatekeeping professions. For her, the methodology she employed served one specific end: furthering her understanding of Puerto Ricans' political perspectives so that she could be an effective ally.

The unconventional path she had forged since leaving South Dakota led Reynolds to funnel her considerable research skills toward anticolonial solidarity work. During this first trip to Puerto Rico, she developed a strong methodology, which, while not based on any formal training, was fundamentally a form of fieldwork. She asked, listened, observed, and documented. As someone committed to her vision of what real solidarity meant, she needed to take the time to understand the situation and the diverse views of Puerto Ricans and their nuances. In other words, understanding her own positionality as part of a colonizing nation meant understanding the diverse effects of US colonialism on the diverse population of Puerto Rico, and she could only glean this information by asking and listening.

Reynolds's methodology was also a sign of how she was grappling with uncertainty over her position in relation to Puerto Ricans who sought independence. Her own growth in the ways that she understood her positionality—as an advocate and as someone who was still learning—manifested as apprehension about the sufficiency of her knowledge about Puerto Rico. As she reflected later in life, "I have no degree, I never studied all this stuff in college, I never got a degree in it. I just didn't feel qualified in a real sense." Developing a methodology based on interviews and close listening not only gave her a sense of direction in the wake of the Tydings hearings; it continued to furnish her with a deep sense of understanding and broad-based perspective on her work. Much later in life, she mused, "I have learned a lot in the last 40 years. . . . I know more about it than most people who have gotten degrees in similar things."[8] The methodology she developed in Puerto Rico in the 1940s became the cornerstone of not only her understanding of political sentiment in Puerto Rico but also her self-understanding as someone with enough information to engage knowledgeably and deliberately as an ally in the fight for independence.

Between October and December 1945, Reynolds traveled to forty-four of Puerto Rico's seventy-seven *municipios* (administrative units that functioned like counties) to ask Puerto Ricans about their nation's political history and aspirations for the future. Reynolds focused on people's views about independence, as well as their views on the two men most closely associated with the contemporary struggle for independence, Luis Muñoz Marín and Pedro Albizu Campos. She arrived with a list of people and contacts she had developed from her contacts in New York and during her time in DC, where her involvement in the Tydings hearings had broadened her introduction to Puerto Rican politics well beyond the Nationalist Party.

For Reynolds the political was also personal. In New York, her private emotional life and social world initially revolved around her pacifist community, quickly expanding to include Nationalist contacts there. Based on a shared commitment to a free Puerto Rico, the "dissident friendships" that Reynolds and Ashram members had established with Albizu Campos and other Nationalists in New York—through visits to Albizu Campos at the hospital and meals at the Ashram—were also expressions of solidarity politics.[9] The trust and mutual respect that had taken root in New York through forms of hospitality had already bridged divides of politics and colonial geography. Such sentiments that furthered a sense of common purpose only deepened in Puerto Rico. Reynolds's home base during her stay, for example, was in Bayamón with the family of Tomás Ongay, whom she had met in New York when both were paying a visit to Albizu Campos at his Columbus Hospital room.[10] As Reynolds recalled from that meeting, "Don Tomás knew that I was struggling to get to Puerto Rico." He had showed her an image of his home, saying, "That house is my home, and it is your home too when you come to Puerto Rico." While Reynolds had initially thought that it was simply an expression, she soon learned that he meant it literally. As she recalled, "I could not go to Puerto Rico without becoming, for a time, a part of the lovely Ongay family."[11]

Meanwhile, during her first night in Puerto Rico, she was invited to the home of José Enamorado Cuesta. "It was his birthday and there was a party at his house in Guaynabo," she noted, "and that was something of an introduction to Puerto Rican society." The festive atmosphere and sense of camaraderie set the tone for her time in Puerto Rico, and she was not insensitive to the gift of welcome she had received. Elaborating on her perception of the political relationships she encountered in Puerto Rico, Reynolds asserted, "In Puerto Rico there [were] no barriers."[12]

Reynolds valued the strong emotions and passions for political work that demanded enormous sacrifice. She funneled a great deal of this emotion into her activism, but she also held space for romance. She was an intensely private person in terms of her romantic life, however, and rarely spoke about courting relationships with men, though there are glimpses of those attachments here and there in her private correspondence and in interviews.[13]

Those glimpses of her romantic life reveal that it was hard to find a partner who accepted or appreciated the ways that her sustained political activism challenged gender roles and expectations. Deeply entrenched societal expectations that married women should prioritize domestic duties above all permeated leftist politics as much as it did dominant society. Most Nationalist men maintained romantic relationships and fathered children while they advanced their political agenda. By contrast, several leading Nationalist women never married or had children. Thelma Mielke, Reynolds's ALPRI colleague, likewise never married. Reflecting on her personal life in a 1986 interview, Reynolds commented on this discrepancy between the men and women in her activist communities. "I was open to the idea" of marriage, she noted, "but not to give up political work because men don't give up their political work when they get married, do they? NO."[14] Those glimpses into her private life also reveal that Reynolds had learned from Albizu Campos that, as she put it, "devotion to your political position comes first, and not your personal desires."[15] That devotion to her political position afforded friendships and connections during this first trip to Puerto Rico that she could build on for the duration of her life.

Indeed, as a result of these connections, Reynolds had broad access to interviewees. When it reported on her presence in Puerto Rico, *El Mundo* included the names of the several prominent individuals she interviewed while there.[16] She interviewed Puerto Ricans of diverse backgrounds. Along with members of the Partido Popular Democrático (Popular Democratic Party; PPD) headed by Muñoz Marín, Reynolds met with leaders from the Republican, Socialist, and Liberal Parties, each of whom held one seat in the insular legislature after the PPD's landslide 1944 electoral victory.[17] She met with leaders of the Congreso Pro-Independencia (CPI) and the Communist Party of Puerto Rico and the Independence Labor Party as well.[18] She also met with Nationalist Party leaders and supporters who rejected electoral politics. Reynolds interviewed across the economic spectrum: agricultural laborers, bankers, tobacco merchants, sugar barons, and residents of San Juan's La Perla and El Fanguito shantytowns, where thousands dwelled in makeshift shanties without running water, electricity, or garbage collection. She solicited the opinions of mayors, religious leaders, union leaders, artists, and writers. She especially sought out government employees "from the top to the bottom of the scale."[19] She also conducted impromptu interviews of fellow passengers as she traveled by *guaguas* (public buses) or with a handful of passengers in *públicos* (public cars) to her destinations on the narrow two-lane roads running along the northern and southern shorelines and connecting the coasts to Puerto Rico's mountainous interior.[20]

Perspectives on Independence, Muñoz Marín, and the Nationalist Party

Much of what she found matched what Nationalists in New York had told her: there was significant pro-independence sentiment and widespread admiration for Albizu Campos. New to her, however, were the nuances of the perspectives on independence that she encountered. Understanding these nuances seemed critical for leading a solidarity group claiming expertise on the topic. Some things did not surprise her. For example, she was not surprised to find strong opposition to independence among members of the diminished statehood movement. Leading pro-statehood figures believed, as Senator Celestino Iriarte Miró angrily shouted at her, "Statehood is independence; it is liberty; it is everything the human heart can hope for." Iriarte Miró erupted when she persisted with the question that she asked all statehood supporters she interviewed: "If you should become convinced that statehood is impossible to attain, which would you prefer—the colony or independence?" While others responded with calm, Reynolds concluded from the conversations with them, "Very few of those who have found great economic profit under the present system are anything but . . . 'estadistas [statehooders].'"[21]

She was, however, intrigued when her line of question revealed pro-independence sentiment among *estadistas* with ties to the laboring class. Most prominent among them was Resident Commissioner Bolívar Pagán. After meeting him, she noted, "Pagán has always advocated statehood. He prefers statehood over independence, but he would fight for independence if doomed otherwise to perpetual colonialism."[22] She further recounted their conversation as such: "I told him that surely after six years in Washington, he must know there is no possibility of statehood. . . . He said he was considering making a statement favoring independence, but that the proper hour had not arrived." Reynolds "urged him to act promptly if he were going to act at all."[23]

Reynolds also met Puerto Ricans who suppressed their desire for independence out of economic concerns. She recorded a banker who explained that "spiritually, all Puerto Ricans desire independence," but he personally opposed independence because he feared that it "would be economically fatal."[24] Others called for a protracted timeline toward independence. Mayagüez school director Elpidio Rivera proposed that Puerto Rico solve its economic problems before pursuing independence, while a PPD senator—who feared that "Puerto Rico could not subsist on its own feet"—suggested autonomy as a step toward independence in twenty to fifty years.[25]

She discovered that many prominent figures within Muñoz Marín's own party, however, were confident in an independence economy that would benefit local industries. Ponce's mayor, Andrés Grillasca, insisted, according to Reynolds's report, that "Puerto Rico could stand on its own feet if permitted to develop her industries normally" and "if not hindered by the tariff."[26] Mayagüez's PPD mayor likewise asserted that "Puerto Rico should have a chance to find out whether it can support itself with independence" and predicted a boom of "liquor traffic, furniture, fisheries, [and] bargaining power" with independence. Mayor Pedro Nelson Colberg of Cabo Rojo said that the city's fisheries had unlimited potential to enrich its residents and thus help to create an independent economy.[27] Reynolds also heard from coffee growers who believed that independence would save their struggling industry.[28] She talked to tobacco growers and dealers who expected to lose the US market with independence but were eager to develop markets in Europe.[29] She met with union leaders who anticipated expanded hiring to meet local demand with independence—for example, in cement and cigarette production.[30] Each one of them was a PPD candidate or supporter at the time.

Reynolds also interviewed aging politicians from the early decades of US control, highlighting consensus among them about independence. Even those who had initially favored US statehood in 1898, she argued, perceived independence as acceptable and even more desirable than US colonialism. Though Puerto Ricans had disagreed as to whether the United States should grant independence or make Puerto Rico a state, "none of them believed that the United States, who had always declared herself opposed to rule of one people over another, would perpetuate a colonial system for fifty years."[31] This was the type of consensus of perspectives that she wanted North American audiences to know.

Most notably, it became clear to Reynolds that Muñoz Marín no longer represented the large pro-independence presence within his own political party. Members of the Congreso Pro-Independencia—the nonpartisan lobbying group peopled mostly by PPD members—vigorously rejected Muñoz Marín's political wisdom. During an interview with the University of Puerto Rico professor and CPI founding member Carmen Rivera de Alvarado, Reynolds made a note: "Is not convinced that Muñoz is God."[32] Another CPI leader characterized Muñoz Marín's emphasis on impending economic doom in his push for a status solution in Congress other than independence as "economic terrorism."[33] United Front for the Establishment of the Republic of Puerto Rico founder Juan Enrique Soltero Peralta denounced Muñoz Marín for mapping an enduring colonial future for Puerto Rico on the basis of existing economic hardships that were themselves the direct result of US economic exploitation. Soltero Peralta asserted, "Small countries can be independent. It is not true that Puerto Rico cannot develop production for a limited domestic market."[34] "To say that PR and the US are now equal before the law," he explained, "is to say that the poor laborer and his rich employer are equal before the law."[35]

At the same time, however, other PPD leaders relayed to Reynolds their unwillingness to break with the politically powerful and enormously popular PPD leader for fear of ruining their own careers—that is, until he spoke publicly against independence.[36] Moreover, she was very surprised to learn that some in Muñoz Marín's own political party were not completely aware of how the senator had undermined the independence bill in Congress the previous summer.[37] In other words, she surmised that Muñoz Marín was facing less scrutiny within his own party precisely because some PPD supporters were either unaware or acting with political expediency. Under these circumstances, then, it looked to her like Muñoz Marín was well positioned to harness the PPD's legislative dominance toward his turn away from independence and toward the "dominion."

At the same time that she solicited such nuanced perspectives on independence and Muñoz Marín, Reynolds was also determined to discover first-hand what the status of the Nationalist Party was in Puerto Rico in the absence of Albizu Campos. Reports from North American religious and pacifist communities suggested "that the Nationalist movement is dead and that Albizu Campos is looked upon by his people now as a sincere man who chose the wrong way of violence and therefore will never again be recognized as a patriotic leader."[38] Notably, these North American communities included some of her Fellowship of Reconciliation colleagues, as well as the personnel of the Civilian Public Service camps established in Puerto Rico during World War II to allow conscientious objectors to fulfill conscription requirements.[39] But, she wrote, "I suspected my friends of being so obviously closely related to the government and approving its current policies to be in a position to hear much contrary opinion."[40] She had to find out the truth through her fieldwork, developing her methodology to do so in real time.

And what she discovered substantially contradicted the reports she had been given. Reynolds found that once she made it known that she admired Albizu Campos, she was "amazed at the flood of confidences . . . and at the number of "abrazos" [embraces] I was enjoined to deliver to [Albizu Campos] in the name of people now earning their salaries in government employ."[41] Reynolds recorded these acquaintances telling her, "He is the only man who can counteract Muñoz." She described them urging her to tell Albizu Campos that "his very presence in Puerto Rico would give tens of thousands the backbone they now lack to speak the truth."[42]

Despite Albizu Campos's decade-long absence from Puerto Rico, Reynolds's fieldwork uncovered widespread admiration for him. Reynolds reported on the enduring relevance and presence of his ideas in the streets and institutions of cultural and political power. "Albizu's friends and enemies agree on one thing," she concluded: "Don Pedro is the greatest orator they have ever heard." As she relayed, "Today the phrases he used are on the lips of the man in the street as he recalls that fearless expounder of the duty of every man to be free and the right of no man to accept slavery."[43] Notably, this admiration came from well-known and unassuming figures both within and beyond the Nationalist Party. Cultural and labor leaders alike expressed confidence in Albizu Campos's leadership. Poet and nationalist Trina Padilla characterized Albizu Campos as the "soul of Puerto Rico." As for Albizu Campos's views on political violence, the head of the pro-independence Central General de Trabajadores "told [Reynolds] that he believed Albizu never desired to stimulate violence, but only courage."[44]

Reynolds also found a Nationalist Party under the leadership of interim president Julio de Santiago that was looking to rebuild after the incarcerations of the 1930s and early 1940s had decimated its membership. Reynolds described de Santiago with great admiration, as someone who "could walk through fire with serenity and poise."[45] Of de Santiago's plans for the party, she noted that "Puerto Rico's experience with the Populares will teach his people once and for all the futility of working 'within the regime, against the regime'" and "the failure once again, of diplomatic means of winning independence." He explained during their meeting that while Puerto Ricans had the right to pursue any method to obtain independence, they were "not prepared to wage war against the United States." He maintained, however, that Puerto Ricans were prepared to advance the struggle for independence by refusing to obey laws imposed on them by the United States and its proxies in the archipelago.[46]

Reynolds well understood the scope of the methods independence supporters were willing to consider—and the dangers they faced in doing so. Before the close of her trip, Reynolds visited five Nationalists who were seven years into twenty-year sentences imprisoned at the Insular Penitentiary in Río Piedras.[47] The five were serving twenty years to life for murder and conspiring to assassinate the American governor of Puerto Rico, Governor Blanton Winship. The assassination attempt, a retaliation for the 1937 Ponce Massacre, had taken place in July 1938 during a Ponce celebration marking the anniversary of the US invasion of Puerto Rico. The governor survived, but a Puerto Rican National Guard colonel standing next to Winship died and dozens were injured; the assassin, Nationalist Angel Esteban Antongiorgi, was killed.[48] As Reynold described it, the visit was "one of the most deeply moving experiences of my life." She wrote, "With difficulty I fought back tears as I saw these boys robbed of their lives on the basis of no evidence whatsoever of having known" of Antongiorgi's intentions.[49]

It was a pivotal meeting for her. The meeting led Reynolds to articulate how her support of Puerto Rico's independence complemented theirs. She told them her activism was a "patriotic duty," in keeping with her rightful loyalty to the United States, which she hoped to "discharge . . . as faithfully as the Nationalists have performed theirs." She described her plans to work for their release and personal reasons for inserting herself in the battle over Puerto Rico's status. "I told them . . . that I believe that when my countrymen know the truth . . . the story will be different." As she explained, "I was working not so much for the Puerto Rican people, much as I love them and deeply distressed as I am over their plight." Rather, she continued, "I was working primarily to clear the honor of my own nation and my own people."[50] A mainstay of her solidarity activism, this was a position that enabled her to voice important criticism in support of independence as an "outsider."

Drafting a Counternarrative

By the end of 1945, Reynolds had developed a thick file of notes from the numerous interviews that she had conducted. They contained an expanded catalog of US abuses in Puerto Rico and extensive evidence that the Nationalist Party's goal of full and unconditional independent sovereignty enjoyed archipelago-wide support and also that the party itself was popular.

Upon her return to the United States, she immediately began drafting her report for the recently founded American League for Puerto Rico's Independence. Far more than a write-up of her experiences and conversations, the finished report was a sophisticated, analysis-driven book manuscript that boldly challenged the US government's representation of itself as an engine of democracy in the Caribbean. Instead, she argued that the United States was a colonizing nation that used the full weight of its economic, legal, and military power over the people of Puerto Rico to maintain that power. Earlier generations of Puerto Rican leaders, she argued, had erred in accommodating US demands and power by conceding independence as a goal. Muñoz Marín was making this mistake again. With this counternarrative, Reynolds sought to enlighten political allies in the US Left of the strong support for independence that she encountered in Puerto Rico and her own conclusion that the Nationalist Party remained the only unequivocal champion of independence.

Her findings were pressing. Back in New York in the winter of 1946, Reynolds learned of two key developments in Puerto Rico. In January, governor of Puerto Rico Rexford Tugwell pardoned the five Nationalists imprisoned in Río Piedras who had moved her so.[51] Then, in February, as Reynolds was in the midst of writing up her report detailing Muñoz Marín's behind-the-scenes work against independence, the PPD leader finally went public with his decision to abandon independence as a goal. In a series of February 1946 *El Mundo* articles, he asserted that the relationship between the United States and Puerto Rico "did not fit the general design of colonialism," and he warned of looming economic catastrophe that would destroy "whatever political freedom is established" if Puerto Rico did not obtain a standard of living capable of reversing population growth.[52] A continued governing relationship with the United States was essential to obtain this political freedom.

Time was of the essence. Reynolds warned ALPRI colleagues, "Puerto Rico was witnessing the beginning of a bitter battle between the true independentistas and those advocating pseudo-liberty under it mattered not which banner."[53] By 1946, Reynolds's solidarity-based support for independence put her and the ALPRI squarely at odds with Muñoz Marín. Reynolds navigated the fraught nature of contesting Puerto Ricans about their political future as an "outsider" by framing her motivation for doing so as a form of patriotism to the United States. She wanted the United States to realize its professed commitment to liberty by giving up rule of its colony.

Toward this end, she geared the report toward demonstrating that although Americans did not like to think of themselves as colonizers, US cultural impositions, economic abuses, and acts of political repression in Puerto Rico were characteristic of colonizing nations around the world. She documented the negative effects of the United States' imposition of English in schools.[54] She explained how US trade and tariff laws transformed Puerto Ricans into a captive market for US products and trapped them into selling commodities and merchandise to the United States. She documented the police killings and unfair trials of Nationalist Party leadership and supporters. Whether or not the US government was behind the police killings, Reynolds asserted, "it certainly upheld its servants," including the US-appointed governor, who contributed to the Ponce Massacre.[55] "The Nationalists," she further noted, "have today, after ten years of unrelenting persecution, sufficient numbers and strength in a single night to kill and destroy the homes of a high percentage of the representatives of the invading power. If they were terrorists some such activity would have been undertaken long since." "But no Nationalist, or other Puerto Rican for that matter," she explained, "contemplates such a program."[56]

Another key part of the report emphasized the singularity of the Nationalist Party in a pattern of accommodationist history that seemed to be repeating itself under Muñoz Marín's lead. As she explained, pro-independence forces founded the Nationalist Party in 1922 upon witnessing "time and again, the decay of the moral fiber of Puerto Rico's own statesmen as they fell under the power of the invading regime." In 1922, after years of US federal pressure, the dominant Union Party abandoned its support for independence for an ill-defined "free associated state"—to no perceivable benefit.[57]

Reynolds argued that Muñoz Marín was making the same mistake of accommodation that the Union Party before him had, blatantly contradicting his own bold pro-independence proclamations in the process, first as a young Liberal Party senator in the 1930s and then in founding the PPD. She characterized him as having once served as "the most outspoken non-Nationalist for independence."[58] She summarized his widely circulated 1936 "Manifesto to the Puerto Rican People," extolling independence as the key to ending US economic exploitation and benefiting from international trade treaties and protective tariffs.[59] "Above all this," the manifesto promised, "independence would create great moral strength, that of a nation that is no longer a colony."[60] Reynolds lauded the effects of these words, saying that "the people, not ready to follow the Nationalists to martyrdom but nonetheless convinced that independence was both their right and their necessity, turned to [Muñoz Marín's] leadership in their hour of deepest sorrow" after the 1937 Ponce Massacre.[61] As Reynolds asserted, Muñoz Marín's "analysis of the evils of colonialism and the necessity for independence" in the manifesto "is quite as valid today as it was then."[62]

But that was the past, and in order to effectively influence policy in Washington, DC, toward independence, potential North American allies had to know what he was doing and how he was doing it. Drawing on firsthand accounts from her fieldwork, Reynolds explained that Muñoz Marín's enormous appeal in Puerto Rico enabled him to deftly and deceptively steer the nation away from true independence. Muñoz Marín had neutralized critics in Puerto Rico. Nationalist Party supporters across the archipelago were subject to surveillance and harassment. Albizu Campos had been released from Columbus Hospital in New York while she was in Puerto Rico, and she presumably consulted him about these ongoing political developments when she was preparing the report. Yet, he was still in New York and far away from the brewing political battle in Puerto Rico. Meanwhile, Muñoz Marín was working behind the scenes with the US government to create a pseudo-independence (at best) or abandon independence altogether (at worst). She was trying to shine a light on the situation for those who might take action, presumably with the US government shaping policy in Washington, DC. There was time to stop him.

Stopping his agenda would be tough, however. As Reynolds explained, Muñoz Marín was tremendously popular—"almost a legendary figure, virtually worshipped as the champion of the masses"—who had built his reputation among the masses through campaign promises of "bread, land, and liberty," and by delivering land reform and industrial development.[63] Facing a daily subsistence struggle, Reynolds explained that "postponement of the issue of freedom until the economic situation has been alleviated was not difficult for the Puerto Rican masses to accept, particularly since the Populares were actually trying to help them secure food."[64]

He was also a master strategist. Reynolds warned that Muñoz Marín had forged a big head start, enacting his agenda by "rupturing every strong independence group except the Nationalists."[65] She analyzed his success destabilizing organized labor and muffling his PPD colleagues during the previous two years. As she explained, Puerto Rico's largest labor union, the General Confederation of Workers (Confederación general de trabajadores, CGT), polarized into rival groups in March 1945 when Muñoz Marín opposed a strike: the majority supported independence and demanded Albizu Campos's release but did not claim allegiance to an electoral party; a minority supported Muñoz Marín and the idea of a plebiscite with various status solutions.[66] Further, within his own party, she explained, Muñoz Marín had convinced party members to forgo discussing status politics during the 1944 election. As Reynolds wrote, the strongly pro-independence party leadership of the PPD "had agreed to this maneuver, trusting that when the proper hour arrived, Muñoz would lead them in demanding genuine independence."[67]

But Muñoz Marín was also vulnerable. She claimed that Muñoz Marín's ability to shape policy in Washington, DC, was uncertain in 1946. He had forged his access to policymakers in Washington during President Franklin Roosevelt's administration. Most important was his collaboration with Rexford Tugwell, the US-appointed governor of Puerto Rico between 1941 and 1946. Tugwell was a prominent New Dealer who worked in concert with US secretary of the interior Harold Ickes and Muñoz Marín to bring a New Deal "modernization" agenda to Puerto Rico.[68] The agenda relied on private US capital and tax breaks for US companies operating in Puerto Rico. It also advocated a commonwealth formula. But, Reynolds explained, "Muñoz may have had influence in Washington, but it was rapidly disappearing." Roosevelt had died in 1945, and "Ickes and Tugwell both appeared to be on the way out." Harry Truman's new policies toward Puerto Rico were still ill-defined, but a new conservatism was likely on the horizon in DC.[69] Moreover, the United Nations had "been established with all of the big powers stained with imperialism; no major victory in the struggle for a just world order would have resulted from its establishment." Given Muñoz Marín's temporary isolation, the new conservative mood in Washington, and the lost international moment, Reynolds insisted that "the strategic time to strike for independence was at hand." As she told an acquaintance in Puerto Rico, "independence comes in 1946 or not until national and international politics again makes the issue a strategic one."[70]

Yet while Reynolds's projection of Muñoz Marín's vulnerability during this time remained to be determined, Reynolds was facing a vulnerability of her own. She remained the target of government surveillance.

FBI surveillance began in New York, almost immediately after Reynolds began regular meetings with Albizu Campos in 1944. It continued in Puerto Rico in 1945. An FBI agent in San Juan monitoring the Nationalist Party reported her arrival and plans to conduct a survey across Puerto Rico under "Miscellaneous Activities."[71] The insular police—who cooperated with the FBI while also maintaining their own surveillance files—had likely created a 4×6" card about her. It was standard surveillance practice when informants or undercover agents identified a new person within the circle of meetings and events among independentistas. Four mentions triggered the insular police to open a formal file of investigation on the individual.[72] Then, back in New York, as Reynolds wrote up her findings of Albizu Campos's enduring popularity in Puerto Rico in 1946, she continued to catch the eye of the FBI agents who were surveilling Albizu Campos. Notably, FBI agents relayed "indications" that Albizu Campos "was losing his popularity among Puerto Ricans in New York" in part because "he was more interested in proselyting among Americans who might back the Nationalist movement, than among his own people."[73] The FBI wishfully saw her allyship with Albizu Campos as a source of weakness.

In fact, Reynolds and her report were assets to the Nationalist Party that expanded the reach and longevity of their struggle in the difficult and urgent political environment. Yet there was a potential cost to circulating her counternarrative, whether it was in print or in person. For at least a decade, the federal government had directed the full force of its many powers toward discrediting and incarcerating Nationalist Party leadership. This machinery was still functioning. Reynolds's solidarity activism had already caught the attention of the US government. By serving as a vocal witness and critical interpreter of the stories of injustice that Puerto Ricans had entrusted to her, however, Reynolds moved closer toward becoming part of that story. In the view of the federal government, Reynolds's sympathetic reporting of a group that it had criminalized called into question the legitimacy of her own activities. The distance separating witness and conspirator narrowed.

Reynolds temporarily escaped this surveillance by writing portions of what became her counterhistory of the United States and Puerto Rico at her parents' home in South Dakota, but she had difficulty staying out of the action. In fact, the report's completion was delayed because of a lobbying effort at the recently formed United Nations. The multifocal nature of Reynolds's solidarity activism entailed mobilizing for independence on multiple fronts, and it was impossible to completely set aside her active engagement in order to write without distraction. On behalf of the ALPRI, Reynolds and Jay Holmes Smith submitted a petition to diplomats gathered at the UN General Assembly in Long Island to address the US government's continued "political and military subjection of the people of Puerto Rico." The petition, they maintained, was a confession for the sins of their nation and an essential step toward ending "the vicious cycle of exploitation and war." It was action she needed to be a part of.[74]

Nevertheless, Reynolds produced a very high-quality draft report. Intriguingly, it appears that she did not formally distribute the full report.

Moreover, Albizu Campos had actually urged Reynolds to publish it as a book, but Reynolds decided not to, considerably limiting the potential influence of the document itself to a larger audience.

But for Reynolds, the act of having engaged in the fieldwork—the solidarity methodology she developed during this first trip—had deepened her understanding of Puerto Ricans' political perspectives in ways that had not been possible in either New York or Washington, DC. Her process of interviewing and writing, and even her apprehension about publishing her findings, also showcased a significant aspect of her developing practice of solidarity: her reckoning with her positionality as expressed through her deliberate efforts to listen to and understand Puerto Ricans' perspectives before claiming any kind of authority or expertise on the subject of independence. As she explained, "My feeling is that I was immature, that I was grappling with things but not understanding them fully. And that it was . . . still a learning experience, but that I was not any authority and shouldn't pretend to be." Years later, in fact, she reflected on the significance of her first trip to Puerto Rico and the subsequent process of committing her new learning to the page: "Now, yes, I'd stand up and yell, and talking—whatever had to be done, but I did not feel that I had put things together completely."[75]

Though she did not "stand up and yell" at the time, Reynolds still managed to bring to light information about the urgency of the moment. She had discussed Muñoz Marín's surprising political actions in the US Congress with many of his pro-independence Puerto Rican admirers. She had also compiled a rich base of documentary evidence that the cause of independence in Puerto Rico was as popular as ever. Her errand going forward and that of her ALPRI colleagues entailed transmitting this fundamental insight to US allies and politicians.

Nearly three years would transpire between this first trip to Puerto Rico and her next one. During those three years, Reynolds and other ALPRI members continued to diligently use the spaces available to them—including congressional hearings and the United Nations—to mobilize for Puerto Rico's independence. When Reynolds did travel again to Puerto Rico in 1948, it was similarly for the purpose of another investigation on behalf of the ALPRI. Her fieldwork methodology, based on interviews and close listening, did not change, but her confidence about publishing her findings did. The price of this confidence that her findings needed to be published would prove to be high.

5 Río Piedras

In the first two weeks of October 1948, Ruth Reynolds regularly walked around the flagship campus of the University of Puerto Rico (UPR) in the town of Río Piedras at all hours of the day and the night. "The campus was pervaded with an atmosphere of fear and suppressed hostility," she observed. "The gaiety of youth, characteristic of any normal university campus, was nowhere in evidence."[1] Three years after her first trip to Puerto Rico, Reynolds had once again come to the archipelago to investigate. This time, she was interested in the ongoing student strike at the UPR and the violent police suppression of student marchers; she could feel the tension in the air. She watched students walking "quietly to and from classes, glancing sideways in passing at the police and detectives" stationed throughout the campus. During one walkabout at 1:30 in the morning, Reynolds counted thirty-one police and detectives in just a block and a half.[2]

From her home base in New York, Reynolds had already tried for months to make leading defenders of civil liberties in the United States understand that the events at the UPR were not a mere conflict between students and university administrators. Rather, they were a full-blown clash over Puerto Rico's future between colonizer and colonized that required significant attention. The American Civil Liberties Union, for example, refused to thoroughly investigate this suppression of students' civil liberties because it saw the campus conflict as a political matter among Puerto Ricans that did not warrant outside intervention. Thus, in late September, when a frustrated Reynolds and other leaders of the American League for Puerto Rico's Independence (ALPRI) learned that police had severely beaten student protesters, the group mobilized. Within a matter of days, Reynolds was on her way to Puerto Rico to investigate on the ALPRI's behalf.

Although Reynolds delayed announcing the investigation, she nevertheless jumped right into gathering information, repeatedly visiting the campus and engaging in casual conversations with students and faculty about the protracted conflict.[3] In mid-October, she moved on to formal interviews. Only then did she go public with the purpose of her visit. With the help of the Puerto Rican press, she issued an open invitation to the Puerto Rican people to come and talk to her about the strike. Anyone wanting to share testimony about recent events at the UPR could find her at the Puerto Rican Athenaeum between 1:30 and 5:30 P.M., Monday through Friday. No appointment was necessary. Reynolds planned to make herself available at this cultural landmark, as one newspaper noted: "As long as necessary, in order to give everyone who is connected in any way with the recent events at the University of Puerto Rico, an adequate and impartial audience."[4]

Reynolds had good reason to delay announcing her presence in Puerto Rico until she was ready to initiate such "formal interviews."[5] She surmised that once word of her investigation spread, she ran the risk of unwanted government surveillance. She had sought a brief window of time to observe campus life without this intrusion. Her assumption was right. One day after Reynolds initiated her Athenaeum interviews, Jorge Camacho Torres, captain of the Internal Security Squad of the Insular Police, prepared a confidential memorandum informing the head of the insular police that "Agents of this Squadron were posted in the surroundings of the Puerto Rican Athenaeum in an effort to obtain information related to the activities of Ms. Reynolds."[6] Camacho's memorandum was among the first documents in *carpeta* (folder) 1340—a secret file devoted to documenting information about her activities in Puerto Rico. Reynolds's investigation exposed the limits of democracy in Puerto Rico, and it made her a target of police surveillance.

The secret dossier on Reynolds was part of the vast surveillance system that the federal government, working closely with the insular government, had built for decades to track the legal activities of Puerto Rican critics of the United States. That system involved multiple agencies and relied on paid community informants alongside police and undercover agents to document the activities of alleged "subversives."[7] The vast majority of Puerto Rican political activists assigned carpetas were independentistas. The total number of carpetas that Puerto Rico's Intelligence Division ultimately produced is unknown, but in 1987, when the Puerto Rico Civil Rights Commission began investigating, there were about 16,000. While some carpetas were slim, many others were thick reams of paper with detailed documentation of the comings and goings of suspected subversives over many decades. Reynolds's carpeta was one of the latter, consisting of several volumes that covered nearly a quarter century.[8]

Reynolds arrived in Puerto Rico intent on running her own investigation into the student protests just a few weeks before Puerto Ricans chose Luis Muñoz Marín, the Partido Popular Democrático candidate (Popular Democratic Party; PPD), as their first elected governor. Since first butting heads with Muñoz Marín in Congress during the Tydings Bill hearings and subsequently traveling to Puerto Rico for the first time to discover whether his views actually represented those of most Puerto Ricans, Reynolds remained suspicious of the politician's motives. Muñoz Marín had, in fact, been quite busy since her last trip. His popular election in November 1948 only further advanced his plans to create Puerto Rico's Free Associated State, or Estado Libre Asociado (ELA) in the name of democratic reform. So too did his party's suppression of the voices of its most outspoken critics. While Muñoz Marín's supporters declared his victory as the first elected governor to be the beginning of the end of colonialism, Reynolds and other pro-independence advocates believed that what appeared to be democratic reform was actually being sustained through the suppression of freedom of expression.

When she arrived, the University of Puerto Rico was ground zero for the battle over Puerto Ricans' right to proclaim their support for independence and to protest Muñoz Marín's evolving status politics. UPR administrators and the police had been silencing pro-independence voices on campus since the beginning of 1948, in an attempt to stifle student support for Nationalist Party leader Pedro Albizu Campos.[9]

Reynolds was convinced that fellow "continentals" would care if they understood that the US government and its insular allies were perpetuating colonialism under the guise of democratic reform. In her view, North American audiences needed to understand the complexities of the UPR conflict because the suppression of student freedoms encapsulated this new phase of colonialism in which the United States relied increasingly on Puerto Rican officials in place of Anglo-American ones to crush the independence movement. This shift in the 1940s made it particularly challenging for outside observers to understand the key arbiters and levers of power over Puerto Rico. Thus, Reynolds was intent on mapping it out for them.

She maintained her position and perspective as an American fighting for US democracy and conceptualized her information campaign as being directed toward fellow non–Puerto Ricans, but her investigation thrust her deeper into the local struggle. The time she spent on the UPR campus put her at odds with the PPD-controlled insular government that favored the creation of the ELA. Local officials categorized her as a subversive, and the insular police watched and recorded her as she watched and recorded government suppression of pro-independence voices. At no other time in her career had her vision for solidarity as an activist been so sorely tested.

Albizu Campos and the 1948 UPR Student Strike

Of all the changes Reynolds encountered since her first trip to Puerto Rico three years prior, perhaps the most significant was the return of Albizu Campos to the archipelago in 1947 after over a decade of imprisonment and probation in Atlanta and New York. Several thousand people—five thousand by one estimate—met him at the dock in San Juan when the boat carrying him arrived in the afternoon of December 15 (see figures 5.1 and 5.2).[10]

Albizu Campos wasted no time in resuming his efforts to mobilize the population toward the cause of independence. The Nationalist Party leader attracted large crowds as he traveled around Puerto Rico giving speeches. In them, Albizu Campos denounced Muñoz Marín's evolving political agenda and insisted that the PPD leader had to be stopped. The PPD leader's evolving agenda would only facilitate US extractive practices and continued militarization of Puerto Rico. At the time, the US military was in the process of expropriating thousands of additional acres of land in Vieques for its Cold War operations. What the US military was doing in Vieques, he warned, "is a practical example of what can happen in the entire territory of Puerto Rico." Albizu Campos assured the crowds that the Nationalist Party would "exhaust all peaceful means in the struggle for independence" but would not hesitate to meet US military force with force.[11] As he promised at a December 1947 press conference, if "the United States decided to stifle the right of Puerto Ricans by force, then the Nationalist Party would resort to force to achieve its objectives."[12] By the spring of 1948, the FBI's regional director in Puerto Rico had notified the FBI director J. Edgar Hoover of intelligence that Albizu Campos was planning an uprising within a few months.[13]

The UPR was the initial site where the PPD mobilized to silence Albizu Campos and his supporters following his return. The government ramped up its policing powers to stem the tide of pro-independence sentiment in Puerto Rico that his arrival had galvanized. In 1948, the UPR administration employed increasingly coercive tactics to suppress students who expressed support for Albizu Campos or an independent Puerto Rico. Meanwhile, Albizu Campos continued to promise that the Nationalist Party would meet any US-backed force with force.[14]

The UPR was an ideal site for the PPD to silence pro-independence voices in Puerto Rico. Founded in 1903, the University of Puerto Rico was an instrument of the US colonial agenda. Its initial mandate called for the production

FIGURE 5.1 A photo of the crowd gathered on December 15, 1947, at the San Juan port and awaiting the return of Albizu Campos to Puerto Rico. Source: "Muchedumbre esperando el regreso de Pedro Albizu Campos, Puerta de Tierra, 15 de diciembre de 1947." Centro de Investigaciones Históricas, Universidad de Puerto Rico, Recinto de Río Piedras, Colección Benjamín Torres, serie: fotografías, caja 4, número 20.

of teachers who would educate Puerto Rico's children to be colonial citizens. At the Mayagüez campus since 1913, and at the Río Piedras campus beginning in 1919, for example, all male UPR students were required to complete ROTC (Reserve Officers' Training Corps) training.[15] Into the 1920s, the majority of UPR professors were Anglo-Americans, and until 1942, the UPR's official language of instruction was English.[16] The UPR, however, was also an incubator of the intelligentsia, including many leading independentista voices of the World War II generation.

By the early 1940s, Muñoz Marín and the PPD held sway over university affairs after legislating expanded powers for the university's highest office of rector (chancellor) over students and faculty and then securing the appointment of a PPD ally to that office. First, in 1941, Muñoz Marín (then senate

FIGURE 5.2 A group identifying themselves as the Nationalist Junta of Río Piedras photographed as part of the large crowd greeting Albizu Campos upon his return in December 1947. Their signs read, from left to right, "The Maestro Arrives after His Exiles"; "Jail Was Your Altar"; and "'Welcome Maestro'/Your People Have Not Forgotten You/Nationalist Junta of Río Piedras." Source: "Regreso de Pedro Albizu Campos, 15 de diciembre de 1947," Centro de Investigaciones Históricas, Universidad de Puerto Rico, Recinto de Río Piedras, Colección Benjamín Torres, serie: fotografías, caja 4, número 25.

president) appointed Rexford Tugwell as UPR rector, but students denounced the choice. Tugwell was a prominent New Dealer in the Franklin Roosevelt administration and an ally of Muñoz Marín. Tugwell resigned within two months of becoming UPR rector, but not because of student protest. Rather, President Franklin Roosevelt appointed him as governor of Puerto Rico in September 1941. In September 1942, Jaime Benítez replaced Tugwell. Benítez, on the faculty since 1931, had been involved in the independence movement for years.[17] In the 1930s, Benítez had been a staunch independentista, even heading the Committee for the Liberation of the Puerto

Rican Political Prisoners that had mobilized for Albizu Campos's release from federal prison.[18] By his 1942 appointment as UPR rector, however, Benítez had become a staunch PPD supporter. His was not an unusual story—Benítez was one of the many independence supporters swayed by Muñoz Marín, through either agreement or fear, to follow Muñoz Marín to his new party. In Benítez's case, he led efforts to transform the UPR into a model of progress as part of the PPD modernization agenda.[19]

Publicly, PPD legislators exalted the rector's expanded powers over students and faculty as a tool for eliminating partisan politics on campus. Privately, they welcomed Benítez's partisan use of those powers to silence their most vocal critics on campus.[20] In fact, the great lengths to which the UPR administration would go to suppress pro-independence voices became clear within weeks of Albizu Campos's return. In January 1948, UPR rector Benítez expelled three students and suspended two others who had marked Albizu Campos's return to Puerto Rico with a very public display. In December of the previous year, they had lowered the US flag from the campus's landmark Franklin D. Roosevelt Tower and raised the Puerto Rican flag in its place (see figure 5.3).[21] Then, in April, Benítez denied the Student Council's request to use the university theater to host Albizu Campos for a talk titled "The Status of Puerto Rico before the United Nations."[22] When the Student Council called for a one-day strike in protest, the UPR administration suspended dozens of students, fired supportive faculty, and closed the university.[23] The government subsequently also issued arrest warrants for those students it had previously suspended for flying the Puerto Rican flag in honor of Albizu Campos's return in December 1947.[24]

By May 1948, the government, the UPR administration, and protesting students were at a standoff. Benítez went so far as to close the university for three weeks. However, he reversed the decision and briefly reopened the university with a ban on student assemblies and demonstrations. During this time, the police beat, tear-gassed, and arrested scores of students who defied the prohibitions. In response, students went on strike again and promised to remain on strike until Benítez resigned. Striking students threatened to boycott final exams. Embattled by the protests, Benítez once again shuttered the university for a second time on May 7—although he still expected students to sit for final exams.[25]

Tensions further escalated on May 8, after Governor Jesús Piñero militarized the conflict by mobilizing the National Guard to San Juan. Military and government officials resolved to contain student protesters and, as one

FIGURE 5.3 "University Students Greet Maestro Albizu Campos," reads a banner that stretches across the Franklin Delano Roosevelt Tower at the entrance to the campus of the University of Puerto Rico at Río Piedras. Students hung this banner and replaced the US flag that was a tower fixture with the Puerto Rican flag. Source: Ruth M. Reynolds Papers. Universitarios saludan al maestro Albizu Campos / University Students Greet Teacher Albizu Campos: RMRe_b04_f02_0001. Archives of the Puerto Rican Diaspora, Center for Puerto Rican Studies, Hunter College, CUNY.

US commander put it, to contain the "outside communist and nationalist guidance" they suspected the students were receiving.[26]

The Gag Law

The full scope of the role that the UPR conflict would play in Muñoz Marín's plans to inaugurate a status for Puerto Rico as neither a sovereign nation nor a US state began to emerge once the Río Piedras campus fell quiet. The majority of students took their final exams in May. Others boycotted exams without further incident. During the summer months of 1948, the strike leaders and protesters, known as the University Crusade, abated their organizing in anticipation of the ACLU conducting an official investigation and delivering its findings.[27] The PPD, by contrast, used its legislative powers to expand its tools for suppressing Muñoz Marín's critics.

During the summer months of 1948, PPD legislators in Puerto Rico employed the student strike to justify enacting a law to crush the Nationalist Party. Insular Law No. 53, also known as the "Gag Law," made it a crime to advocate the overthrow of the insular government by force and violence. It was modeled on the US Alien Registration Act of 1940, or the Smith Act, that made it a felony to advocate the overthrow of the US government. The US government enacted the Smith Act to prevent wartime subversion and, after World War II, used it to prosecute Communists and other leftists across the United States.[28] As senate president, Muñoz Marín insisted on the necessity of Law 53 to prevent any obstruction of the upcoming historic elections. Critics argued that the law's real purpose was to intimidate the independence vote and Nationalist Party supporters.[29] One dissenting lawmaker complained during the legislative process, "We do not favor the university strike but condemn that it be used as a pretext to oppress thought, to choke the conscience and to suppress speech."[30]

Despite piercing criticisms, the PPD-dominated Legislative Assembly passed the Gag Law under a cloak of secrecy of closed late-night sessions and with the intent of silencing Albizu Campos and his supporters. Governor Piñero signed the bill into law on June 10.[31] Muñoz Marín had been moving away from a pro-independence position since at least 1945. With this law, all the pieces were in place for him to formally announce that he had given up on independence in July.[32] Understanding that the Nationalist Party was the law's primary target, Albizu Campos promised that the Nationalist Party was prepared to respond to state violence with violence.[33]

The new academic year began in August 1948 with a heavy police presence in Río Piedras, the new Gag Law in place, escalating tensions between Albizu Campos and Muñoz Marín and their respective supporters, and the future of hundreds of students in jeopardy. Forty-eight students were under injunction not to enter the campus, and more than 600 others remained suspended for boycotting their final exams. The University Crusade commenced picketing, and some students were arrested for violating the injunctions.

In late September, police dispersed students marching through the streets of Río Piedras to commemorate the eightieth anniversary of the Lares rebellion against Spanish rule of Puerto Rico. They did so by beating students, at least two of them to the point of unconsciousness.[34] It was this event, and the American Civil Liberties Union's refusal to respond to it, that precipitated Reynolds's second trip to Puerto Rico in 1948. Upon receiving the news of the police actions against students celebrating the Grito de Lares on September 23, Reynolds and other ALPRI board members Jay Holmes Smith, Rachel Davis DuBois, Lula Peterson, and Richard Walsh quickly convened and resolved that Reynolds should launch an investigation.[35] By the time she arrived in Puerto Rico on September 29, students had already called for an indefinite strike.[36]

Reynolds Investigates

Well before Reynolds arrived in Puerto Rico in the fall of 1948, she had already expressed deep fear that the buildup could result in a deadly police attack on students similar to the massacre of civilians in Ponce on Palm Sunday, 1937. Prior to that incident, the governor of Puerto Rico had similarly suppressed free speech and assembly for months. And in the days and hours immediately preceding the police shooting of unarmed marching Nationalists and bystanders in the streets of Ponce, the government had amassed and heavily armed a police force presence in the southern coastal city. With soldiers patrolling Río Piedras in 1948, Reynolds wrote President Truman and Governor Piñero, warning that they would be held "personally responsible in the event of any repetition of the Palm Sunday Massacre of 1937."[37]

Watching tensions unfold from New York that spring and summer, Reynolds's concerns mounted. She turned to the ACLU for help. In 1937, the ACLU had conducted an extensive investigation into the circumstances surrounding the police attack in Ponce and issued a report blaming US-appointed governor Blanton Winship for the massacre. Reynolds alerted ACLU staff counsel that Governor Piñero's mobilization of the National

Guard suggested that "the Government is seeking to provoke an incident, on the basis of which the Nationalist and student leadership could once more be incarcerated on conspiracy charges, following the pattern of the Winship Era of the 1930s."[38]

At the same time, Reynolds urged the ACLU to understand that the UPR conflict was ultimately a struggle between Puerto Ricans' right to demand national sovereignty and the federal government's efforts to eclipse that freedom. She noted that it was difficult for outsiders to see it as more than "a simple disagreement between a group of students and the rector" because all involved, including the governor, were Puerto Rican. Since the ACLU's 1937 investigation, she argued, "the United States Government has followed a policy of appearing to relax its tyranny without making any basic change at all"—especially by putting Puerto Ricans into local offices previously reserved for North Americans. She pointed first and foremost to the office of the governor. At the time, Piñero was the archipelago's first appointed Puerto Rican governor. In November, Puerto Ricans would elect a governor for the first time. "Now that a determined movement of non-cooperation is once more developing in Puerto Rico," Reynolds asserted, "the government is replying with a new wave of terrorism, this time seemingly directed by Puerto Rican officials, who are under the complete control of the federal government."[39]

Reynolds had already firmly rejected the notion that electing a governor was a step toward self-rule when the issue first arose in Congress in 1947. Testifying on behalf of the ALPRI before a US House subcommittee in May 1947, Reynolds had argued that the Elective Governor Bill (also known as the Crawford-Butler Act) that was then before the committee "changes the empire-colony relationship between the United States and Puerto Rico not at all. It merely transfers from the President of the United States to the people of Puerto Rico the questionable privilege of selecting one more servant of empire." As she testified to Congress, "The master-slave relationship cannot be disguised, gentlemen." "A ruffle here, a patch there," she continued, "may fool a few Puerto Ricans and a few Americans for a short while, but it will not fool anybody very long."[40] Nevertheless, both houses of Congress passed the Elective Governor Bill, and in August 1947, President Truman signed it into law. It was widely assumed that Muñoz Marín would emerge victorious from the November 1948 elections as Puerto Rico's first elected governor.[41]

When Reynolds reached out to ACLU leadership, it was her greatest hope that its leadership would send an investigating commission. Although it is difficult to determine whether her lobbying swayed them in any meaningful way, there was initially some reason to hope. In late May, UPR students who had traveled to New York to meet with ACLU leadership announced that the ACLU had promised to send an investigating commission to Puerto Rico.[42]

In the end, the ACLU ignored Reynolds's concerns. Her assessment that many outsiders were unable to recognize the US government's sleight of hand proved truer than ever. Indeed, after consulting with Rector Benítez again, the ACLU issued a subsequent statement affirming its decision not to get involved because the conflict was primarily one among Puerto Ricans and not between US officials and Puerto Ricans. The ACLU called for a complete ban on all partisan meetings at the UPR as the solution to the conflict; it would be less controversial if the university denied all partisan student groups access to campus facilities, rather than just one.[43]

Reynolds began to read the writing on the wall. A new strategy was needed, and this is how she came to be walking around the campus, ready to conduct her own investigation that October. This reconnaissance may have been unannounced, but she likely stood out during these early morning walks, especially because Nationalist Manuel Negrón Nogueras (whose family she was living with) accompanied her.[44]

After her initial unannounced reconnaissance around the UPR campus, Reynolds employed the fieldwork methodology of asking questions and careful listening that she had refined on her previous investigative trip to Puerto Rico. Under the shadow of government surveillance, she embarked on interviews at the Athenaeum. After assigning detectives to the site, Captain Camacho Torres of the Insular Police's Internal Security Squad relayed to his boss, "Very few people have visited this lady, so she intends to personally visit those who have an interest in the matter."[45] Some students and other eyewitnesses weathered the intimidating gaze of detectives pacing outside the Athenaeum in order to sit for an interview with the ALPRI investigator from New York. Others met with Reynolds in secret or provided information during chance encounters. Reynolds likewise called on government officials and Río Piedras campus administrators for interviews.[46] While Benítez and a few UPR administrators met with her, they refused to cooperate with the investigation. Not discouraged by officials' admonishments to stop interfering in Puerto Rican affairs, Reynolds promised to carry out the investigation with or without officials' help.[47]

In early 1949, after conducting numerous interviews over a period of four months, Reynolds aspired to write up an impartial report that no one could question because its claims were backed by the wealth of evidence that she gathered.[48] After all, this was the strategy she had engaged in to bring the findings from her first trip to Puerto Rico to light in 1945. "An honest imperialist and an honest anti-imperialist," she insisted, "could reasonably be expected to discover the same facts through an investigation, however different their interpretations of and attitudes toward those facts might be."[49] Reynolds believed that she had identified those facts. She aimed to put them in the context of US imperialism in Puerto Rico in order to "convey to the American people a full sense of the educational tragedy resulting from our complete domination over Puerto Rican life."[50]

Indeed, Reynolds had a head start because she was able to draw on the sophisticated but unpublished manuscript she had prepared in 1945 to evaluate Puerto Rico's economic and status struggles under the US flag. She also had the assistance of the Nationalist Party, which provided "office accommodations." Reynolds resolved to work on her new report in Puerto Rico—a marked shift from when, after her 1945 investigation, she wrote up her findings at her home in New York and her parents' house in South Dakota.[51]

However, she commenced her work under continued police surveillance and dwindling support from important North American allies. Without Reynolds's presence in New York to lend steadfast leadership, the ALPRI had started to collapse.[52] The ACLU had already declined involvement altogether. And tensions flared between Reynolds and Fellowship of Reconciliation (FOR) leadership.

Lilian and Bob Pope—the North American pacifists heading the FOR in Puerto Rico with whom Reynolds lived for eight and a half months—became exasperated with her Nationalist Party sympathies and "bitter feelings toward Americans, toward Puerto Rico government officials, and toward Independentistas."[53] "Referring to the Christian-inspired FOR ideology for resolving conflict, the Popes complained to a colleague that "it was clear that she was making no attempt at reconciliation."[54] After many discussions on pacifism, violence, and Puerto Rico's status politics, Reynolds and the Popes parted ways. Reynolds moved out in July 1949.[55]

Over a decade later, Reynolds described the situation as such: "Paradoxically, most pacifists in Puerto Rico enthusiastically embrace United States imperialism there, and denounce those who struggle against it. The only pacifist couple I knew who [stood] against colonialism and [were] Gandhian in outlook had never become acquainted with the Nationalists to any degree, and I could not waste time trying to convince them of the imminent danger and the need for sacrificial action." Under the circumstances, she concluded, "Whatever I was to do I would have to do alone."[56] At that moment in her radical solidarity journey, allyship meant increasing isolation from North American allies at a moment when their support would be most helpful.

Confronting Violence

When Reynolds's ties with North American allies strained, new and long-standing friendships with Nationalists were more important than ever for Reynolds's investigative efforts. After leaving the Popes and with little to no funds at her disposal, Reynolds was welcomed into a string of Nationalist homes: the Ciales farm of Carlos Vélez Rieckehoff and Luisa Guadalupe de Vélez Rieckehoff; Juan Alamo Díaz's home in Bayamón; Isolina Rodón's place in Río Piedras; and eventually the small cottage that Paulino Castro maintained behind the family's home in Cataño.[57] At the same time, Reynolds finally met Laura Meneses de Albizu Campos, who after years of residing in Cuba and Peru returned to Puerto Rico to join her husband.[58] Forged in the shadow of escalating tensions and constant surveillance, Reynolds and Meneses de Albizu Campos's friendship developed as a close and enduring one that facilitated their shared political goal of a free Puerto Rico.

As Reynolds worked on her manuscript between 1949 and 1950, the insular police continued to log her often daily visits to Nationalist Party headquarters in San Juan. Detectives reported seeing her on February 5, 1950, at the Capitol Building taking notes on US ambassador to the United Nations Warren Austin's speech there, and the next day attending the federal trials of Nationalists who had violated the Selective Service Law. They reported her attendance in mid-April 1950 at a student rally commemorating the second anniversary of the UPR student strike, and in May at a labor demonstration organized by Communist Party leadership. They also documented her attendance at Nationalist Party events: in Fajardo, Aguada, and Arecibo in the fall and winter of 1949, and in 1950 in Ponce on March 21, in Cabo Rojo on April 8, in San Juan on April 16, in Manatí on June 11, in Guánica on July 25, in Lares on September 23 (see figure 5.4), and in Farjado on October 26.[59]

Reynolds, however, was also watching them. In late October, her observations tested her pacifism and made her a witness to the first wave of government arrests that triggered the 1950 Nationalist insurrection. On October 25, Reynolds informed Albizu Campos of an assassination plot against him planned for the following evening in Fajardo. Albizu Campos

FIGURE 5.4 The insular police took this photo of the September 23, 1950, Grito de Lares celebration in Lares. Reynolds (*no. 1*) is among the four individuals identified by number on the reverse side of the photograph. The others (*left to right*) are Nationalists José Bermúdez (*no. 4*), Juan Alamo Díaz (*no. 3*), and Pedro Albizu Campos (*no. 2*). Also clearly visible here is Isabel Rosado Morales. She appears in the bottom left, holding the flag and looking directly at the camera. Source: Archivo General de Puerto Rico, Archivo de fotografía, fondo: Departamento de Justicia (Tarea 90–29), serie: Documentos Nacionalistas. "Conmemoración Grito de Lares, 23 de septiembre de 1950." Fondo: Departamento de Justicia (Tarea 90–29), serie: Documentos Nacionalistas, item 84, fotografía número 176.

was scheduled to speak at the Nationalist-sponsored event in Fajardo honoring nineteenth-century independentista and native son Antonio Valero de Bernabé.[60] While dining at a popular San Juan restaurant on the evening of October 25, Reynolds overheard a group planning the assassination and recognized among them a detective regularly stationed outside Albizu Campos's residence at Nationalist Party headquarters. Thus, she assumed that the would-be assassins were government agents or proxies. She lowered her gaze to avoid recognition as she listened. She then rushed to Nationalist Party headquarters to tell Albizu Campos what she had heard.

Reynolds struggled with how to align her pacifism with the potential consequences of her personal actions when Albizu Campos requested that she travel to Fajardo to identify the would-be assassins. What if identifying the men resulted in their deaths? In a 1961 statement that Reynolds prepared at the request of Laura Meneses de Albizu Campos to ensure a written record of the 1950 plot, Reynolds reflected, "Just as I could not stand idly by and let my friend be killed without warning, and had therefore told Don Pedro what I had heard, neither could I conscientiously point out his enemies as targets for death."[61]

Albizu Campos remained steadfast in his views on just war theory and armed resistance. But he did make her a promise: "'We will not provoke bloodshed tomorrow,'" she quoted him telling her, "'but if violence is started against us, we must act according to our own philosophy.'"[62] After much introspection and despite the tension with her personal philosophy on violence, Reynolds went to Fajardo. "I knew I was the only person who could identify them," she wrote in 1961, "and therefore the only person who could prevent Don Pedro from being killed." She was confident that Albizu Campos would not initiate bloodshed. If the government did, she was prepared to die in order to shield Albizu Campos and also live up to her pacifist principles. She believed that "the proper Gandhian method of dealing with this situation would be . . . for pacifists to surround both the would-be killers and the chosen victim, and shield him from his murderers with their own bodies." But she was alone. "I knew," she wrote, "that, in case I should see any one of them prepared to act before I could point them out to the Nationalists, the only proper course of action would be for me to block their target from them with my own body." Thus, she explained, "I went to Fajardo hoping and praying that, in this eventuality, I might have both the valor and the agility to do so."[63]

The FBI file on Albizu Campus makes clear that police detectives were present at the plaza in Fajardo to document the event, as they were at all of Albizu Campos's public speeches.[64] The group Reynolds had overheard in San Juan, however, did not show. Reynolds speculated that the government abandoned its plan because the police knew that Albizu Campos knew of them. According to Reynolds, she had seen Albizu Campos make sure of it the previous night by asking the detectives stationed outside his home about the plot.[65]

It was on the journey home that Reynolds experienced firsthand the early stages of the government crackdown on the Nationalist Party. Shortly after midnight, a group of Nationalists and the police who constantly trailed them began the several-hour drive back to San Juan. Reynolds traveled by *público* (a taxi for multiple passengers) with three Nationalists, Rafael Burgos Fuentes, Eduardo López Vázquez, and José Mejías Flores.[66] In a second car, Nationalist Antonio Moya Vélez drove five others as he accelerated, stopped, and swerved on the narrow road trying to frustrate the three police cars trailing the third vehicle carrying Albizu Campos.[67]

As the carloads of tired travelers neared the end of their journey shortly after 3 A.M. on October 27, police attempted to block them, separating the convoy. Responding to an early morning tip that the group was transporting arms, Santurce police stopped Moya Veléz's vehicle, and shortly after in Río Piedras, a larger group of police surrounded the *público* carrying Reynolds. The police confiscated multiple firearms, bombs, rounds of bullets, and a submachine gun. They charged Moya Vélez, Burgos Fuentes, and López Vázquez with violating the law to carry arms. The police interrogated Ruth Reynolds and other passengers—Ana Rita Pagan, Gladys Barbosa, and José Mejías Flores—at Hato Ray police headquarters.[68] In a separate incident earlier that same day, police also had pulled over a car carrying Albizu Campos but did not arrest him.[69]

Confronting violence put her pacifism at odds with her allyship. She resolved to embody her radical solidarity through her own suffering. It was the beginning of a new phase of allyship for her.

Returning to Her Work

After her harrowing adventure with Albizu Campos and the journey to Fajardo, the police released Reynolds several hours later without charging her. Exhausted from the experience, Reynolds returned to the Cataño cottage behind Nationalist Party leader Paulino Castro's home, where she was living by the fall of 1950.[70] There in the cottage sat her completed typewritten book titled *Training for Treason: A Study of the University of Puerto Rico, 1942–1950*. By this point, *Training for Treason* was a dense 600-page manuscript and appendix in three parts. Each of the three parts had titles corresponding to stages of a familiar natural disaster in Puerto Rico: "The Gathering Storm," "The Hurricane," and "The Aftermath."

Collectively, the book chronicled the human disaster of a transforming US imperialism that during the 1940s increasingly relied on Puerto Ricans to maintain their own subjugation under the fraudulent guise of self-rule. It detailed how the US government relied on the mutually constitutive levers of cultural, economic, and political power it had linked to the archipelago's premier educational institution to control student politics both on and off campus. Her detailed treatment of how these levers of power reinforced each other and gave rise to the student protests were meditations on how totalizing power operates and the challenges of resisting it.

The manuscript included examples of these levers at work through the university. Covering the roughly two decades prior to the 1948 strike, "The Gathering Storm" discussed the US "economic and physical terrorism" that led onetime independentistas like Benítez and Muñoz Marín to quash the pro-independence voices of fellow Puerto Ricans.[71]

Her detailed account of "The Hurricane" on campus that erupted in the spring of 1948 likewise explored the profound political, economic, and social pressures that worked against defying the US government and its allies. She explained that the majority of students sat for their final exams, despite vowing to boycott them, because students and their families, like nearly all residents of Puerto Rico, faced limited opportunities for upward mobility beyond the aspirations tied to college education.[72]

In "The Aftermath," Reynolds wrote that the responsibility for the empire "rests on you and on me—citizens with full rights of government and full responsibility for government in the United States of America." She insisted, "Let not Americans who believe that they believe in democracy evade any longer this responsibility." She further asserted, "Let us not plead ignorance—for to plead ignorance is to confess to indolence and indifference. It is worse—it is to confess to a pagan sense of racial and national superiority, for, while we have been ignorant of the details of American rule in Puerto Rico, we have not been ignorant of the fact of American rule in Puerto Rico."

For Reynolds, radical solidarity was not just about expressing allyship. It was also about self-emancipation. "Let us free Puerto Rico," she wrote, "and in doing so begin to free ourselves from the racial and national arrogance that is making our nation a curse in the earth." She urged that "for the sake of the American people, primarily, and secondarily, for the sake of the Puerto Rican people, let us recognize immediately Puerto Rico's right to constitute her own free and independent government."[73]

Also threaded through the manuscript were Reynolds's meditations on the differences between collective and individual violence. She inverted US government formulations back on themselves, pointing out the "absurdity of singling out the Nationalists to condemn for violence when the system they oppose is solely based in violence and is supported by the most powerful armed forces in the world." She criticized the military requirement for Puerto Rican men studying at the UPR directed toward serving in the US Army Reserves: "No university that requires all its male students to train for violence can properly make non-advocacy of violence a pre-requisite for the use of its facilities."[74] A hallmark of her allyship was focusing attention away from individual transgressions and toward state violence.

• • • • • •

By the fall of 1950, Reynolds was arranging to publish her book. Whatever apprehensions had prevented her from publishing her ALPRI report as a book in 1946 had been replaced with greater confidence in her role as an outside expert. She was in conversation with Peacemakers colleague Dave Dellinger to publish with his Libertarian Press in New Jersey, which had already printed several radical pacifist books since Dellinger founded it in the late 1940s.[75] She was pursuing funds to cover the costs of roughly 6,000 copies of *Training for Treason* in both English and Spanish to place free of charge in libraries across the Americas, but particularly the United States. Reynolds explained the importance of this errand to Félix Benítez Rexach in requesting a "large contribution" from the Dominican Republic–based Puerto Rican businessman. Benítez Rexach had provided financial support to the Nationalist Party in the past, most recently welcoming the Albizu Meneses family to reside without charge at his well-known Normandie Hotel in San Juan.[76] She wrote, "I know from painstaking personal search that a conscientious American of good faith can go through the best libraries in the country looking for information on Puerto Rico and encounter nothing but lies, lies, and more lies."[77]

Reynolds, however, sought to avoid government notice of such publication plans. As she advised Dellinger, "Since the contents of this manuscript are tropical in temperature, it is best that as few people as possible know about it before printing arrangements are completed."[78] She had dedicated over two years of her life to the project, experienced the surveillance and threats of state violence on the archipelago, and yet persisted in her work—committed to revealing the real situation in Puerto Rico to other "continentals" who seemed to take the US government at face value in its promises of democracy.

She hoped the book would open people's eyes and increase support for unqualified independence. And support was needed more than ever. In her absence, the ALPRI had begun to disintegrate. The ACLU had turned a blind eye. No one, it seemed, was listening. Driven by the intensity of her convictions, Reynolds remained an optimist in her estimation that an evidence-driven book like the one she had just completed could convince more allies like herself.

However, Reynolds's hopes for her book's future were dashed. Once again, she had written up her extensive documentation of a firsthand investigation in Puerto Rico only for the project to unravel at the last minute. In this case, the momentum that Reynolds had generated toward publishing the book came to a complete halt in the early morning hours of November 2, 1950. This was the day she was arrested.

6 La Princesa

....

On September 7, 1951, a San Juan judge sentenced Ruth Reynolds to two to six years of hard labor for conspiring to overthrow the government of Puerto Rico. The conviction stemmed from the 1950 Nationalist Party uprising in Puerto Rico and assassination attempt of the president of the United States in Washington, DC. Hours after sentencing, Reynolds met with her lawyer, Conrad Lynn, at the San Juan District Jail where she was being held. Despite its wretched condition, the jail was widely known as La Princesa because of its location on a promenade built for the mid-nineteenth-century visit of Spain's future queen. Reynolds told Lynn she was being tortured.

In the weeks immediately after, Reynolds wrote a full accounting of her mistreatment at La Princesa and smuggled it out of the prison. Her charges of suspected radiation poisoning and other abuses paralleled those made by Nationalist Party leader Pedro Albizu Campos.[1] In her covert memorandum, Reynolds included a postsentencing conversation with Lynn: "I told him . . . that I believed that the government was trying the same stuff on me that it had used on Albizu Campos. I told him that I, being no scientist, didn't know what it was all about, but that I was being spoken to by unseen voices." She documented Lynn's response: "Then Albizu Campos is right." She urged Lynn to share her explosive accusation only with a select few, because most people "would naturally only consider me crazy."[2] Even without such allegations, Reynolds's proximity to Nationalist Party members had already cost her many political allies.

Incarceration marked a new stage of Reynolds's radical solidarity. This stage was forged in the shadow of revolutionary and colonial state violence. Reynolds experienced firsthand the brutality of US empire that previously she had only heard about. Both La Princesa and the Arecibo District Jail—where Reynolds actually spent the majority of her pre- and post-conviction incarceration—functioned as extensions of the United States' colonial apparatus in Puerto Rico. Prior to her arrest, Reynolds employed nonviolent tactics to confront commonwealth proponents in the halls of government in San Juan and Washington, DC. She also empathized with the patient suffering of Nationalist Party supporters who endured government persecution because of their political views. After her arrest, Reynolds embodied radical solidarity through her own suffering and bearing witness to the pain of others.

Though the number of Reynolds's US allies shrank dramatically in the wake of the Nationalist uprising, her entrance into a unique community of women political prisoners expanded her activist world. Reynolds's embodied solidarity took shape amid the harsh prison conditions she experienced alongside Nationalist women at La Princesa and the Arecibo District Jail. This new sense of solidarity endured after her release from prison because she did not carry alone the memories of how the colonial state attempted to silence her ally-oriented pacifism. She shared these memories with a community of Nationalist women whom commonwealth proponents had likewise tried to silence by criminalizing their politics. The cognitive and physical imprint of such collective trauma fueled Reynolds's decolonization and political prisoner defense efforts going forward.

The 1950 Insurrection

Reynolds's embodied solidarity started to take shape at the close of her second year in Puerto Rico. At the time of her arrest, she was completing her investigation of the University of Puerto Rico's (UPR) suppression of student strikers, an investigation that she had initiated in 1948 (see chapter 5). During that time, she had had come to understand the UPR's heavy-handed response to pro-independence student strikers as emblematic of an entirely new phase of colonialism—one defined by the United States' increasing dependence on Puerto Rican officials to crush the independence movement.

Reynolds viewed the 1950 Puerto Rico Federal Relations Act as an extension of this new phase of US policy of relying on Puerto Ricans to shore up their own colonial status—this time by voting in favor of the constitutional details of their own colonial status. Governor Luis Muñoz Marín and Puerto Rico's resident commissioner in Congress shepherded the bill, also known as Public Law 600, through the House and Senate. Congress approved Public Law 600, and President Truman signed it into law on July 3, 1950.[3]

Public Law 600 outlined the steps for inaugurating a new constitution that had the potential to expand local governance but otherwise did not fundamentally change the colonial relationship between the United States and Puerto Rico: first, Puerto Ricans would vote in a special referendum to approve or reject Public Law 600. Approval of Public Law 600 would authorize Puerto Rico's legislators to call a constitutional convention to draft a new constitution. Puerto Ricans would then go to the polls again, this time to vote on the new constitution. Voter approval of the new constitution would authorize President Harry Truman to transmit the document to Congress if the president determined that it conformed to the parameters of Public Law 600 and the US Constitution. If Congress accepted the new constitution, it would then go into effect.[4]

Public Law 600 did not provide a pathway for Puerto Ricans to vote for either complete independence from the United States or further incorporation into the United States as a state. While Congress lauded the bill as "a concrete demonstration to the nations of Latin America and the world, and especially the people of Puerto Rico, that the United States translates its principles of democracy and self-determination into action," members of Congress also publicly promised that any new constitution "would not change Puerto Rico's fundamental political, social, and economic relationship to the United States."[5]

Nationalist Party president Pedro Albizu Campos was at the forefront of dissent. He urged followers to defeat the process outlined in Public Law 600—not with their votes but rather through armed rebellion.[6] On September 23, he made a speech in the town center of Lares to commemorate a rebellion against Spain that had taken place there in 1868. Drawing on the anti-imperial symbolism, Albizu Campos insisted to the crowd that Public Law 600 "must be challenged and it must be challenged only as the men of Lares challenged despotism, with the revolution!"[7] He planned for the rebellion to begin six weeks later in November, when the process for implementing Public Law 600 was scheduled to begin.

Albizu Campos originally called on supporters to rise up against the government of Puerto Rico and its implementation of Public Law 600 in Puerto Rico on November 4, 1950, when voter registration opened. Puerto Ricans who sought to participate in the referendum to accept or reject Public Law 600—scheduled to take place in June 1951—had to first register.[8] Several days ahead of the opening of the two-day voter registration period on November 4, however, insular police launched preemptive raids against Nationalist strongholds, disrupting Albizu Campos's plans.[9]

Tensions between the police and Nationalist supporters escalated quickly from there. During the next two days, a large group of incarcerated Nationalist men were among those who escaped from the notorious Insular Penitentiary in Río Piedras (widely known as the Oso Blanco) amid a prison revolt. In Ponce and Peñuelas, police confiscated stockpiles of weapons that Nationalist Party members had accumulated in preparation for the rebellion.[10]

As police raids of Nationalist property and arrest of its leadership expanded, Albizu Campos instructed followers to revolt in their own towns on October 30 rather than wait until November 4. He instructed them to shut down their town's municipal operations and then retreat collectively to the central mountain town of Utuado. Utuado was strategically positioned and rich in agriculture, and Albizu Campos envisioned that pro-independence forces could sustain the resistance for an extended period from that site. Perhaps putting too much faith in the United Nations, some Nationalist leaders believed that such a public display of resistance would prompt the United Nations to demand the end of US imperial rule of Puerto Rico once and for all.[11]

Police and Nationalists battled between October 30 and November 1. Both Nationalists and insular police lost their lives and were among the injured in Peñuelas, Ponce, Arecibo, Jayuya, Utuado, and San Juan. US National Guard fighter planes bombarded Nationalist positions in Jayuya and Utuado. Ground troops armed with machine guns advanced on Jayuya. In Utuado, members of the National Guard summarily executed Nationalists.[12] Through overwhelming force, the government prevented the planned convening there.[13] The United Nations took no action.

The government also thwarted Nationalist efforts in Arecibo to declare the Republic of Puerto Rico over the radio and to plant the Puerto Rican flag atop city hall.[14] In Jayuya, however, Blanca Canales, a social worker and Nationalist Party member since 1931, famously eluded government forces and raised the Puerto Rican flag high in the town center, announcing the Republic of Puerto Rico. There, Nationalists held government forces at bay for two days and damaged the police station, the post office, and the Selective Service Office, symbols of US power in their city.[15]

On October 31, Puerto Rico's leading newspaper, *El Mundo*, featured on its front page an image of the lifeless bodies of two Nationalists splayed on the courtyard of Muñoz Marín's residence, La Fortaleza (see figure 6.1). Five men had rushed and opened fire on the official residence of Puerto Rico's architect of the commonwealth. Only one survived the rain of bullets from the insular police.[16] Muñoz Marín was not injured, but three police officers were. Local radio also broadcast live a multihour firefight in San Juan's Barrio Obrero.[17]

The uprising was not restricted to Puerto Rican soil, however. On the afternoon of November 1, Nationalists Oscar Collazo and Griselio Torresola approached President Truman's temporary residence at Blair House and opened fire. Upon learning about the uprising, the two decided to travel from their New York homes to Washington, DC, in lieu of returning to

FIGURE 6.1 This photograph of Carlos Hiraldo Resto's and Manuel Torres Medina's lifeless bodies in the courtyard of La Fortaleza on October 30, 1950, appeared on the front page of *El Mundo* the following day. Source: Ruth M. Reynolds Papers. Crime Scene: RMRe_b39_f02_0008. Archives of the Puerto Rican Diaspora, Center for Puerto Rican Studies, Hunter College, CUNY.

Puerto Rico to join their comrades. According to Collazo, the two men sought to upend US reporting on the uprising as an exclusively internecine struggle between Puerto Ricans when they attacked Truman's residence. Guards and secret service agents returned fire and rushed to block access to Blair House. Collazo shot one guard. Torresola shot another several times and mortally wounded a third officer. In his final moments, the officer killed Torresola with a shot to the back of the head. By the end of the battle, Nationalists and officers had exchanged an estimated thirty shots. Collazo survived, but with a bullet wound to the chest. Truman heard the shooting from inside Blair House but was not injured.[18]

The government's response was swift and far-reaching. In the hours and days that followed, the insular police, the National Guard, and FBI agents

FIGURE 6.2 A photo taken during the mass arrests in 1950. Source: Ruth M. Reynolds Papers. Soldiers Rounding People Up: RMRe_b39_f02_0006. Archives of the Puerto Rican Diaspora, Center for Puerto Rican Studies, Hunter College, CUNY.

fanned out across Puerto Rico and detained thousands: Nationalist Party members, their family members, members of Puerto Rico's small Communist Party, and, as *El Imparcial* reported, "anyone who seems suspicious due to the relationships they may have or have had with the Nationalist Party" (see figure 6.2).[19] This included local leaders of the Puerto Rican Independence Party (Partido Independentista Puertorriqueño; PIP), the second-largest electoral party and primary opposition to Muñoz Marín's Popular Democratic Party in the insular government.[20] Gilberto Concepción de Gracia, PIP president and lawyer to Albizu Campos in the 1930s, vehemently denounced the arrest of his party's local leaders. Although he opposed Nationalist violence, he affirmed the Nationalist Party's right to seek independence.

In some areas, the unrest did not fully abate despite widespread repression. In Mayagüez, for example, Nationalist supporters scuffled with the police and National Guard for several more days until November 6—one day after voter registration closed. The insurrection came to an end on November 10 in Naranjito, when the leader of that mountain town's Nationalist insurgents finally surrendered to police.[21] The Nationalists nevertheless failed to halt the registration process. Voter registration took place as scheduled on November 4 for women and November 5 for men. Approximately 75 percent of the adult population—779,695 Puerto Ricans—registered.[22]

Not surprisingly, commonwealth champions declared the two-day registration period a triumph of democracy over terrorism. "Firing prospective votes instead of bullets," the *New York Times* reported on November 5, "this island outpost of democracy in the Caribbean repeated today the unexpectedly high registration of yesterday."[23] Muñoz Marín similarly assured journalists, "The registration results are the democratic response of the people against gangsterism, violence and terrorism." *El Imparcial* quoted him telling the press, "In reality, Puerto Rico, is not a colony" or a possession or even a territory but rather a new form of government "adaptable to the North American model."[24]

The self-congratulations were misleading. When the referendum that Puerto Ricans had registered for in November 1950 finally took place on June 4, 1951, less than half of Puerto Rico's adult population actually went to the polls. Among them, 75.6 percent approved Public Law 600—or approximately 37 percent of the adult population (17 percent of the entire population).[25] The PIP unsuccessfully demanded that the Insular Board of Elections nullify the results.[26]

Soon after, on August 27, 1951, just 43 percent of the archipelago's registered voters went to the polls again, this time to elect delegates for a constitutional convention. The PIP refused to participate in an election that thwarted independence and was taking place under the shadow of widespread government surveillance and harassment of PIP supporters. With the PIP boycott, seventy-two of the ninety-two delegates were members of Muñoz Marín's PPD. On September 17, 1951, they convened in San Juan to write a constitution unlike any other in the history of either Puerto Rico or the United States.[27]

Ruth Reynolds and Support from the Continental United States

The insular police's temporary detention of Reynolds on October 27 as she traveled from Fajardo to San Juan was part of the government's preemptive raids against Nationalists to prevent disruption of the upcoming voter registration.[28] Her formal arrest on November 2 was one of the roughly 2,000 that police made during their dragnet across Puerto Rico following the assassination attempt against President Truman (see figures 6.3 and 6.4).

FIGURE 6.3 The National Guard detaining people in 1950 at the San Juan District Court in Puerta de Tierra. Reynolds appears in the center of the line of detainees. Source: "Guardia Nacional y personas en fila en la Corte de Distrito de San Juan, Parada 8, Puerta de Tierra," Centro de Investigaciones Históricas, Universidad de Puerto Rico, Recinto de Río Piedras, Colección Benjamín Torres, serie: fotografías, caja 10, número 12.

FIGURE 6.4 This image provides a closer view of Reynolds in the line.

Within a few days of her arrest, the ALPRI announced its dissolution. On November 6, ALPRI officers Jay Holmes Smith, Lula Peterson Farmer, and A. Philip Randolph issued a statement that, while acknowledging "Reynolds's remarkable devotion to the work of the League," disavowed any connection with her because of her alleged membership in the National-ist Party. Without suggesting when or how, these officers expressed a bland "hope that a fresh approach to the problem of Puerto Rico's political status may soon be effected, with new forces taking an active part."[29] ALPRI offi-cers Thelma Mielke and Richard Walsh apparently did not participate in the decisive meeting to break with Reynolds.[30] Decades later during an interview, Reynolds suggested how this decision intersected with gender ideologies privileging male voices. If Smith as ALPRI chair had "held his ground" against scrapping the group so quickly, she asserted, "we would have had greater success, not only because he did have some talents, he was not untalented, but because he was male, he was listened to more."[31] In the days immediately after her arrest, however, Reynolds's attention was focused elsewhere on helping her family understand what was going on.

On November 13, 1950, Reynolds spelled out for her parents her daunting situation. "I have been accused of 'conspiring to overthrow the Government of Puerto Rico by force and violence,'" she wrote. "I am not guilty," she asserted; "I have never believed in killing for any purpose, and have had no part in planning or executing the violence of the past week here." Nevertheless, Reynolds prepared her parents for an uncertain future. She warned, "In the trial I may be exonerated, and I may not. I have tried my best to help avoid the things that have come to pass, but they have come anyway." Though expressing regret for their pain, Reynolds also explained her acceptance of her imprisonment by invoking a revolutionary history they appreciated: "When Puerto Ricans are in jail for wanting liberty, I belong there with them. After all, I had ancestors who fought in the American Revolution. If they had not won, they would be in jail."[32]

Her parents were devastated by her arrest, and, as her younger sister recalled, both were "upset that she would bring this on her parents" and worried that "they had failed in bringing her up." Along with a son-in-law, they reached out to US senators to help obtain her release. Reynolds refused one offer promising that "if she would return west of the Mississippi and never go east again, that she would be released." As her sister recalled, "And of course, she wouldn't agree to any stipulation of that sort."[33]

Reynolds's longtime political interlocutors in New York formed a Ruth Reynolds Defense Committee (RRDC) by the end of the year, with the goal of raising money to pay for a lawyer and publicizing her case among US leftist communities. Thelma Mielke served as the committee chair, and Julius Eichel as its treasurer. Other members, spread across the Northeast, included prominent pacifists such as Dave Dellinger, Rachel DuBois, Conrad Miller, A. J. Muste, and James Peck. Collectively, this group drew from her multiple political communities—the Ashram, the defunct ALPRI, the Fellowship of Reconciliation, and the recently formed pacifist group, the Peacemakers.[34] An RRDC flyer that likely dates to July 1951 warned that the atmosphere of government intimidation and repression in Puerto Rico was such that only a few attorneys "associated with the Nationalist Party" would serve to defend detainees. "Two or three men," they wrote, would be "carry[ing] the whole load of a defense of over four hundred persons." This would prove accurate: the same lawyers who represented Albizu Campos—Francisco Hernández Vargas and Juan Hernández Vallé—also traveled all over Puerto Rico to represent Nationalist Party members, to their own financial detriment.[35]

The RRDC warned of a "danger of grave miscarriage of justice" should their fundraising fail to procure better legal representation for Reynolds.[36] Conrad Lynn stepped in. Reynolds knew Lynn from Ashram events, and in 1942, they were both part of a nonviolent interracial group that had walked from New York to Washington, DC, to protest racism in the United States.[37] By the time Lynn began attending Ashram events in the mid-1940s, he was a lawyer committed to a range of social justice causes. As Lynn recalled in his memoirs, "Even before I passed the bar examination[,] I had promised myself to handle cases in which social issues were involved."[38]

Lynn had worked with pacifists and liberals; he was neither.[39] He had been a member of the Young Communist League and the Communist Party during the late 1920s and 1930s, until the party expelled him in 1937 for criticizing its abandonment of striking oil workers in Trinidad in the face of British violence.[40] Since that time, he continued to pursue antiracist activism, participating, for instance, in the first freedom ride to desegregate interstate bus travel in the South in 1946.[41] He had also continued to build a modest law practice that sometimes carried him beyond his financial means. "My client list was hardly dotted with corporations and rich individuals who kept me on large retainers," Lynn recalled. He described asking his sister for a loan that would enable him to keep working on a case. As he observed, "A client generally gets the justice he or she can financially afford, and seldom can the poor invoke all the remedies of the law."[42]

Lynn was well aware that the relationship between the married, mixed-race leader of the Nationalist Party and Reynolds, a single, white North American woman, made her an easy target for prosecutors who might employ sexual innuendo as a stand-in for evidence. The cultural well associating transgressive female sexuality with political instability ran deep in the United States and Puerto Rico. In the immediate post–World War II years, US media and government celebrated the white patriarchal family consisting of a breadwinner husband and dependent wife and mother tasked with purchasing modern conveniences to fuel the economy. In Puerto Rico, the PPD also harnessed such an idealized image of women's domesticity toward the promises of economic mobility at the heart of its colonial populism.[43] As Lynn recalled, "a good deal" of the defense's investigation was spent on preparing to contest implications that the unmarried Reynolds and the married Albizu Campos had a sexual relationship, which motivated her to advocate violence out of love for him.

Lynn was also Black, and both Reynolds and Albizu Campos understood that their affiliation challenged intersecting racial and gender norms. According to Lynn, Reynolds and Albizu Campos "were aware that the symbol of a black lawyer defending a white pacifist woman and a brown-skinned Puerto Rican revolutionary would be highly significant." Although Lynn did not serve as Albizu Campos's lawyer, in representing Reynolds, Lynn defended Albizu Campos's politics as well. Lynn knew that supporting them would likely harm his career. Still, as he recalled, "I was thrilled by the opportunity" Reynolds's trial presented.[44] However, not everyone who knew Reynolds wanted Lynn to support her.

Fault Lines among US Pacifists

Reynolds's incarceration forced North American pacifists to grapple with the nuances of expressing solidarity with liberation movements that condoned armed resistance. A small but impressive list of pacifist colleagues in the United States stuck with her. Very few of these supporters, however, actually endorsed the type of anticolonial solidarity that she practiced. They focused instead on the contradictions of radical pacifist and Nationalist ideologies when defending Reynolds, while simultaneously and vehemently distancing themselves from the Nationalist Party. Other colleagues dismissed Reynolds altogether as a wayward pacifist hanging out with the wrong crowd, at best; at worst, she was a dangerous criminal deserving of conviction.

Some pacifist members of the Ruth Reynolds Defense Committee (RRDC) supported Reynolds but not her vision of common cause with the Nationalist Party in advancing a shared critique of US colonial state violence. RRDC treasurer Julius Eichel, for instance, defended Reynolds's right to campaign for Puerto Rico's independence, but he stood firm in his conviction that pacifists like himself had to distinguish between political goals and movements. "While a pacifist may see his way clear to support those who agitate for independence," Eichel held, "he is not always ready to support an independence movement." In his estimation, the RRDC could "denounce American imperialism and attempt to help the victims of it" but should "not endorse the Nationalist Party or its methods."[45] RRDC fundraising flyers promised that contributions did "not commit anyone to support of the

Nationalist Party or to any position with respect to political problems of Puerto Rico."[46]

A minority of North American pacifists, however, fervently opposed detaching Reynolds's defense from her solidarity politics. Notably, the "Gano Peacemakers"—as they were known because of their location in Gano, Ohio—urged the RRDC to highlight Reynolds's pro-independence work as a first step toward repairing long-standing pacifist neglect of the independence movement.[47] Like Eichel and Reynolds, the five members of this interracial Ohio collective—Juanita and Wallace Nelson, Marion and Ernest Bromley, and Lloyd Danzeisen—were Peacemakers. Founded in 1948, Peacemakers practiced tax resistance in an effort to deny US military funding, either by maintaining incomes below tax rates or refusing to pay federal taxes altogether.[48] In "the eyes of the Nationalists," the Gano Peacemakers surmised, "it must seem that the pacifists were not really for their freedom."[49] Chiding the RRDC, they contended that Reynolds was "practically the only pacifist who has really made this struggle a primary thing," while other efforts floundered. "Every time pacifists got interested in the cause," they clarified, "much was made of the fact that the Nationalist Party was not pacifist, and after some talk and some investigation interest died down."[50]

In defending the authenticity of Reynolds's pacifism, the Gano Peacemakers practiced radical solidarity themselves—championing allyship grounded in common opposition to state violence rather than in strategic conformity. They broke with colleagues, like fellow Peacemaker Dorothy Hickie, who accused Reynolds of participating in the insurrection. In the *Peacemaker* newsletter, Hickie, a North American missionary residing in Mayagüez, denounced pacifist support for Reynolds unless she had a "mental deficiency." Yet Hickie was an exception among the Peacemakers. In the same issue, Gano group member Lloyd Danzeisen defended Reynolds as "one of the leading exponents of Gandhian nonviolence on the American scene" without backing away from her ties to Albizu Campos and his supporters. "There is no doubt that her sympathies and activities are in support of the Nationalist Party," Danzeisen wrote, "but she does not advocate nor do we believe she would participate in armed violence."[51] "We believe," he continued, "as we think Ruth believes, that true independence will come to Puerto Rico only through non-violent soul force."[52]

Gano member Marion Bromley turned the tables on Reynolds's critics to expose their own unexamined ties to political violence in Puerto Rico. To Hickie's argument that a true pacifist would have tried to stop the uprising, Bromley retorted, "If Ruth is to be so severely criticized from something she did *not* do, what about the rest of us, including Dorothy Hickie, who did not prevent the violence, and apparently did not even speak out for independence for this subject island?" If Hickie was "a true lover of freedom," Bromley challenged, she "would be at least disturbed by the terroristic activities of the Government as those of the Nationalist Party." "All are guilty," Bromley charged, "for not taking an early, and strong, stand for the freedom of Puerto Ricans and for not working hard to make the resistance to American aggression in Puerto Rico a resistance of the Gandhian kind."[53]

Reynolds's arrest catalyzed wide-ranging debate among her allied pacifist communities, testing where anti-imperialism and nonviolence ideologies could meaningfully intersect. By the time Reynolds's trial date approached, no firm consensus had been reached.

The Trial

Over nine months after her arrest, Reynolds went on trial in late August 1951 for two Gag Law violations tied to transporting arms and taking an oath in support of the insurrection. She was the only non–Puerto Rican defendant in the slew of Gag Law trials that occurred between 1951 and 1952. Reynolds was tried simultaneously with Rafael Burgos Fuentes, Eduardo López Vázquez, and José Mejías Flores, the three Nationalist men with whom she had been detained during the October 27, 1950, ride back from Fajardo to San Juan. The men faced the same arms-related charge as Reynolds. Only Reynolds, however, faced the charge of taking the oath. There were other differences at trial. The judge denied Reynolds's request for a separate trial in English when the men waived their right to a trial by jury. Reynolds's fate was determined by jury and the three Nationalists by a judge only.[54]

The timing of Reynolds's court date signaled the weight that the government placed on the trial for the success of pending Gag Law prosecutions. Only Albizu Campos's court case preceded the joint trial of Reynolds, Burgos, López, and Mejías.[55] A few days before jury selection got underway for Reynolds, a separate jury found Albizu Campos guilty of violating twelve counts of Insular Law 53. Each of these counts was connected to speeches that Albizu Campos had given between 1948 and 1950 and that prosecutors identified as accelerants that ignited the insurrection. A judge sentenced Albizu Campos to twelve to fifty-four years in prison.[56]

Puerto Rico's legal community closely watched Reynolds's trial—possibly even more than Albizu Campos's case—as a barometer of the Gag Law's full reach in criminalizing dissent. Both Albizu Campos's and Reynolds's trials were about the legal boundaries of free speech and association in the revolutionary moment. Prosecutors pointed to Albizu Campos's words as the source of the uprising. They pointed to Reynolds's proximity to such words and Nationalist Party members as proof of her subversive guilt. The defense, by contrast, championed the constitutionality of free speech and association that grounded the revolutionary moment in foundational US political and legal philosophy.

In the first count, Reynolds was charged with pledging willingly to give her life in armed revolution to overthrow the insular government of Puerto Rico. She faced this charge alone at trial. It stemmed from a December 1949 Nationalist Party meeting she had attended in the northern coastal town of Arecibo, nearly a full year before the 1950 insurrection. There, 500 Nationalist Party supporters had gathered to raise funds to support the appeal cases of Nationalist Party members incarcerated for refusing the Selective Service Act.[57] Undercover police informants and FBI agents were scattered among the crowd. They assiduously wrote down license plate numbers and the names of known attendees. They also took notes on Albizu Campos's speech reprimanding Nationalists for not donating enough or doing enough for the cause of independence. They recorded him exclaiming, "Stand up! All who are Nationalists—true Nationalists—those who are ready to give their lives and fortunes for this cause, stand up!" Nearly all of the hundreds of attendees stood.[58] Reynolds acknowledged being present but claimed she did not stand, presumably because she was not a Nationalist Party member.[59]

The second count, which charged Reynolds, Burgos, López, and Mejías with being in possession of firearms and bombs with the intent of inciting revolution as part of a separatist movement, tested the boundaries of free association. This charge stemmed from Reynolds's October 27 detention after police found firearms and bombs in the car in which she was riding with her three codefendants.[60]

The government used the trial to quash dissent not only among defendants but also among anyone who might lend public support for them. As court proceedings got underway, police set about to intimidate observers with the threat of increased government scrutiny by snapping photos of the audience every few minutes. Lynn persuaded the judge to put an end to the photos. Still, unwilling to take the risk of further police surveillance, very few spectators returned to watch the trial.[61]

Among those who continued to attend regularly were Wallace Nelson, Ralph Templin, and Ernest Bromley, the three-person Peacemakers delegation that had traveled to Puerto Rico to observe the trial. Templin and

Bromley were Reynolds's former Ashram colleagues; Bromley and Nelson were part of the "Gano Peacemakers." Within the pacifist debates over appropriate anticolonialisms that Reynolds's arrest had sparked, the three men stood firmly in the camp of supporters who defended her allyship with the Nationalist Party. The emptied-out courtroom made the large presence of detectives, marshals, and heavily armed police that much starker and, as the Peacemaker delegation reported, "made one feel that here was a case upon which the government was concentrating heavily, and did not want to lose."[62]

During the several weeks that they spent in Puerto Rico, the Peacemaker delegation also put together a damaging picture of civil liberties being trampled, as well as indifference among US pacifists in Puerto Rico, to report on to colleagues. During a ten-day fast, Bromley made himself available daily at a local plaza for impromptu meetings with Puerto Ricans, publicized through *El Mundo* and *El Imparcial*. The delegation also met with US pacifists; they were shocked at the "bias, bitterness, and lack of knowledge regarding Ruth and her case" that they encountered among them.[63]

All the US pacifists they met in Puerto Rico opposed independence. Many defended the Gag Law. "It was an upsetting experience for us to realize," the delegation reflected, "that so many were casting their efforts strongly on the side of the oppressor, as against the individual." As they reported, "Guilt by association is a dominant reality as well as a fear. People stay away from some others whom they personally like because there is no need to run unnecessary risks." They realized as much from their conversations with Puerto Ricans—the PIP leader who explained the tremendous courage that it took for someone to admit membership in the party, or the professor who withdrew from political life out of fear of imprisonment after being fired for his pro-independence stance. They also started to more fully understand the risks of a pro-independence stance by witnessing Reynolds's trial.[64]

Prosecutors attempted to erode juror empathy for Reynolds by putting the violence of the revolution itself on trial, using photographs of the dead and injured. They had already pursued this strategy at Albizu Campos's trial by showing jurors large caches of firearms, dramatic images of the dead and maimed, and even the actual remains of a Jayuya officer who died in a fire ignited by Nationalists.[65] Albizu Campos had remained stoic throughout his trial.

At her trial, Reynolds cried when prosecutors showed these images and upon hearing police officers recount their suffering during testimony. She sat quietly as police witnesses exhibited machine guns, rifles, revolvers, dynamite, and Molotov cocktails.[66] In the estimation of the Peacemaker delegation, the prosecution's strategy "to show that violence had occurred and that Ruth Reynolds had associated with Nationalists" failed to prove the charges, much less prosecutors' assertions that Reynolds was a Nationalist Party leader with advance knowledge of the insurrection.[67]

By contrast, the defense championed Reynolds's constitutional right to criticize the government and associate with its most vocal opponents. Reynolds did so on her own behalf by refusing to retreat from her beliefs under cross-examination. She responded to prosecutors' efforts to link her to the insurrection's killings and arson with a careful exhortation of the principles of radical pacifism that had guided her allyship. When prosecutors asked why she had not worked "with the pacifist party in trying to get independence," she rebuffed that "there is no pacifist party in Puerto Rico." Thinking they had boxed her in, prosecutors pointed to the PIP, but Reynolds—whose initial contact with the cause of independence in New York resulted from ties between Nationalist Party and pacifist draft resisters— explained the consistency of her pacifism by unmasking the assumptions behind the line of questioning. As she responded, "A pacifist is opposed to killing, and war. Most of the Independentist young men of draft age that I knew registered for the draft and went into the [US] army." In other words, from her radical pacifist perspective, militarism shaped the strategies (withdrawal from or participation with the US government) of both the revolutionary and electoral wings of the independence movement.

When prosecutors probed about advance knowledge of Albizu Campos's plans for revolution, Reynolds asserted, "Long ago I said that I expected violence to break out into the open at any time." "But I also said," she retorted, "that the basic violence is the imperialism of the United States, and the Insular authorities who help enforce it."[68]

Reynolds's courtroom supporters were profoundly moved by the praxis of radical solidarity that they witnessed. In a letter to her family, Lynn described Reynolds taking the stand: "Immediately the courtroom was infused with a fresh atmosphere. Instead of the stoolpigeons, detectives and police there was a young woman composedly telling her life work."[69] The Peacemaker delegation similarly reported, "We came from the courtroom feeling that we had witnessed one of the most significant things of our time—the indomitable will of one young person pitted against one of the most crushing empires the world has yet seen."[70]

Reynolds's calm display of her ideological convictions on the stand belied her profound suffering. Though Reynolds spent the majority of her incarceration at the Arecibo District Jail, the weeks that she was held at La Princesa during her own trial in 1951 were among the most difficult of her life. Reynolds variously experienced mental anguish, exhaustion, an inability to eat, uncontrollable trembling, and difficulty speaking. During cross-examination, she recounted, "I was so weak that when the interpreter asked me to speak more loudly I found that I could not do so."[71]

Reynolds pointed to psychological and physical torture as the weapons of colonial power behind her suffering at La Princesa. She described verbal mind games and electromagnetic waves from the office below and the roof above the cell that she occupied for the duration of the trial.[72] Reynolds suspected an orchestrated campaign designed to break her will and to turn her state's witness.

From directly below her cell, Reynolds heard seemingly staged conversations and rhythmic chants in English at all hours of the day and night that left her sleepless and confused. She believed they were primarily from two FBI agents. One had a Southern US accent. They threatened, "She doesn't know yet what we've got planned for her. She's going to work for *us*, and right here in Puerto Rico." A third, "fatherly sounding figure" who identified himself as an FBI agent, promised her help and urged repentance for promoting the insurrection: "'Don't you think it encourages [Nationalists] to know a girl like you will support them all the time no matter what they do? And even though you tell them you disapprove of even *their* violence, they also hear you say that theirs is 'insignificant when compared to that of the empire?'"[73]

The psychological weapons of colonial power that Reynolds described also included racist and sexual verbal abuse intended to humiliate her. She heard racial epithets in reference to Lynn and Albizu Campos, and accusations that she had an abortion. She heard many sexually degrading conversations about herself and other Nationalist women prisoners. "Sometimes they would spend an hour saying that I was in love with Albizu Campos," she described, "and the next hour saying I didn't care about him at all. They would say the same thing, with less frequency, about my affection for Conrad Lynn. They would express the same vacillation in regard to the feelings of these gentlemen towards me." She quoted the suspected FBI agents calling the Ashram a "fucking comradeship" and calling her "Albizu Campos's mistress." "They repeated over and over and over again," she quoted them saying, "'Ruth M. Reynolds didn't come to Puerto Rico to write a book at all; she came here to fuck with Albizu Campos.'"[74]

Reynolds also regularly felt strong vibrations that left her with headaches. She described "vibrations from what I took to be an electric motor in the offices directly below me . . . especially when I was trying to nap." She elaborated: "I had a sensation that they were being directed precisely at my head, and they caused what resembled a mild electric shock. When I slept in the opposite direction my feet felt the shock more severely than my head." "The 'electric charges' or whatever they were at the base of my skull were very strong, so strong that once or twice I had to brace myself against the head and foot of the bed to keep from crying out." "Sometimes," she also documented, "I would hear a 'click, click,' on the roof above me, as though a photograph were being made."[75]

In the midst of her suffering, Reynolds struggled with the certainty of truth and the faith that constituted the bedrock to her politics. She questioned her ability to distinguish facts from lies and temporarily lost her ability to pray.[76] Still, Reynolds reassured herself that she "would neither be killed nor driven insane, because the Government knew that it could never hide permanently from the knowledge of [her] friends what had happened to [her]."[77]

It is entirely possible that the US government intentionally exposed Reynolds and Nationalist prisoners to radiation or other biological weapons. In the 1950s, the Central Intelligence Agency (CIA) was engaged in developing diverse forms of "no-touch" torture, including sensory deprivation and electric shock.[78] Between the 1940s and 1970s, the US government supported human radiation experiments and intentional exposure upon tens of thousands across the United States.[79] Since the early twentieth century, US researchers had used Puerto Rico as a laboratory for social science and medical research—for instance, dispensing a female oral contraceptive to women there without informing them that the contraceptive was still being tested for safety.[80] Ultimately, while it is unclear if state actors exposed Reynolds and the women with whom she was incarcerated to radiation, there is no doubt that the women confronted isolation and malnourishment. This mistreatment made Reynolds's time at trial very challenging.

At trial, Lynn faced different challenges in mounting his powerful defense. The difficulty of his task increased when Reynolds rejected his witness plan for ideological reasons. Lynn proposed subpoenaing commonwealth supporters who were well acquainted with Reynolds to testify in her defense. These included Governor Luis Muñoz Marín, former governor Jesús Piñero, and University of Puerto Rico chancellor Jaime Benítez. "I saw clearly the legal and political validity of this approach," Reynolds described, "but I was not enthusiastic about it because it involved obliging them forcibly to help me." She concluded that "it was to me extremely distasteful to use the machinery of the courts to oblige those who oppose the independence of Puerto Rico to speak in my defense."[81] Ultimately, Lynn settled for calling Templin and Bromley, two of the Peacemaker delegates attending the trial, as character witnesses for Reynolds.[82]

Despite this significant adjustment in strategy, Lynn advanced a defense of civil liberties that was made even more challenging by the US Supreme Court's June 1951 *Dennis v. United States* decision affirming the constitutionality of the 1940 Smith Act that had served as the basis for convicting leaders of the Communist Party USA.[83] Insular Law 53 was known not only as the Gag Law but also as the "Little Smith Act" because it was based on and nearly verbatim to the 1940 Smith Act. Many in Puerto Rico justifiably speculated that the prosecution deliberately delayed Gag Law trials until after the *Dennis* decision that essentially facilitated government repression.[84]

Lynn pressed on with a civil liberties defense without the support of the American Civil Liberties Union. The ACLU was an organization that Lynn had worked with in the past—as a cooperating attorney and during his own brother's court challenge of segregation in the US military during World War II. In the midst of preparing for Reynolds's court case, Lynn urged the ACLU not to "avert its face" from the over 800 Nationalists awaiting trial in Puerto Rico. He urged the ACLU to form a "Committee on the Prosecution of the Puerto Rican Revolutionaries" to generate support for these defendants and monitor their rights. As Lynn speculated in a letter to ACLU staff counsel Herbert Levy, "I am sure, that most liberals regard the revolution as having been foolhardy," given the slanted and superficial coverage of the insurrection in the American press. "At the very least," Lynn asserted, "the Union owes to the American people the opportunity to read the facts" about the uprising and thus use the ACLU's sway with the "great liberal sympathies of the American people" to the benefit of Nationalist defendants.[85]

The ACLU declined to set up such a committee so as to avoid entanglement in the cases. ACLU leadership did not view the Gag Law as vulnerable to a civil liberties challenge. As Herbert Levy wrote ACLU founding member Roger N. Baldwin, Nationalist violence had made such a challenge moot, "since there would seem to have been a clear and present danger of an attempt to overthrow the government resulting from the advocacy."[86] Levy went further, however, suggesting that even if the uprising had not taken place, recent ACLU policy rejected Nationalist Party members' calls to overthrow the colonial government as protected free speech. The ACLU had opposed the passage of the Smith Act, but the Supreme Court's 1951 *Dennis* decision had a chilling effect on its willingness to take up similar free speech convictions.[87] As Levy reminded Baldwin, the ACLU has just "agreed not to oppose laws which would make criminal the teaching of acts designed to overthrow the government, on the theory that such teaching in itself presents a clear and present danger."[88]

Nevertheless, Lynn attempted to secure Reynolds's freedom by challenging the Gag Law's constitutionality. He pinned some of this strategy on the possibility that the Supreme Court would interpret *Dennis* and not use it as precedent for Insular Law 53. Writing to Herbert Levy of the ACLU the day after asserting its unconstitutionality at trial, Lynn explained, "My feeling is that if the US Supreme Court is to limit the holding in *Dennis et al. vs. US* it may very well do it while passing on some Little Smith Act."[89]

In opening arguments closely watched by the legal community in Puerto Rico, Lynn asserted a powerful defense of free speech that grounded the revolutionary moment in Puerto Rico in foundational US political and legal philosophy.[90] The Declaration of Independence itself, Lynn argued, recognized that "under a certain circumstance—an unresponsive government— it was legal, indeed necessary to overthrow the government," and "that such a circumstance existed in Puerto Rico."[91]

He also attempted to secure Reynolds's freedom by rooting the legitimacy of Albizu Campos's revolutionary ideas in two landmark free speech Supreme Court cases preceding *Dennis*. He quoted from Justice William Douglas's 1949 majority opinion in *Terminiello v. Chicago*: "The purpose of free speech should be to incite people to anger against their oppressors." He also invoked Justice Oliver Wendell Holmes's 1925 minority opinion in *Gitlow v. New York*: "When the ideas of a revolutionary are held by the majority of the people, those ideas should be the law." As Lynn recalled, "I argued that Albizu's ideas were the sentiment of the majority" in Puerto Rico.[92]

On September 5, just a few weeks after the trial's start, and a two-and-half-hour deliberation, the jury of eleven men and one woman convicted Reynolds of the first charge of violating Insular Law 53 by taking a pledge at the October 30 Nationalist Party meeting in Arecibo. They acquitted her of the second charge related to traveling in a car with firearms and incendiary bombs, even as they convicted two of her traveling companions.[93] In Lynn's opinion, the guilty verdict had been "foreordained."[94]

However, he did not stop fighting. Lynn argued for an arrest of judgment on the basis that Reynolds's conviction rested solely on a pledge she denied taking, which the prosecution alleged had taken place almost a year before the uprising and about which witnesses offered conflicting accounts.[95] The judge was not swayed. On September 7, Reynolds was sentenced to two to six years of hard labor.[96] Lynn appealed on September 10, but the judgment held.[97]

Embodied Radical Solidarity

Incarceration marked a new chapter in Reynolds's radical solidarity. Experiencing the weapons of imperial power to silence opponents from the inside was different from reporting on them from the outside. Before her arrest, Reynolds's resolve to work for Puerto Rico's independence steadily deepened with each account of Puerto Rican suffering at the hands of US empire. After her arrest, she embodied radical solidarity through her own physical pain and her witness to the pain of others. Embodied solidarity meant sacrificing her own liberty and physical welfare, just as those with whom she claimed allyship had done. Losing her freedom amid the government crackdown expanded what Reynolds held in common with them. From that point on, radical solidarity with Nationalist Party supporters revolved around not only the demand of independence and a shared critique of US militarism but also the collective experience of state repression.

Reynolds's new sense of solidarity took shape amid the harsh prison conditions she experienced with seven Nationalist women also incarcerated at the San Juan and Arecibo District Jails: Leonides Díaz Díaz, Juanita Ojeda Maldonado, Carmen María Pérez González, Isabel Rosado Morales, Doris Torresola Roura, Monserrate del Valle del Toro, and Olga Viscal Garriga. The eight women forged a community informed by shared trauma and shared resilience.

They also forged powerful memories. Researchers have shown that the release of neurotransmitters during moments of extreme stress contribute to vivid memories of those moments. Reynolds's body carried the memory of the trauma, isolation, and malnutrition she experienced at La Princesa and the Arecibo District Jail.[98] But she did not carry these memories alone. She became part of a cohort of women political prisoners with shared recollections of mutual support in the face of profoundly difficult conditions.

Reynolds already knew several of them from the networks of her dissident friendships and from the investigative work she had done before her arrest. In 1945, for instance, Reynolds had interviewed and reported on the conviction of del Valle del Toro's husband, Tomas López de Victoria, for the 1938 assassination attempt on the governor.[99] She met Rosado Morales during Isabel's 1946 trip to New York.[100] Reynolds and Rosado Morales developed an abiding friendship that included visits with Rosado Morales's family in Ceiba and with her coworkers at the Humacao school where Rosado Morales taught once Reynolds returned to Puerto Rico in 1948 to investigate the UPR strike. Viscal Garriga was among the students whom the UPR expelled in response to that strike. Pérez González was part of the inner circle of Nationalists who peopled party headquarters, where Reynolds had a typewriter set up to write her book manuscript that police subsequently confiscated during her arrest.[101]

Reynolds found herself among a group that ranged in age, marital status, class, and racial status; Reynolds was thirty-four years old, highly educated, unmarried, and from a middle-class Anglo family.[102] Díaz Díaz was the oldest at fifty years of age; she was also an Arecibo homemaker, mother of six, and longtime Nationalist. Monserrate del Valle del Toro was the mother of two young daughters. Rosado Morales and Ojeda Maldonado, both in their mid-forties, were unmarried; so were twenty-eight-year-old Torresola Roura and the youngest among them, Pérez González and Viscal Garriga, who were both twenty-one. The group's formal education ranged from college, as was the case for Rosado Morales, to primary school, as was the case with Díaz Díaz.[103] Those who appear in the US censuses of Puerto Rico were listed as either white or "mulatto."[104]

Each woman's path to the Nationalist Party was tied to generationally defining moments of government repression and party building during the 1930s and 1940s. State-sanctioned violence against Nationalists propelled the 1930s generation of Díaz Díaz, Rosado Morales, and Ojeda Maldonado toward heightened commitments to the party. Rosado Morales, a teacher and social worker from Ceiba, for instance, was a lifelong advocate of independence. However, she only began her formal involvement with the party in 1937 as part of her outrage over the police shooting of Nationalists that year, which became known as the Ponce Massacre.[105] A decade later, Pérez González, Viscal Garriga, and Torresola Roura were inspired by Albizu Campos's riveting critiques of colonialism, which they heard at Nationalist events organized across Puerto Rico.[106]

In some cases, the commitments of these women to the Nationalist Party had also been nurtured within pro-independence families. Torresola Roura's family had supported Albizu Campos since her childhood in the 1930s. In 1950, the Torresola family paid a heavy price for their leadership in the uprising. One of Doris's brothers, Griselio, died in a hail of capital police bullets at Blair House while attempting to assassinate Truman. Another brother, Elio, led the attack on the Jayuya Selective Service and post offices. He served eighteen years in prison for his actions. Her cousin was Blanca

Canales, who had led the uprising in Jayuya.[107] Díaz Díaz's husband, two sons, and brother faced multiple charges in connection with the insurrection. Her nephew died while attacking the Arecibo police barracks—an assault that also resulted in the death of four policemen.[108] By contrast, Viscal Garriga, like Reynolds, had defied family wishes through her politics. Viscal Garriga's parents, with whom she lived in San Juan at the time of her arrest, favored the Muñoz Marín government and strongly disapproved of Olga and her sister Irma's involvement with the Nationalist Party.[109] In 1951, Viscal Garriga's father testified that Reynolds had once showed up at their home alongside three armed Nationalists and accused the family of maltreating their daughter. He also criticized Olga's older sister, Irma, for conducting "love affairs" with a Nationalist man.[110]

Along with a shared commitment and experiences of hardship, each of their political lives had been similarly shaped by gendered ideas about male leadership and feminine morality. As with the civil rights and pacifist movements where Reynolds got her start, men, with few exceptions, led the Nationalist Party and women took on informal leadership roles. Some did so in the women's sections of the Nationalist Party, which emerged in 1930.[111] Nationalist women regularly conducted unglorified behind-the-scenes labor essential to the Nationalist Party's function, much like Reynolds's efforts at the Harlem Ashram. As Carmen María Pérez González described in a 1998 interview, "Not enough women were appointed or elected to leadership positions in the Party, though they were the ones who kept it going while the male leaders were in prison."[112]

The eight women had each found a political home within an organization that simultaneously emphasized women's unique moral authority and their shared obligations with men. During a February 1950 speech in Utuado, for instance, Albizu Campos characterized "woman [as] the custodian of our existence as a mother" and urged women to revolt, along with their husbands, with "a machete, a stick, and a gun to defend the honor of [their] country." He similarly told a March 1950 Ponce audience, "The power of the salvation of the country [patria] belongs to the women. If the women are weak, then we will all be weak."[113]

Even though its formal leadership was predominantly male, the Nationalist Party was the political community in which Reynolds and the women with whom she was incarcerated carved out revolutionary political lives that transgressed broader society's demands of female adherence to the cultural and political status quo. Several, including Reynolds, overtly recognized Albizu Campos for taking them seriously as political agents. In a 1998 interview, Pérez González credited Albizu Campos with giving "women the opportunity to lead, and treat[ing] them as equal partners in the struggle." As she recalled, Nationalist Party men who held less favorable views about women's leadership "always respected us because of Don Pedro."[114]

Alongside these gendered experiences, the group of eight shared an abiding commitment to patient suffering for their political beliefs that sustained them both individually and collectively. Reynolds's understanding of patient suffering was grounded in Gandhian nonviolence, Christian doctrine, and admiration for Nationalist Party emphasis on personal sacrifice. Nationalist women recognized their own incarceration as the praxis of the "courage and sacrifice" animating their movement. Albizu Campos had first iterated the oft repeated phrase *"La patria es valor y sacrificio"* ("Homeland is courage and sacrifice") in 1932 after the Nationalist Party's lackluster showing at the polls (the party's one and only try in the electoral arena). Upon taking charge of the party in 1930, Albizu Campos—himself a convert from Protestantism to Catholicism—developed what one scholar calls a "Christian social ideology" that fused religion and economic justice as inspiration for taking on personal sacrifice.[115]

The colonial judicial system tested each woman's willingness to sacrifice for their politics. The group bore witness to each other's encounters with the painful fallout of affiliating with the Nationalist Party. Like Reynolds, the Nationalist women with whom she was incarcerated faced prosecution for whom they knew, meetings they had attended, or what they said. For instance, del Valle del Toro had been arrested, in essence, because she was married to an insurrection leader and not because there was evidence of her collaboration; her only charge was one Gag Law violation.[116]

Together, the eight women experienced miserable prison conditions at La Princesa and Arecibo. Following her arrest, Reynolds spent nine days at the San Juan police headquarters where the FBI interrogated her before guards moved her to La Princesa. There, she spent several days in a dark and foul-smelling unventilated cell with Pérez González, Viscal Garriga, and Torresola Roura. Torresola Roura was recovering from a gunshot wound to the neck and grieving her brother Griselio; she remained behind when authorities initially transferred Reynolds, Viscal Garriga, and Pérez González from La Princesa to the Arecibo District Jail. It was the first of several heavily guarded trips for them back and forth between the two prisons.

The government periodically transferred Reynolds and Nationalist women prisoners approximately forty miles from the Arecibo District Jail to San Juan to facilitate court proceedings (see figure 6.5).[117] A January 1951

FIGURE 6.5 Reynolds during a court proceeding next to lawyers Francisco Hernández Vargas (*left*) and Juan Hernández Vallé (*right*). Source: "Izq. A der. Lcdo. Francisco Hernández Vargas, Ruth M. Reynolds, Lcdo. Juan Hernández Vallé durante el juicio 1951–1952," Centro de Investigaciones Históricas, Universidad de Puerto Rico, Recinto de Río Piedras, Colección Benjamín Torres, serie: fotografías, caja 6, número 37.

photo of Reynolds, Viscal Garriga, and Pérez González sitting handcuffed together was taken during one of these court proceedings (see figure 6.6).[118] It shows Pérez González on the left staring directly at the camera, along with Viscal Garriga and Reynolds as they waited in court for their arraignments. The women's refined appearances in neat print dresses belied the grim living conditions in Arecibo where they were immediately returned at the close of proceedings. Handcuffed together that day, they took in details about the government cases against each of them. Pérez González was charged with attempted murder and violating the Gag Law.[119] Because she had visited New York in the spring of 1950, authorities suspected Viscal Garriga of relaying orders from Albizu Campos to Oscar Collazo and Griselio Torresola

FIGURE 6.6 Carmen María Pérez González, Olga Viscal Garriga, and Ruth Reynolds (*left to right*) during their arraignments on January 3, 1951. Source: Photograph taken by Luis de Casenave, Colecciones de la Universidad de Puerto Rico, Recinto de Río Piedras.

to assassinate Truman, though they did not have any evidence.[120] Reynolds learned during the arraignment that the government planned to portray her as a leader with prior knowledge of the uprising.

Reynolds alternately experienced isolation and overcrowding at the Arecibo District Jail, where she spent the majority of her incarceration. For nine months before her trial, Reynolds, Pérez González, Viscal Garriga, Torresola Roura, and Rosado Morales were housed in the two *calabozos* (solitary confinement cells) in the women's section of the Arecibo District Jail, sometimes one to a cell, sometimes two or three people to a cell.[121] They were permitted one hour a day outside the small hold, in the jail's courtyard. Each calabozo was about 5½ by 11 feet with a small toilet and faucet, a slot Reynolds used to peer out onto the jail patio, and an out-of-reach window through which, she remembered, "you could see the sky once in a while and the moon, if the moon wiggled in the right direction."

The calabozos were hot. A single *bombilla* (bulb) burned twenty-four hours through the night.[122]

After conviction, uncomfortable overcrowding replaced the cramped isolation of solitary confinement when Reynolds and her calabozo cellmates were moved to one of the Arecibo District Jail's *galerías*, which housed over 120 female prisoners. There, prisoners slept in closely packed bunk beds in stacks of three—two in the bed and the third on the floor below. An adjacent room had open toilets and showers. These difficult living conditions were alleviated when the warden moved Reynolds and the seven Nationalist women to a separate ten-by-ten-foot room.[123]

At both La Princesa and the Arecibo District Jail, the tight-knit community of eight women political prisoners turned to each other for emotional support. Reynolds's outsider status was an asset. Reynolds and Pérez González, for instance, prepared to leverage Puerto Rican authorities' unease over detaining a North American toward supporting Viscal Garriga. As Reynolds recounted matter-of-factly in the 1980s about their calabozo assignments, "Olga was a very high-strung person and had a history of epilepsy, and I said to Carmín [as Carmen was also known] 'it is better for you to be alone and I will stay with Olga.'" "I was older than Carmín," Reynolds explained, "and also I already recognized that the administration was a bit uptight about having this North American around and I felt that they would listen to me more than to Carmín in case of an emergency with Olga."[124]

Reynolds's cellmates returned the favors of compassion and companionship during some of her darkest moments. While Reynolds was suffering terribly during her trial, her isolation lifted when authorities moved Torresola Roura, Pérez González, and Viscal Garriga to a La Princesa room separated from her cell only by chicken wire. Reynolds recalled, "We could easily see and visit with one another."[125] Likewise, the Nationalist women housed in the general population at the Arecibo District Jail regularly visited those held in the calabozo, opening the slot in the door to chat.[126]

Ironically, the group of eight's physical isolation in prison amplified their collective access to a transnational network of supporters. Each of the eight tapped into personal circles to the benefit of the entire group. Ojeda Maldonado, for instance, helped Reynolds smuggle letters out of the prison to circumvent government censors. In a 1985 interview, Reynolds described Ojeda Maldonado's underground network: "The people who were not from the San Juan area were always with the other prisoners. And so she knew them all, knew when they were leaving and so on and so forth." As Reynolds described, "So I'd just write a letter, wad it up tightly and say 'Could you get this out?' . . . She says, 'I think so.' So, either that weekend or the next weekend she'd tell me it's gone. And I never knew who took it."[127]

Reynolds's networks also benefited the group. The Ruth Reynolds Defense Committee in New York successfully lobbied federal officials and the governor's office in Puerto Rico to investigate after receiving a letter from Reynolds detailing her declining health.[128] They found her severely malnourished. Reynolds negotiated a larger separate room for the entire group after the warden offered it to her for her own use as well as permission to use her own funds for a weekly delivery of groceries. She refused unless the other seven women could join her.[129]

Both before and after the move, each woman shared deliveries from family and friends to supplement the group's staple prison diet of rice, beans, coffee, and bread.[130] In her memoirs, Rosado Morales recalled the monthly groceries from Viscal Garriga's father and the fruit that Pérez González's father brought his daughter from their Lares farm.[131] Rosado Morales also described the small luxuries that lifted their spirits: papaya sweets from her sister in Ceiba, cakes from Reynolds's family in South Dakota, and other sweets from the Ojeda Maldonado, Torresola Roura, and the Díaz Díaz families. "And, those letters that Alfredo, Doris's brother-in-law, sent to the prison," Rosado Morales recalled, "made us laugh until we could not laugh anymore."[132]

Both Reynolds and Díaz Díaz leveraged networks of trusted supporters toward feeding the group of eight. With her new privileges, Reynolds used funds sent by her defense committee in New York to purchase a two-burner plate, a daily quart of milk, and a weekly *compra* (grocery order) for the group: steak, canned sardines, Vienna sausages, Spam, and fruit. A contact of Díaz Díaz in her hometown of Arecibo did the purchasing and deliveries.[133]

Reynolds's presence alongside them also mattered to Rosado Morales, and by her account, to the six other incarcerated Nationalist women. In a 1979 interview, Rosado Morales remembered Reynolds telling the Nationalist women that it was an honor for her to be incarcerated with them. "And we were proud," Rosado Morales told the interviewer, "to have with us a North American who defied the laws of her empire."[134]

Finally, in June 1952, Reynolds was released on bail, with her appeal pending. Reynolds suspected that, after months of waiting, the Department of Justice in Puerto Rico finally granted her the option to post bail in March because the perceived threat from pro-independence voices had passed.[135]

Less than 60 percent of eligible voters in Puerto Rico had approved the commonwealth constitution in March 1952. Truman had transferred it to the US Congress for approval in April. The Ruth Reynolds Defense Committee in New York prepared to transfer funds to pay for Reynolds's bail, but Nationalist Party lawyer Hernández Vallé insisted that Puerto Ricans perform that task, thus conveying the significance of Reynolds's personal sacrifice to the movement. Three independentista businessmen with close ties to the Nationalist Party set aside the threat of government reprisal to quickly put their own property up as collateral to pay her bond.[136]

On the afternoon of June 21, 1952, Reynolds walked out of the Arecibo District Jail to Nationalist Party leader Paulino Castro's waiting car—still bullet-riddled from the uprising. Reynolds, Castro and his wife, Carmen, their adult son Luis, and Hernández Vallé traveled toward San Juan, passing through Manatí, where Castro's son pinched a pineapple from the fields for the group to share.[137] The group's trip ended where Reynolds's journey through Puerto Rico's criminal justice system had begun in the early morning hours of November 2, 1950—the Castro family home. Reynolds took up residence there again for nearly three weeks before she boarded an overnight Pan Am flight to New York.[138]

Much had changed. Reynolds's significant weight loss showed the effects of incarceration. She now had firsthand knowledge of what it was like to be a political prisoner. This knowledge deepened her empathy for the political prisoners and fueled her seemingly tireless advocacy for those who remained imprisoned.

"Liberty, it is wonderful!" Reynolds wrote to Lynn on June 22, 1952. Noting the many changes during her incarceration, Reynolds described, "Hernández Vallé's two oldest sons have changed from boys into men, Paulino has acquired two grandchildren." Still, some things had remained the same and perhaps were made even sweeter with freedom. Referring to the Old San Juan diner known for its coffee and *mallorcas* (Puerto Rican sweet bread), Reynolds enthused, "But the coffee at the Bombonera is the same as, if not better than, ever." "After a perfectly frivolous twenty-four hours," she wrote, "I promise by tomorrow to have settled down to a serious contemplation of the future, and to start trying to collect my scattered thoughts."[139]

Once she did, Reynolds's focus remained on the plight of friends she had left behind at the Arecibo District Jail. Among the Nationalist Party women incarcerated with Reynolds at Arecibo, only Rosado Morales was also free. Rosado Morales had been convicted of violating the Gag Law in April and sentenced to the fifteen months she had already served.[140] After a year and a half of incarceration, Viscal Garriga's trial had just ended in May 1952. Viscal Garriga was convicted of violating Insular Law 53 and sentenced to one to ten years, plus an additional 930 days for thirty-one contempt citations during her trial.[141]

The timing of Reynolds's release in June enabled her to attend Torresola Roura and Pérez González's joint July trial in San Juan, despite friendly exhortations to stay away. As Reynolds described, "I walked up the street and people came running out of buildings telling me not to go to that court. 'Don't go, don't go!' 'Why not?' 'You might be picked up again.' 'So what? These are my friends, they're on trial. I'm going.'"[142] Pérez González was acquitted. Torresola Roura, who had earlier been acquitted for illegal weapon possession and attempted murder, was sentenced to one to two years for violating Insular Law 53. Among the others, del Valle del Toro was eventually acquitted.[143] Ojeda Maldonado was convicted but, like Rosado Morales, sentenced to time served and released almost immediately. Díaz Díaz, who had previously been given multiple life sentences for murder and attempted murder convictions (all later overturned), was sentenced to an additional two to ten years for an Insular Law 53 violation.[144]

During this period before she departed for New York, Reynolds also typed up her memorandum about the torture—or "Experiences Phenomenal," as she titled it—that she experienced while incarcerated. This was the typewritten version of the memo she had originally drafted in prison and surreptitiously handed to lawyer Hernández Vallé in early December 1951 to smuggle out.[145] With this documented record of her experiences, Reynolds looked to the Supreme Court of Puerto Rico and to the United Nations as sites to appeal her case and to fight for the freedom of other political prisoners—and for Puerto Rico itself. She brought something new to this work: her own firsthand experiences of the brutality of US colonialism.

Part III

7 Desbrosses Street

Peering across the subway at riders' reading materials on March 1, 1954, Ruth Reynolds saw headlines of a shooting in the US Capitol. She rushed to buy a newspaper.[1] Earlier that day, she discovered, Lolita Lebrón had led a group of three others to the "ladies gallery" of the US House of Representatives. Lebrón gave the command to open fire, raised the Puerto Rican flag, and yelled, "Freedom for Puerto Rico now!" The group wounded five congressmen.

The four Nationalists considered the action an attack on the legislative body directly responsible for the creation of the commonwealth and the decimation of the independence movement.[2] The final straw for them had been the decision of the United Nations to release the US government from its obligation to submit reports on Puerto Rico, as it was no longer a colony.[3] The group expected it to be a suicide mission and hoped it would make the world pay attention to US efforts to prevent self-governance in Puerto Rico. However, they survived. They were arrested and eventually convicted to decades of incarceration.

Reynolds's first reaction to what she read was fury.[4] The attack on the US Capitol came nearly two years after she had been released from prison and had returned to the United States. During this time, she had lobbied at the United Nations for Puerto Rico's liberation. She had worked for the release of Puerto Rican political prisoners, including the imprisoned leader of the Nationalist Party, Pedro Albizu Campos. She was technically still a political prisoner herself, out on bail with a pending appeal. Authorities could return her to prison at any time. But that did not stop her from pursuing her work on behalf of Albizu Campos and all those whose fates so closely mirrored her own experience of torture and incarceration following the 1950 Nationalist uprising.

Only a handful of others had joined her during many months of hard work—and it had now been brought to an abrupt halt. Indeed, while Lolita Lebrón and her Nationalist allies saw their attack as a last-ditch attempt to make the world pay attention to what the United States was doing in Puerto Rico, Reynolds could see that the shooting in Congress would prevent the scientific investigation she had been spearheading into the radiation torture that Albizu Campos had experienced in prison.[5] Reynolds's surmise was correct. The momentum of the investigation halted. Worse, Puerto Rico's governor Luis Muñoz Marín revoked Albizu Campos's 1953 pardon.[6]

Although no doubt frustrated at the turn of events in relation to the Albizu Campos case, Reynolds still shifted her work on behalf of Nationalist prisoners to encompass Lebrón and the three others. The group's attack on Congress did not align with her personal ethos of pacifism, but Reynolds still put into practice her own particular mode of radical solidarity in order to help defend them. In doing so, she took bold steps in a direction few were willing to go. The already high price of advocating for an independent Puerto Rico—government surveillance and prosecution—became even steeper after 1954. The insular government intensified its use of the Gag Law under which it had prosecuted Reynolds and others in 1950 to silence those in Puerto Rico who continued to publicly advocate independence in the wake of the attack on the Capitol.

Reynolds's experience in prison had only sharpened her keen intellect and moral compass. She would need this kind of conviction, experience, and unwavering commitment as the struggle for Puerto Rico's independence entered its bleakest years. For many in the United States and the international community, the Commonwealth of Puerto Rico "resolved" the case of Puerto Rico in 1952 without compromising US democratic principles. With the commonwealth's inauguration, the United Nations concluded that Puerto Rico was no longer a colony—thus, an independence movement seemed to be an anachronism. During this time, and especially after the Nationalist attack on Congress in 1954, the government and mainstream media dismissed convicted Nationalists as deranged fanatics and largely forgot about them.

Reynolds, however, did not forget the Nationalists or the goal of independence, even as few fellow North Americans joined her at the time. She embarked on a new phase of her solidarity activism that required defining solidarity during the most discouraging of times. As much as she, as a pacifist, disagreed with Nationalist Party tactics during the 1950 uprising and the 1954 attack on Congress, Reynolds's expansive definition of solidarity activism encompassed supporting their aims if not their means.

For Reynolds, solidarity activism meant not only protesting the US empire but also doing the work of supporting colonized subjects resisting that empire. Rather than dwell on the contradictions of radical pacifist and Nationalist ideologies, Reynolds emphasized their confluence: a shared critique of US state violence and colonialism. In the process, she mapped out a vision of solidarity activism for non–Puerto Rican US citizens like herself that recognized the possibility of collaboration across strategic differences. In that support, North American allies could pick their own protest tools, but they should not tell Puerto Ricans what tools to use in their struggle for national sovereignty. Her concern was US colonialism, and on that count, she was unwavering.

With this approach to solidarity activism, Reynolds focused on two main areas after leaving prison: mobilizing for the release of political prisoners and lobbying for the United Nations to apply its international authority toward the decolonization of Puerto Rico. Albizu Campos's health and welfare were other concerns of hers. To advance these multiple endeavors, she filed writs of habeas corpus—legal petitions to determine unlawful imprisonment. She also organized defense committees, petitioned the United Nations, and lobbied UN delegates. From her New York apartment on Desbrosses Street, she produced copious and detailed correspondence with a large cast of characters—prisoners, their families, exiles, lawyers, judges, journalists, clergy, heads of state, revolutionaries, pacifists, scientists, and intelligence officials—who were spread across the Caribbean, Latin America, and the United States.

Collectively, these efforts contested the triumphant narrative that democracy had prevailed with the commonwealth's establishment, and they redirected focus away from individual transgressions by Nationalist Party members and instead toward state violence. Despite the loneliness of her crusade, Reynolds was steadfast in her commitment to freedom for Puerto Rican political prisoners and for the independence of Puerto Rico itself.

Defending Oscar Collazo and Critiquing State Violence

In 1952, having only just returned to the United States from Puerto Rico and her own political incarceration, Reynolds set to work on the cause of Oscar Collazo, a Nationalist prisoner facing execution for his part in the 1950 assassination attempt on President Harry Truman. Reynolds was in prison in 1951 when a US district court in Washington, DC, sentenced Collazo to death for killing a policeman during the Truman assassination attempt.[7] His execution date was scheduled for August 1.

Without hesitation, Reynolds wrote the president directly in an effort to stop Collazo's execution. "After twenty months of enforced silence," she wrote Truman, "I return to my duty of working through educational and political channels for the Independence of Puerto Rico and the release of all Puerto Rican political prisoners."[8]

Reynolds knew Collazo and his wife, Rosa Cortés Collazo, from the overlapping political networks of 1940s New York. The Collazos were among the hundreds arrested for involvement in the 1950 Nationalist uprising, which had led to Reynolds's own arrest. Rosa was released after nearly two months in the Women's House of Detention in Greenwich Village, when a judge determined that there was insufficient evidence that she had plotted with her husband to assassinate President Truman in 1950.[9] Reynolds and Rosa Collazo were part of a tight-knit network of those incarcerated and subsequently released in relation to their support of Puerto Rican independence. In fact, Rosa Collazo was among the small group who met Reynolds's airplane when it arrived in New York from Puerto Rico in mid-July 1952.[10] It was the international campaign of Rosa Collazo and *El Diario/La Prensa* journalist Luisa Quintero to stop Oscar Collazo's execution that Reynolds joined as soon as she arrived back in the United States.[11]

With Collazo's scheduled execution just days away, the situation was bleak. Still, Reynolds drafted a letter to Truman that demonstrated her commitment to radical solidarity. Indeed, in advocating for Collazo and other Nationalist prisoners, Reynolds drew upon what set her apart from them as much as what they held in common. While Nationalist prisoners refused to engage the US government and its legal remedies to end their own incarceration, Reynolds positioned herself as a non–Puerto Rican US citizen making demands on her own government for the release of Puerto Rican prisoners—and doing so in the best interest of US democracy. Reynolds also drew on her pacifism, using the seeming contradiction of a pacifist defending individuals supportive of the use of political violence to critique, above all else, US state violence.

The letter called upon Truman to pardon Collazo "for the sake of that for which both you and I should be willing to live or die, for the sake of the honor of the United States of America." She warned Truman of a backlash when Americans learned about "the aspirations for liberty of the Puerto Rican people, and the contempt in which your administration has held those aspirations."[12] She also argued the ideological hypocrisy of the planned execution by contrasting her pacifism to both Collazo's and Truman's shared views about killing and patriotism. "Being myself of pacifist persuasion," she wrote, "I need only to know that Oscar Collazo is a human being created in the image of God to believe that his life ought not be cut short by other human beings or by the state."[13]

While positioning herself as a pacifist allowed Reynolds to call on a higher moral authority in opposition to Collazo's execution, she nonetheless under-

stood the utility of addressing Truman on the plane of state-sanctioned violence—ironically, an ideological space where Truman and Collazo had more
in common with one another than Reynolds did with either man. "Neither
you nor Oscar Collazo is a pacifist," she wrote, "and I must appeal to you on
other than pacifist grounds if I wish to be seriously considered." As she explained, "Non-pacifists distinguish between kinds of killing on the basis of
degree of provocation and unselfishness of motive" and "consider killing
quite proper if it is done for patriotic reasons, for the good of one's country. . . .
In our country," she wrote, "all young men are subject to being 'selected' for
military training and service, which involves killing other young men, and
women and children, in whatever part of the world the governmental authorities consider it to our national interest to send them." Her critique drew
in the contemporaneous context of the ongoing US conscription of citizens,
including Puerto Ricans, for the Korean War. "Persons who refuse to engage
in such killing missions," Reynolds pointed out, "are subject to five years
imprisonment as felons."[14] In other words, Reynolds was alerting Truman
to his own participation in patriotic killing and to the shared logic behind
state-sanctioned war and anticolonial revolution.

In the end, it is unclear whether Reynolds sent the letter to Truman—
and whether she would have felt a need to. The letter was dated July 25,
1952, but Reynolds likely learned that Truman had, in fact, commuted
Collazo's sentence to life in prison while she was finishing her last draft.
The announcement was made on July 24 by the *New York Times*. While life
in prison was a far cry from achieving Collazo's release, it fundamentally
changed the requirements—and timeline—of protest. On July 25, the very
same date Reynolds had intended to send her letter, the *New York Times* reported that Puerto Rico had officially become a commonwealth of the
United States.[15] The commonwealth would prove a major obstacle for carrying forward the struggle for independence.

The State Department, for example, forecast that the commonwealth
status would cut off independence-minded Puerto Ricans and their allies
from international support. Just weeks before the commonwealth became official, a US State Department letter to the Senate promised that
"the achievement of self-government by Puerto Rico will be a matter of
great interest to Members of the United Nations in their discussions of
the political progress of non-self-governing territories." As the letter enthused, the new commonwealth constitution would serve to rebut critics
"who have charged the United States Government with imperialism
and colonial exploitation."[16] It was clear that the United States sought to

forestall international critique—and oversight—of its new relationship to Puerto Rico: colonialism under the guise of commonwealth.

Yet even as US officials prepared to shut down international criticism, Reynolds was at work putting together a new North American solidarity group called Americans for Puerto Rico's Independence (APRI) that would challenge the rosy narrative that the commonwealth had extended the full blessings of liberty upon Puerto Ricans. The group was a successor to the American League for Puerto Rico's Independence (ALPRI), which had fallen apart during Reynolds's incarceration because of internal disagreements about her relationship to the Nationalist Party. Years later, however, Reynolds characterized the new APRI membership as "the old radical bunch." In addition to herself, the APRI included Julius Eichel, Thelma Mielke, Roger O'Neil, Jean Wiley, Abraham Zwickel, Charlie Wellman, Ruth Miller, Conrad J. Lynn, and Yolanda Moreno. Some had lived at the Ashram during the 1940s. Most had participated in the ALPRI.[17] All had remained supportive of Reynolds throughout her confinement ordeal, even as other colleagues distanced themselves from her and her solidarity work.

The task before them was immense. This "old radical bunch" established the APRI when the political environment was far less conducive to introducing newcomers to the independence cause. During the early 1940s, Reynolds had encountered in New York a migrant community awash in pro-independence sentiment, but virulent Cold War anticommunism had taken its toll on public support for independence in Puerto Rican migrant communities. In 1950, Congress made the House Un-American Activities Committee into a permanent standing committee that Senator Joseph McCarthy used to investigate perceived subversives and create a "culture of fear" that discouraged dissension. Anyone challenging the political and social status quo of Cold War America risked accusations of disloyalty. Immigrants, sexual minorities, labor activists, and opponents of racial segregation, colonialism, and sexism alike—whether tied to the Communist Party USA or not—caught the eye of red baiters, and often with devastating consequences, including social ostracism, job loss, and violence. Leftist Puerto Rican leaders in New York were the targets of congressional investigations and the FBI and the victims of anti-leftist purges.[18]

In contrast with the previous decade, this changed political environment blunted pro-independence sentiment for Puerto Rico and made it more difficult for outsiders to access activists who favored independence, much less develop a politics of solidarity around it. However, the "old radical bunch" was able to quickly forge ahead. These APRI founding members had already learned how the United States acquired a colony in Puerto Rico and about the exploitations of continuing US rule. They had supported Reynolds as she endured prosecution and incarceration.[19] Their shared history created a powerful context for a solidarity campaign to reignite among this small group. Building from the defunct ALPRI, Reynolds and the few stalwart holdovers created the APRI as the new organizational site to carry forward solidarity work for the independence cause for Puerto Rico during a time many had abandoned it—or worse, gleefully considered it vanquished.

The newly formed APRI announced its plans to support Puerto Rican independence in a press release it issued on the day of the commonwealth's inauguration on July 25, a move that—along with its call for the liberation of all political prisoners—signaled its membership's continued dedication to Puerto Rican independence. It denounced the antidemocratic practices behind the commonwealth's creation: "We deplore the fact that [the Commonwealth] 'Constitution' has been written and instituted while hundreds of Puerto Rican patriots have been kept in prison, thus being deprived of the opportunity to expressing themselves in Puerto Rico or outside in relation to it."[20] As a strategy for amplifying the APRI's contribution, its press release promised that the APRI would "maintain friendly relations with but complete independence from all Puerto Rican organizations working for the same end." This included the Nationalist Party. Its modus operandi was working "through educational and political channels."[21]

Reynolds and other APRI founders saw such organizational autonomy as a framework for collaborating with other pro-independence groups that used different protest methods and representing alternative standpoints from within the colonial relationship between the United States and Puerto Rico. It was, in effect, a manifestation of Reynolds's own approach to activism—an approach to solidarity beyond (and despite) the nuances of difference within the independence movement. Privately, APRI members also hoped that their new organization might work more nimbly than their predecessor organization, able to spring into action where there was work to be done. Amid those organizations devoted to Puerto Rican independence, Reynolds hoped that APRI members could "make a contribution that was not being made by anybody else."[22]

A Former Political Prisoner at the United Nations, 1952–1953

The United Nations quickly became the site of the APRI's first lobbying effort, as Reynolds and colleagues worked to expose the gap between creed and promise in the case of Puerto Rico. Reynolds stepped firmly back into this familiar space of lobbying—one she had occupied prior to her own incarceration—at the very same time that she was agitating on behalf of Nationalist Party members who remained incarcerated after the 1950 uprising.

It was a critical moment. Puerto Rico had just become a commonwealth, and the United States was boasting that the status of Puerto Rico had been "resolved" democratically. Moreover, the United States was swiftly trying to remove Puerto Rico from being a topic of any concern to the world body. Despite what may have seemed to her like an insurmountable challenge, Reynolds and her small community of solidarity activists persevered in their efforts to convince the global community that democracy had not, in fact, prevailed.

The foundations for Reynolds's postincarceration engagement at the United Nations were laid in the years immediately before her arrest. From the United Nations' formation in 1945 until her arrest in 1950, Reynolds and her colleagues had gained a foothold at the United Nations by using the spaces available for nonstate actors there. Reynolds did so by speaking on behalf of the ALPRI, while Thelma Mielke held a formal role as the Nationalist Party's UN observer.[23]

Before the commonwealth, Reynolds, Mielke, and other ALPRI members had sought to harness the United Nations' international authority toward interrogating the United States' relationship with Puerto Rico. Practically, this meant demanding US compliance with the UN Charter's "Declaration Regarding Non-Self-Governing Territories." Article 73(e) of the declaration obligated UN member nations to promote the well-being and self-governance of territories under their control and also to submit regular reports on conditions therein. Puerto Rico was one of seventy-two territories that the General Assembly included on the initial list of "non-self-governing territories" that it drew up in 1946.[24] Puerto Rico's inclusion on the list amounted to UN recognition that it was a colony—a significant tool for pro-independence advocates seeking to advance their cause at the international level.

Before traveling to Puerto Rico in 1948 and then being imprisoned for conspiring to overthrow the government there, Reynolds had also worked with colleague Jay Holmes Smith to submit a petition to the United Nations on behalf of the ALPRI. The petition denounced Congress's failure to promote free political institutions in Puerto Rico as mandated in Article 73(e) and urged commensurate "appropriate action" at the United Nations. The members of the ALPRI emphasized their political standing by characterizing the petition as "perhaps the first instance of citizens of a great power appealing to *the United Nations* to take action of the domination of their own nation over another."[25] Reynolds and Smith also traveled by train from her home in Manhattan to Long Island, where the UN General Assembly was located, to observe meetings of the ad hoc committee charged with implementing article 73(e) and to lobby its delegates.[26]

Until 1950, while Reynolds was in Puerto Rico, Mielke continued her work in New York as the Nationalist Party delegate to the United Nations. Those efforts came to an abrupt halt that year. Upon learning about the government crackdown on Nationalist supporters, Mielke urged the United Nations to take up the case of Puerto Rico for discussion. She argued that the events unfolding in Puerto Rico—that is, "a non-self-governing territory under the administration of the United States of America"—"as in any colony, [were] not merely a domestic matter." She pointed to precedents—such as Indonesia and Korea—when the United Nations had taken up discussion about the "administering power's" treatment of inhabitants in non-self-governing territories.[27] Rather than take up this request, the United Nations withdrew her accreditation without giving a reason. Reynolds noted that though Mielke might have technically violated UN procedure for nongovernmental observers, her expulsion "was, no doubt, because the United States didn't like Thelma's action in calling upon the security council."[28] By the fall of 1950, Mielke and the Nationalist Party had been kicked out of the United Nations. By then, Reynolds was incarcerated in Puerto Rico.

In 1952, Reynolds—now out on bail and back in New York—stepped into the battle to ensure that Puerto Rico *remained* on the list of non-self-governing territories. The vote for a commonwealth gave the United States leverage to declare the status of Puerto Rico resolved democratically. The stakes were high. Whereas before in 1946, the UN had recognized Puerto Rico as a colony, after the commonwealth vote, it might come off the list of non-self-governing territories. Removal was tantamount to UN recognition that Puerto Rico was no longer a US colony and would constitute a major obstacle to the independence movement. Reynolds denounced the United States for using UN forums to hold on to Puerto Rico as a colony by another name: commonwealth.

But Reynolds and the newly formed APRI faced challenges in their UN organizing. The APRI's message of a gap between creed and promise at the United Nations ran directly opposite larger cultural and political shifts in the United States away from World Word II rhetoric promising a world free of colonial relationships. After World War II, dominant US political culture pivoted toward an emphasis on global security dependent on defeating communism.[29] As postwar anticolonial sentiment around the globe contributed to a spate of decolonization processes in Africa and Asia, the United States worked to maintain its own colonial holdings. It also further expanded its global reach with the aim of preventing Soviet influence in newly independent nations. The US Cold War security state prosecuted "subversives" such as Reynolds, who challenged enduring US colonialism, as well as those critical of the United States' interventions in national liberation struggles across the globe in the name of defeating communism.

Despite the daunting odds, the APRI dove right into lobbying for Puerto Rico to remain on the list of non-self-governing territories. In the fall of 1952, Reynolds and Lynn urged the UN Committee on Information from Non-Self-Governing Territories to keep Puerto Rico on the list of colonies. In a preemptive move, Reynolds and Lynn filed their own petition on behalf of the APRI, requesting that the UN Committee on Information "disallow any petition of the United States Government for the removal of Puerto Rico" and also to "appoint an investigating commission on Puerto Rico." As the petition outlined, such a UN investigating commission would make

> a detailed documentary analysis of the juridical relationship of
> Puerto Rico to the United States Government; and . . . an on-the-spot
> investigation of the treatment accorded the independence movement
> of Puerto Rico, and especially the Nationalist Party of Puerto Rico,
> including a study of the juridical processes by which hundreds of its
> members have remained incarcerated during the period in which the
> Puerto Rican Constitution has been promulgated and proclaimed,
> and including a study, which shall not exclude testimony of the
> Puerto Rican political prisoners themselves, of the events leading
> up to their detention and of their treatment before, during, and
> after trial.[30]

Reynolds invoked the UN's *own* reclassification standards in a lengthy brief, titled "Why Puerto Rico Can Not Be Removed from Classification as a Non-Self-Governing Territory by the United States." This document, along with a brief by Lynn on the legal relationship between the commonwealth and the United States, accompanied the formal petition to the United Nations. In her brief, Reynolds asserted that the people of Puerto Rico had not freely chosen to associate with the United States—a hurdle for reclassification from "non-self-governing" to "self-governing"—either at the time of the

1898 US invasion or at any time thereafter. Puerto Rico had not been self-governing *before* voters agreed to the commonwealth's limited sovereignty. The elections themselves were therefore deeply flawed: pro-independence voters boycotted elections, the government suppressed Nationalist Party opposition, and the less than 50 percent of voters who did cast ballots only had the option of for or against the commonwealth. She invoked US representatives' own 1950 promises to each other that any new constitution "would not change Puerto Rico's fundamental political, social, and economic relationship to the United States."[31]

The preemptive battle of 1952 shifted to an offensive one in 1953. As Reynolds had expected, in January 1953, the United States officially notified the UN secretary-general that because the creation of the commonwealth had ended Puerto Rico's status as a non-self-governing territory, the United States would no longer transmit information about Puerto Rico to the secretary-general as required by Article 73(e). In other words, the United States proclaimed that its 1952 report on Puerto Rico was its last.[32]

In this new context, both the APRI and the Nationalist Party sought to sway UN deliberations away from accepting the United States' decision. Neither had the opportunity.

The Nationalist Party was denied a hearing with the UN's Committee of Information (COI), which was deliberating the case of Puerto Rico. Writing to the COI chair on behalf of the Nationalist Party, Pinto Gandía warned that the US petition should "be not considered unilaterally and on the sole basis of the exclusive information from the administering power, lest a grave injustice be done [to] 2,400,000 people who since the 18th century have been struggling, as they still are, for their right to freedom and independence."[33] Pinto Gandía alerted the COI chair that the petition was misleading in its representation of Puerto Rican support for the commonwealth. This new campaign in the United Nations was merely "the last effort before that international organization to perpetuate free from all supervision the more than a half century (1898–1953) of military intervention of the United States over Puerto Rico."[34]

The United States continued to lock the Nationalist Party out of participating in UN conversations. Mielke, who had served as the Nationalist Party's UN observer between 1947 and her expulsion amid the 1950s uprising, had already been denied an appeal to restore her Nationalist Party's observer credential.[35] The United Nations also rejected Pinto Gandía's request to present "ample information and legal arguments to contest the allegations of the Government of the United States."[36]

Locked out of formal CIO deliberations, Nationalist Party members tried other tactics. Pinto Gandía, as well as the Puerto Rican Independence Party leadership, directly lobbied the COI nonaligned members, such as Cuba and Ecuador, to speak for the Nationalists in UN deliberations. A small group of Nationalist Party women took to the streets, opting for direct protest. Dressed in elegant white pencil skirts and black blouses and holding signs denouncing US imperialism, about eight Nationalist Party women (including Rosa Collazo and Lolita Lebrón) peacefully picketed and passed out flyers demanding a hearing with the UN's Committee of Information. They were arrested and eventually convicted for "disorderly conduct."[37]

Efforts to sway the United Nations were not going well.

Embattled on All Sides

While the Nationalist Party was denied a hearing, Reynolds was preoccupied. Unfortunately, the timing of the debates over Puerto Rico's removal from the list of non-self-governing states coincided with an uptick in Reynolds's own freedom struggle. Reynolds's attention was focused on her appeal. In early 1953, Conrad Lynn had submitted an appeal to the Supreme Court of Puerto Rico to overturn Reynolds's Gag Law conviction. Though out on bail, Reynolds was still a convict and remained free at the discretion of federal authorities. Reynolds's appeal to the Supreme Court of Puerto Rico and the UN deliberations about removing Puerto Rico from its list of non-self-governing territories had been on parallel but separate tracks through much of 1953. That changed in November 1953, when Reynolds's efforts to vacate her conviction and her efforts to block US manipulations at the United Nations merged.

When the COI forwarded the issue to the General Assembly without making a recommendation of action, the battle to block the US petition began anew. But in the critical early weeks of November, when the General Assembly's Fourth Committee was debating removal, both Lynn and Reynolds were in Puerto Rico to attend her appeal hearing. It seemed that the US government was manipulating her court date—a move that Reynolds interpreted as an effort to "silence" her. She suspected that pro-commonwealth forces in the United States and Puerto Rico had intentionally pushed back her appeal court date several times until November 5 in order to, as she put it at the time, "incapacitate" both Lynn and her from lobbying Fourth Committee members during this critical debate.[38]

Reynolds reported the use of other familiar silencing tactics aimed at Nationalists. There was a crackdown on the Nationalist Party members in New York and Chicago in the two weeks before the United Nations removed Puerto Rico from the list of non-self-governing territories.[39]

Whether this strategic targeting had any real effect on the outcome of the debate is difficult to say, but when the UN General Assembly approved Puerto Rico's removal, Reynolds was unequivocal in pointing out its dire consequences for the fight for independence. The year 1953 was the first time that the United Nations voted on the removal of territories from the list of non-self-governing territories. But while Puerto Rico was one of three cases considered (along with the Netherlands Antilles and Suriname), it was the first and only territory removed from the list.[40] At the very least, this signaled that the international body no longer perceived the United States as a colonial power in Puerto Rico. More forebodingly, it sent a message that the United Nations would allow the United States to use UN institutions as a cover for perpetuating its colonial power.

The writing was on the wall. "In addressing the Plenary Session yesterday," Reynolds wrote in one of her many correspondences at the time, the US Ambassador to the United Nations "stated that Eisenhower had authorized him to say that he, Eisenhower, will request Congress to grant Independence to Puerto Rico whenever the Legislative Assembly of Puerto Rico asks for it." This was a "safe statement to make," she argued, since the Puerto Rican Legislative Assembly was, in her view, "an instrument of Washington." "It will ask for Independence whenever its boss, Mr. Eisenhower, tells it to," she wrote. "Thus what Mr. Eisenhower was really stating was that he will ask Congress to grant Independence to Puerto Rico whenever he feels like it!"[41] This, she determined, would be no time soon. "There is no more a chance that the Popular Party today will request Independence than there is that Joe McCarthy will join the Communist Party. In fact there is less chance. . . . The people of Puerto Rico do not express themselves through the colonial election but, to the contrary, through noncooperation with them." She concluded that President Eisenhower had chosen the authorized wording very carefully. Ending with a flourish, she stated, the US ambassador "did not say he would request independence whenever the Puerto Rican people express themselves for it (as they had been doing repeatedly for decades) but only when the colonial legislature requests it."[42]

While in Puerto Rico, Reynolds personally delivered the news to Albizu Campos that the UN had removed Puerto Rico as a non-self-governing territory. "He looked at me and said, 'Well, eight years of work down the drain,'" she reported. When she suggested that perhaps she should have stayed in New York rather than attending her court date in Puerto Rico, he said, "No. Nothing you or anybody else of our friends could do could have stopped this. You and we did all we could."[43]

Reynolds was able to meet with Albizu Campos in person because he had just been released from prison in September 1953, shortly before she had returned to Puerto Rico for her appeal hearing. The APRI had been calling for his release since the group's formation, and in September 1953, APRI founding member Conrad Lynn filed a petition for a writ of habeas corpus for Albizu Campos as a "next friend"—a legal move that allows a person to act legally on behalf of another person in a court of law. Reynolds favored this approach, as opposed to requesting a pardon or amnesty, because a writ of habeas corpus by its very nature challenged the legality behind Albizu Campos's imprisonment as well as the conditions of his imprisonment.[44] The approach taken by Reynolds and this small community of activists complemented the Nationalist Party's own nonengagement policy with the US government—Albizu Campos refused to petition a government that he did not recognize, and he opposed Puerto Ricans doing so on his behalf.

The APRI put all the limited resources at its disposal toward assisting Albizu Campos. In this legal role of "next friend," Lynn stood in place of Albizu Campos before the court. The Ruth Reynolds Defense Committee (RRDC) diverted funds from Reynolds's defense to cover Lynn's legal fees.[45] Albizu Campos had refused to petition the government that he did not recognize since his first incarceration in the 1930s, but North Americans could petition their own government to remedy its unjust incarceration of Puerto Ricans—which is exactly what Reynolds and the APRI set out to do.

Increased energy to obtain Albizu Campos's release was driven by reports of his rapidly declining health, which were furnished by his lawyers and eventually found their way into the Puerto Rican press between 1951 and 1953. In February 1952, El Imparcial published a press release in which his lawyer, Juan Hernández Vallé, quoted Albizu Campos's explosive assertion that the government was attempting to murder him in prison through radiation poisoning. By September 1953, rumors were circulating that Albizu Campos was near death. When the court nevertheless denied Conrad Lynn's writ, Lynn appealed, at which point Governor Luis Muñoz Marín, responding to mounting pressure to prevent Albizu Campos from dying in prison, pardoned Albizu Campos.[46]

Although Albizu Campos left prison alive, he was still suffering the lingering effects of the incarceration. Reynolds practiced solidarity by bearing witness to the corporeal evidence of his mistreatment in prison and his enduring pain. Reynolds saw the brown spots that physicians had diagnosed as burns when she visited Albizu Campos at Nationalist Party headquarters in Old San Juan, where he was bedridden after his pardon. Reynolds did not witness the unusual beams of light and strong vibrations that Thelma Mielke, Ruth Miller, and several others reported on their visits with the Nationalist Party leader, but she amplified their concerns.[47] Their witness provided firsthand evidence against skeptics.

Even after the pardon, the APRI continued to search for justice for the abuse. They did so in order to counter government propaganda that Albizu Campos's claims of radiation poisoning were a sign of mental illness and of the madness of his political ideas writ large. It seemed to Reynolds that the future reception of his brilliant ideas about struggle, law, human rights, and sovereignty were tied to demonstrating that he had indeed been the victim of government abuse. By early 1954, Reynolds and Mielke had been working for months to find well-respected scientists who would conduct an independent investigation on the cause of the burns on Albizu Campos's body. Albizu Campos's attorney had already been waiting over a year for the United Nations General Assembly to respond to his petition for an investigation.[48]

For their part, Mielke and Reynolds helped to form a committee of North Americans to lobby for an official inquiry.[49] By the spring of 1954, they were hopeful that the photographs of Albizu Campos's burns and the witness testimonies—including Reynolds's own firsthand experiences at La Princesa—that they had forwarded to the Society for Social Responsibility in Science (SSRC) had convinced the group, which opposed military research, to accept their request to investigate.[50]

But on March 1, 1954, Lolita Lebrón led Rafael Cancel Miranda, Andrés Figueroa Cordero, and Irvin Flores Rodríguez in the Nationalist Party attack on the US House of Representatives that resulted in a new wave of trials and incarcerations, effectively bringing the APRI's defense of Albizu Campos to a standstill. Further, Muñoz Marín summarily revoked Albizu Campos's 1953 pardon.[51]

Between the disappointments at the United Nations and the simultaneous frustrations on the legal front for both Reynolds and Albizu Campos, it had been a difficult couple of years. Yet even as circumstances forced Reynolds and the APRI to pivot their focus and resources from Albizu Campos's case once again, she persevered with her unique approach to supporting the cause of Puerto Rican independence.

An Outsider in the Wake of the 1954 Attack on Congress

Ruth Reynolds's solidarity activism meant she had to persevere during the most discouraging of times. And in the next phase of her efforts on behalf of political prisoners and Puerto Rican independence, when discouragement pressed in on all sides, she did, indeed, persevere. Ruth Reynolds stuck with solidarity activism in the wake of the 1954 attack, even though she disagreed with their actions, and even when "guilt by association" forced her to the fringes of political activism.

In the aftermath of the attack on Congress, the US and commonwealth governments immediately stepped up surveillance and arrested dozens of Nationalists and Communists in Puerto Rico, New York, and Chicago.[52] US-friendly Latin American dictatorships in Cuba and Venezuela also increased surveillance and arrests, including assigning a police detail to watch Albizu Campos's wife, Laura Meneses de Albizu Campos, who was living in Cuba.[53] Reynolds was one of ninety-one people subpoenaed in New York to appear before three federal grand juries on March 8.[54] It was the first of her many court appearances. Reynolds recalled that another witness, Nationalist Juan Carcel, made a joke about the irony of the government bringing together the people it had previously prosecuted for meeting with each other.[55]

In response to the wave of arrests and incarcerations, Reynolds and A. J. Muste were among the small number of non–Puerto Ricans who helped establish a new committee to assist Nationalist defendants: the Committee for Justice to Puerto Ricans (CJPR). However, disagreements over how to address potential political fallout of "guilt by association" tainted the new committee's structure. The members of the RRDC, who were still awaiting the result of Reynolds's appeal to the Supreme Court of Puerto Rico, formed the nucleus of the new group. Muste, in particular, opposed Reynolds's and Mielke's formal membership, and a majority of the other members agreed. By Reynolds's account, he convinced colleagues to deny membership in the CJPR due to her incarceration and due to her personal acquaintance with the accused.[56] They also voted against Mielke's membership due to her acquaintance with the accused.

The CJPR's decision to deny membership to Reynolds and Mielke might have been motivated by the public they hoped to win over. Muste believed that the CJPR's only hope in attracting support rested in a strategy emphasizing the injustices of imperialism, the right of the accused to a fair trial, and the CJPR's nonaffiliation with the Nationalist Party.[57] On this last point, he saw Reynolds and Mielke as liabilities. He reasoned that their very public ties to the Nationalist Party would undermine the CJPR's legitimacy as impartial and good faith actors among supporters and critics alike. Muste wrote Dave Dellinger three weeks after the shooting at the House of Representatives, "Ruth Reynolds and Thelma Mielke will of course sit in and serve as consultants of the committee but they will not be members so that there will be no basis whatever for saying this is just [an] N. P. [Nationalist Party] set up."[58]

Muste's concerns were not unfounded. They spoke to the challenges that Reynolds faced in mobilizing solidarity activists in the United States after her release from prison. As Reynolds was no longer incarcerated, her reputation was nevertheless tarnished by accusations of violence that surrounded Nationalist Party members, as was Mielke's reputation because of her former role representing the Nationalist Party at the United Nations.

Reynolds privately criticized the shooting in the House of Representatives as "counterproductive."[59] Publicly, she refused to denounce the four or distance herself from them. To fellow organizers, she insisted that knowing someone did not mean "complete agreement" with them. She denounced the CJPR's consideration of her incarceration in assessing her membership. Reynolds characterized Muste's position against her membership in the CJPR as "immoral." Ruth Miller, who served with Reynolds and Mielke on the APRI's organizing committee, gave up her membership in protest.[60]

Ultimately, Reynolds and Mielke did not let different views on strategy prevent them from behind-the-scenes fundraising, assisting defendants' families, monitoring the treatment of Nationalist prisoners, and confronting ongoing government scrutiny and economic hardship. The cost was high. Both were fired from their day jobs and had difficulty obtaining work because of frequent court appearances and trailing FBI agents.[61]

Overall, the CJPR had difficulty raising funds to launch its defense of a large group of defendants. By May 1954, the government had indicted seventeen Nationalists, most for seditious conspiracy.[62] Years later Reynolds recalled, "We got enough money, not to mount a *proper* defense, but to mount *some* defense."[63] Political repression and government intimidation of independentistas made it nearly impossible to raise money from Puerto Ricans outside Nationalist circles. Any hint of pro-independence advocacy could elicit government scrutiny that included accusations of communist sympathies.[64] As the historian Margaret Power has documented, the United States and commonwealth governments quickly used the attack on Congress to further associate the Nationalist Party—and independence sentiments more generally—with communism. "Tying the Nationalists to the Communists," Power explains, "allowed both the US and Puerto Rican governments to dismiss the Nationalists' claims that Puerto Rico remained a US colony as nothing more than anti-U.S. Communist propaganda."[65]

Some civil libertarians and communists had been supporting Nationalist causes since the 1930s. However, Reynolds identified the key donors to the CJPR as pacifists who gave because of their opposition to US colonialism and insistence on a fair trial.[66]

An Enduring Radical Solidarity

Even when forced to the margins of a network she helped to build, Reynolds continued to think about what was needed to support prisoners and their families. In addition to fundraising, Reynolds took on a special role of serving as a point person for defendants' families who contacted her for all kinds of assistance—from navigating the legal system, to sharing their pain and fears, to completing daily tasks that required English or literacy. Many of these families were bereft with the arrest of their breadwinner and person who had taken care of quotidian household transactions that required English. Reynolds reflected on why these families trusted her: "Because people felt rightly or wrongly, that I knew more about how to get things done than anybody else, that I was not afraid, and I wasn't. You take a position, you take the chances that go with the moral position you take. I knew I was vulnerable [to arrest] all the time, but you run that risk."[67] In Reynolds's view, the personal sacrifice that she made for that moral position had cemented Laura Meneses de Albizu Campos's confidence in her. As Reynolds recalled, "The people [*doña* Laura] trusted were few. I happen to be one of the privileged. My feeling is she didn't trust me fully until after I'd been in prison and passed through the test."[68]

Reynolds was also a fierce advocate for how their incarcerated family members were treated in prison. The momentum that Reynolds and Mielke had generated into an investigation of whether the government had radiated Albizu Campos stopped with the attack on Congress, but Reynolds's push to monitor prison conditions continued in the CJPR, including the conditions of her former cellmates at La Princesa. Isabel Rosado Morales and Doris Torresola Roura had been arrested and convicted in the wake of the 1954 attack. Muste likewise wrote Muñoz Marín, as well as the superintendent of prisons, for information on those arrested in Puerto Rico.[69] As Muste explained to the superintendent of prisons, "From newspaper reports we understand that scores of persons arrested on March 6th and following . . . are being held incommunicado. This would seem to involve being treated as convicts even before they are indicted." Muste continued, "We are deeply concerned about the health of Don Pedro Albizu Campos. . . . It is also reported to us that he is being held in solitary confinement."[70]

Albizu Campos had already been returned to prison after Muñoz Marín revoked his pardon. Between July and October 1954, thirteen of the seventeen indicted Nationalists involved in the attack on the US House of Representatives were also convicted and sentenced to at least six years in prison. The four directly involved in the US Capitol shooting received maximum prison terms for their involvement in the shooting: Cancel Miranda, Figueroa Cordera, and Flores Rodríguez received twenty-five to seventy-five years; Lolita Lebrón received sixteen years and eight months to fifty years (she had shot into the ceiling, so she faced one fewer charge).[71] On October 26, 1954, a federal judge in New York handed down six-year sentences for seditious conspiracy to Lebrón, Cancel Miranda, Figueroa Cordera, and Flores Rodríguez and to nine others, including Rosa Collazo, Julio Pinto Gandía, and Carmelo Álvarez Roman. The four others, including Lebrón's brother, had pleaded guilty prior to the trial and received six-year suspended sentences and five years of probation.[72]

Amid all this disappointment, one note of good news had to do with Reynolds's own case. On November 17, 1954, the Supreme Court of Puerto Rico reversed the lower court's decision and acquitted Reynolds, concluding that the prosecution had not provided sufficient proof to convict Reynolds of violating Insular Law 53. As Justice Pedro Pérez Pimentel wrote in the unanimous decision, "Neither the oath taken by Ruth Reynolds nor her affiliation with the Nationalist Party, nor her attendance at particular meetings held by the said group can be classified as criminal acts under clause 1 of Law 53 which we are discussing."[73] It was only the second time that the courts had reversed a Smith Act–related conviction. The first had taken place only several months earlier in January 1954, when the Pennsylvania Supreme Court overturned a Smith Act conviction.[74] In overturning Reynolds's conviction, however, the Supreme Court of Puerto Rico was careful to reaffirm the legitimacy of Insular Law 53 itself, a position the court noted that the justices had already taken in the decision they rendered on Reynolds's codefendants several months earlier.[75]

Ironically, while Muste had erased Reynolds from the CJPR's outward face by successfully lobbying against her membership, he placed her front and center in a December 18, 1954, letter to supporters announcing the news.

In it, he announced that Reynolds's appeal victory in the Supreme Court of Puerto Rico was a good sign for the CJPR's next stage of work: appealing the sentences of the Nationalist resistance fighters. Muste asserted that Reynolds's appeal victory was a "remarkable tribute" to Conrad Lynn's legal ability and a sign that the "CJPR has been vindicated in showing an interest" in the cases of Nationalist defendants.[76]

A vindicated Reynolds continued her solidarity work all the while the legal foundation for Insular Law 53 itself—the Smith Act—fell apart. Insular Law 53 was known as the "Little Smith Act" precisely because it was nearly verbatim to the 1940 Smith Act, which the US government used to prosecute sedition cases against members of the Communist Party USA. During 1956 and 1957, however, the US Supreme Court ruled against multiple Smith Act cases, overturning multiple convictions. Under these circumstances, Puerto Rican legislators repealed Insular Law 53. But the damage of the Gag Law to the independence movement was profound.[77]

It was especially because of this ongoing damage of US rule that in December 1958, Reynolds joined nine other Peacemakers in Puerto Rico for a multiday "Peace and Good Will Walk." "We oppose US military and congressional domination in Puerto Rico," read one sign. "Pacifists Walking from Guanica to San Juan," read another sign, announcing the group's symbolic path from the coastal town where US troops invaded in 1898 to the capital city location of the United States' military command in Puerto Rico (see figure 7.1). Along the way, they passed out thousands of flyers. "We come on foot," the flyer read, "so that there may be no barriers between us and those we meet along the way." The group concluded with a silent protest in front of the headquarters because US intercontinental ballistic missiles in Puerto Rico, their flyer also explained, made Puerto Rico a prime target in Cold War hostilities (see figure 7.2).[78]

At the same time, the US Supreme Court's rulings against the Smith Act and the successes of anticolonial movements across Africa and Asia seemed to portend well for the campaign to free the remaining Nationalist prisoners. From Reynolds's perspective, this shifting legal and geopolitical environment made it the perfect moment to strike. Acutely aware of this more supportive domestic and international environment, Reynolds had encouragingly speculated in a 1961 letter to Lynn, "Since we now have a wider range of anti-imperialists to draw upon than in the past and since the fear of McCarthy's ghost is not as strong as it was ten years ago, I believe that it will be much less difficult now than then to raise funds" for a new habeas corpus campaign [for Albizu Campos].[79] Indeed, fundraising to cover legal

FIGURE 7.1 Reynolds at the front of the Peacemakers Walk across Puerto Rico in December 1958. Behind her stands Wally Nelson and then Ralph Templin. Source: Ruth M. Reynolds Papers. Peacemakers marching down the road: RMRe _b37_f07_0003. Archives of the Puerto Rican Diaspora, Center for Puerto Rican Studies, Hunter College, CUNY.

fees was a primary activity for defense committees. It was a bellwether of the amount of public support for Nationalist prisoners and the idea of an independent Puerto Rico itself.

In the early 1960s, there was still no mass movement for Puerto Rico's independence in the United States with which APRI solidarity activists might collaborate in their prisoner work. Years of government oppression had pushed the expression of support for independence behind closed doors. Reynolds and her colleagues also found that the end of Insular Law 53 did not benefit Nationalists convicted for taking up arms in 1950. As a 1963 APRI flyer put it, "The people who rebelled against the hundreds of unconstitutional arrests in 1950 are still in prison."[80]

FIGURE 7.2 A silent demonstration in front of Old San Juan's Casa Blanca, which served as headquarters of the US military command for Puerto Rico. Reynolds and Wally Nelson appear in the middle with signs. Pictured as well are Ralph Templin (*third from left*) and Thelma Mielke (*third from the right*). Source: Ruth M. Reynolds Papers. Peacemakers: RMRe_b01_f07_0001. Archives of the Puerto Rican Diaspora, Center for Puerto Rican Studies, Hunter College, CUNY.

Under these circumstances, Reynolds tried once again to win Albizu Campos's freedom. Between 1962 and 1964, Reynolds stepped up the pace of her visits, making multiple trips to Puerto Rico—for a few days to a week at a time—to serve as Albizu Campos's "next friend" in a revitalized APRI habeas corpus effort to bring his case to light. Lynn was Reynolds's legal counsel, and lawyer Carlos Carrera Benítez (a longtime Nationalist) also eventually joined the case (see figure 7.3). They argued that Albizu Campos had been illegally incarcerated since March 1954, when Muñoz Marín had summarily revoked his earlier gubernatorial pardon without due process.[81]

In response to various court delays in 1963 and then again in 1964 to her writ of habeas corpus as a "next friend," Reynolds, Ruth Miller, and a hand-

FIGURE 7.3 At the Supreme Court of Puerto Rico in 1964 appealing Albizu Campos's writ of habeas corpus. Reynolds appears in the middle alongside lawyer Carlos Carrerra Benítez. In front (*right to left*) are Lynn and Yolanda Moreno (Albizu Campos's former nurse, an APRI activist, and Lynn's spouse). Source: Ruth M. Reynolds Papers. Tribunal Supremo Colonial: RMRe_b37_f03_0002. Archives of the Puerto Rican Diaspora, Center for Puerto Rican Studies, Hunter College, CUNY.

ful of other North American pacifists demonstrated outside the hospital treating Albizu Campos, the prisons housing about two dozen Nationalists, and the Supreme Court of Puerto Rico.[82] They carried signs in Spanish charging, "Judges Awaiting Death of Albizu Campos to Resolve Habeas Corpus" and "Until Today Albizu Campos Habeas Corpus Unresolved for 702 days" (see figure 7.4). They distributed Spanish and English leaflets denouncing the injustice of the enduring incarceration of Nationalists who had revolted in 1950 against a law that was no longer valid, and who in 1954 had defended themselves against "the police who had bombarded them with machine gun fire and tear gas."[83] Though they were a small group, their picketing generated coverage in *El Mundo* and *El Imparcial*.[84]

FIGURE 7.4 Reynolds and Miller protesting in Puerto Rico on August 21, 1964, against court delays on Albizu Campos's writ of habeas corpus. Source: "Ruth M. Reynolds y Ruth Miller cargando carteles de protesta, 21 de agosto de 1964," Centro de Investigaciones Históricas, Universidad de Puerto Rico, Recinto de Río Piedras, Colección Benjamín Torres, serie: fotografías, caja 8, número 35.

Before the Supreme Court of Puerto Rico rendered a decision on her "next friend" writ, Muñoz Marín pardoned Albizu Campos on November 1964 for a second time. Muñoz Marín did not want Albizu Campos to become a martyr by dying in prison on his watch. Reynolds denounced the US and commonwealth governments for lacking "the courage and honesty to free him through juridical process" but nonetheless celebrated Albizu Campos's freedom.[85] She also began to raise funds. As Reynolds wrote APRI supporters, non–Puerto Rican US citizens like themselves had a special obligation to raise the $2,000 needed monthly for Albizu Campos's care because their government had "broken" his health.[86]

· · · · · ·

Albizu Campos died on April 21, 1965. Reynolds joined the mass march for Puerto Rico's independence that took place in 1965 in San Juan during ceremonies connected to Albizu Campos's funeral. She published an article in

FIGURE 7.5 Reynolds next to Laura Meneses de Albizu Campos at the Santurce, Puerto Rico, funeral home where Albizu Campos's body lay in state for forty-eight hours in April 1965. Source: "De izq. A der. Ruth Reynolds, Laura Meneses en la Funeraria Jensen Home, 24 de abril 1965," Centro de Investigaciones Históricas, Universidad de Puerto Rico, Recinto de Río Piedras, Colección Benjamín Torres, serie: fotografías, caja 9, número 9.

the *Peacemaker* that attempted to convey to readers the importance of Albizu Campos's life for many Puerto Ricans by detailing what she called the "pageant of spontaneous homage" that erupted upon his death. As she explained, "the filthiest journalism of the century" had "defamed" Albizu Campos's character such that "his 'public image' in the United States has become the precise opposite of what he really was." She described a "constant stream of admirers" who passed by to pay their respects as Albizu Campos's body, which lay in state first at a funeral home in Santurce (see figure 7.5) and then at San Juan's cultural institution, the Ateneo Puertorriqueño, for a total of seventy-two hours, as well as the massive crowd of 100,000 who accompanied the coffin to the burial site in San Juan's "Old Cemetery."

FIGURE 7.6 A large crowd gathers to witness the interment of Albizu Campos in 1965. Source: Centro de Investigaciones Históricas, Universidad de Puerto Rico, Recinto de Río Piedras, Colección Benjamín Torres, serie: fotografías, caja 9, número 40.

(see figure 7.6). The crowd was so large, she said, that she and the close family and friends of Albizu Campos with whom she was walking "could hardly see the beginning of the procession entering Old San Juan, and the end of it was not visible at all." "The tribute paid him by his own," she asserted, "demonstrated the futility of money and greed and the military and economic oppression [the US government] employ[s] to destroy his place in their affections."[87]

About twenty-one years had passed between the first time Reynolds and Albizu Campos had met in February 1944 at his New York hospital room and Albizu Campos's death in San Juan in April 1965. In 1944, Reynolds had just recently taken an interest in the struggle for Puerto Rico's independence, alongside her civil rights and Free India activism. By 1965, she was a seasoned independence activist who had developed a distinct vision of solidarity work guided by what she saw as pacifism's priorities and the ob-ligations of non–Puerto Rican US citizens. After years of defending herself and assisting Nationalist defendants and prisoners, Reynolds knew well the strategies, politics, and legal framework for challenging such incarcera-tions. She also was a repository of knowledge about the government's re-pression of pro-independence voices in the years before and after the commonwealth's inauguration. She harbored memories of her own arrest and ill treatment in prison, and she had heard such stories from others, in-cluding Albizu Campos. Her political expertise and firsthand knowledge were valuable in a new era of unprecedented Puerto Rican diasporic mobili-zation. She carried his vision forward in her radical solidarity and became a vital link between activist generations.

. . . .

In late October 1977, Ruth Reynolds typed out a letter to Dolores (Lolita) Lebrón from her Manhattan apartment, inquiring whether Lebrón would welcome another visit. Lebrón, the Nationalist Party's former US delegate, whom Reynolds had known since the early 1950s, was serving her third decade of a fifty-year prison sentence for participating in an armed Puerto Rican Nationalist attack on the US Congress in 1954. Reynolds had already visited her at the Federal Correctional Institution for Women in West Virginia earlier in the year. Now, as Reynolds explained in her letter, she wanted Lebrón's feedback on the US Committee to Free the Five Puerto Rican Nationalists (USCFF), a newly formed group lobbying for the liberty of five political prisoners—including Lebrón.[1]

"My own concern in work of this kind," Reynolds wrote Lebrón, "is that we do nothing contrary to the wishes of the persons most involved—the prisoners themselves." She explained that her acquaintance with the five prisoners prompted other members of the USCFF to ask her to visit all of them "to discuss with you our plans and see whether or not you approve—what you think we should and should not do."[2] To this end, Reynolds also wrote the other four prisoners: Oscar Collazo, who was serving a life sentence for the 1950 Truman assassination attempt, and Rafael Cancel Miranda, Irvin Flores Rodríguez, and Andrés Figueroa Cordero, who had all joined Lebrón in the attack on Congress. They were each serving over seventy years in federal prisons.[3]

Lebrón wrote back immediately: "You are always most welcome at any time and for any purpose you would wish to consult me. It is very wonderful to see you again!"[4] Cancel Miranda likewise wrote back: "One thing is for sure, Ruth, I would be very happy to see you! I know about the new Committee and I think it's already doing a good job."[5] The others may have written as well.

Of course, it was not so simple. Late in October, another group—the similarly named Committee to Free the Five Puerto Rican Nationalists—had dramatically draped a massive Puerto Rican flag from the crown of the Statue of Liberty while occupying the landmark for several hours.[6] Based on the similarity of the groups' names, the warden at the US penitentiary in Marion, Illinois, assumed that Reynolds was affiliated with the protesters and denied her request to visit Cancel Miranda. She had to set the record straight, that there was no connection to the "recent takeover of the Statue of Liberty." The existence of multiple groups working for Nationalist prisoners' release (Reynolds knew of four) was "only natural, since [the] feeling is increasingly widespread that these people should be freed."[7] Yet the warden still denied her request, insisting that any business with Cancel Miranda could be conducted by mail.[8]

By the late 1970s, the political landscape had altered with the emergence of multiple groups working for the release of the remaining Nationalist prisoners. In the 1950s, few people in the United States and Puerto Rico risked the government repression that came with such advocacy, but by 1977 there were enough groups to make the news with their protests and cause occasional confusion. Reynolds persisted with her own work alongside and in cooperation with these multiple groups. They brought the fight right to Washington, DC, which was unusually attentive to global human rights under the administration of President Jimmy Carter. Here, they found success at last. Carter commuted the prisoners' sentences, paving the way for them to walk free on September 10, 1979, after twenty-five years in prison.

For Reynolds, this victory was particularly sweet after decades of often lonely solidarity advocacy for Puerto Rican independence and the release of imprisoned Nationalists. While Reynolds's activities remained the same, the world had changed around her. The Cuban Revolution (1953–59) replaced a US-backed military regime with a revolutionary government that was highly critical of US colonialism and supportive of Puerto Rico's struggle for independence. In Puerto Rico, a vocal pro-independence Left emerged in the form of the Pro-Independence Movement (MPI or Movimiento Pro-Independencia) in 1959, which then became the Puerto Rican Socialist Party (Partido Socialista Puertorriqueño; PSP) in 1971. Meanwhile, at home in the United States, the legacy of the recent anti–Vietnam War movement and the ongoing work and recent successes of the civil rights movement galvanized young activists. Suddenly, Reynolds had a lot more company in her independence work thanks to this new wave of social engagement.

In the 1970s, a new generation of multiracial activists in the United States joined her in making independence for Puerto Rico a priority. They identified with the Third World and applied anticolonial critiques developed there to the inequalities that they experienced as marginalized peoples within the United States. The Puerto Rican Young Lords, in particular—strong in Chicago and New York—focused on Puerto Rico's colonial status to understand their own subordinate plight in the United States. Across the globe, the induction into the United Nations of dozens of newly independent nations from Africa and Asia also made the international body a more amenable site for Reynolds and other pro-independence advocates to press the colonial case of Puerto Rico at the international body. These former colonies demanded UN attention to end colonialism where it endured.

Surrounded by new allies and a changed United Nations, Reynolds's commitment to solidarity activism placed her in a position to further Pedro Albizu Campos's vision of pursuing Puerto Rico's independence on the international stage. It also allowed Reynolds to carry forward his political thought—as it sat in her syncretic anticolonial strategy—into this new era of decolonization. Radical solidarity meant playing a long game. Reynolds had been patiently mobilizing for Puerto Rico's independence for decades. Now, she was able to apply her ideas about allyship toward working not only with longtime allies but also with a new generation of activists. Between the 1940s and 1960s, she had endured surveillance, incarceration, and political isolation with no guarantee that her personal suffering would result in a sovereign Puerto Rico. But the changed political environment of the 1970s made a more immediate breakthrough seem promising. In this new context, she sustained her long-standing work on behalf of independence and Nationalist prisoners while linking a new generation of activists to the earlier era of nationalist activity.

Third World Activism and New Alliances

During the 1970s, Reynolds encountered a new generation of radical activists committed to a range of intersecting anticolonial, antiracist, and anticapitalist liberation agendas. Reynolds developed a working relationship with a broad array of these radical activists between 1970 and 1975, when she mobilized for the freedom of Puerto Rican prisoner Carlos Feliciano. The mass protests that surrounded the Feliciano case during this five-year period made it a different organizing experience than the earlier ones Reynolds had participated in. For the first time in her years of working for the release of Nationalist prisoners, a mass movement had formed, and it was being fueled by a new generation of youth activists.

Feliciano was a longtime Nationalist Party supporter from Mayagüez. He had been incarcerated for violating Insular Law 53 in connection with the 1950 uprising. Like with Reynolds, the Supreme Court of Puerto Rico overturned the conviction—in his case, after he served four years of a five-year sentence at La Princesa. He relocated to New York and married. Beginning in the mid-1950s, nearly as soon as he moved to the United States, the FBI began surveilling his family at their home.[9]

In May 1970, authorities arrested and charged Feliciano with attempted arson, reckless endangerment, conspiracy, and unlawful possession of explosives in connection with a series of bombings in New York City that authorities believed were the work of the Movimiento Independentista Revolucionario Armado (MIRA; the Independent Armed Revolutionary Movement). The MIRA claimed ties with revolutionary Cuban nationalism and belonged to the most radical separatist wing of the Puerto Rican independence movement. Between 1969 and 1972, members set fire to and bombed hundreds of buildings associated with the US government and corporate activities.[10] Although Feliciano denied membership in the MIRA and any involvement with the bombings, he was caught in the crossfire. Over the course of 1970 to 1971, Feliciano was indicted for attempted arson of the General Electric Building, for attempted arson of the United States Armed Forces Recruiting Station, and for making false statements when applying for a firearm permit.[11]

Once again, Reynolds was navigating unpopular territory that did not outwardly seem to align with her pacifism. Her radical solidarity and dedication to Puerto Rico's independence, however, guided her choices. Though Reynolds and Feliciano had operated in similar political circles for years, at the time of Feliciano's 1970 arrest, Reynolds did not personally know him. Yet within a few months, Reynolds was one of four officers leading the Carlos Feliciano Defense Committee (CFDC) and its planning meetings at St. Mark's Church in-the-Bowery—the "Third World revolutionary church of New York," as St. Mark's' priest and CFDC president David García characterized it. Since the 1960s, it had provided meeting space for the Young Lords, the Puerto Rican Student Union, and the Black Panthers.[12] She joined as an individual when the APRI decided not to take up the cause as an organization, determining that its members would be most effective by working with the CFDC and other involved organizations in whatever ways they could on their own.[13] Along with García, St. Mark's young Mexican American priest, Puerto Rican Nationalists Luis Sosa and Epigmenio Martínez joined Reynolds as officers heading the CFDC's multiracial political coalition.[14]

In the process of mobilizing for Feliciano's freedom, Reynolds deepened ties with the radical Puerto Rican youth movements emerging in the United States while maintaining crucial ties to an older generation. At the time, she was intrigued by the revolutionary youth movements in New York and Chicago that demanded Puerto Rico's independence—from the Young Lords, to the Puerto Rican Student Union, to the US branches of the archipelago-born Puerto Rican Socialist Party (PSP), the radical Left pro-independence party that had taken the mantle from the Puerto Rican Pro-Independence Party (MPI) in 1971. Among those who followed the rise in youth activism with satisfaction was Reynolds's dear friend and Albizu Campos's widow, Laura Meneses de Albizu Campos. "One thing doña Laura said to me," Reynolds noted in a 1986 interview, was, "'There are two things that have happened I never expected. One is the liberation of Africa and the other is the rise of an independence movement among the youth, the young Puerto Ricans of the United States.'" Reynolds remembered Meneses saying, "We had virtually written off with a few individual exceptions, the second and third generations."[15]

Reynolds's own journey toward radical solidarity had begun in the 1940s, when she encountered the vibrant political community that the migrant parents and grandparents of the current generation of young activists had forged in New York. Since then, these Puerto Rican communities had grown significantly and become younger demographically because of the massive and notably young migration of Puerto Ricans to the United States between the 1950s and the 1970s. During these years, the government of Puerto Rico sought to end unemployment in the archipelago by promoting labor migration to the continental United States to fill industrial and agricultural jobs.[16] As a result, outmigration from Puerto Rico rose to nearly a third of the archipelago's population.[17] New arrivals joined second and third generations, whose lives, though they were born in the continental United States, were shaped by lasting coloniality—in the form of low wages, discrimination, and marginalization. By the 1970s, this lasting coloniality also meant limited job opportunities in both Puerto Rico and the continental United States. The structural limitations of the US-dependent commonwealth economy rooted in labor outmigration, private US capital investments, and tax breaks for US companies operating in Puerto Rico became glaringly apparent amid the era's financial crises.[18]

Within this context, the youth of the massively expanded Puerto Rican communities of New York, Chicago, and other cities came to occupy a unique "social location." As the historian Johanna Fernández explains, "The social location of the children of the Puerto Rican migration—as translators and cultural interlocutors between their parents and America's hostile bureaucracies—gave them a second sight."[19] Politicized by the Black civil

rights movement and the anti–Vietnam War protests and the cultural tur-
moil of the moment, they translated their unique point of view into a radical movement in opposition to colonialism.

Migration and repression played key roles in the politicization of this generation and in the creation of their own cross-movement alliances—a
"Third World Left"—during the late 1960s and 1970s. So did proximity.
Growing Black and Brown communities expanded up against each other in
urban spaces like New York and Chicago, leading to new solidarities and
common cause. Modeled on the Black Panther Party, the Young Lords, for
example, was a revolutionary Puerto Rican youth group that emerged in
Chicago in 1968 and then quickly spread to New York. Its continental US-
based members demanded independence for Puerto Rico and mobilized
against discrimination in the United States.[20]

Reynolds encountered this generation of Puerto Rican youth activists in
different ways. In the case of the Young Lords, the most visible of these
groups, she sought them out shortly after their emergence in New York. In
the winter of 1970, Reynolds headed to their storefront headquarters to find
out "what they were all about." When they occupied East Harlem's First
Spanish United Methodist Church (FSUMC) in December 1969, she noted
that they had "stirred up the church community of the establishment in a
way that nobody else had ever been able to do."[21] They had done so, notably, after the FSUMC and other churches had denied them space to run a
free breakfast program for local children.[22] Reynolds interviewed several
Young Lords in early 1970 and found them "utterly captivating in their zeal
and dedication, in their giving of themselves and of their slender economic
resources to meet the basic needs and resolve basic problems of their fellow Puerto Ricans in New York City."[23]

In an expression of the radical solidarity that had guided her support of
Puerto Rican–led activism, she joined the Young Lords' mass walk through
the streets of Harlem to protest the suspicious death of an incarcerated
Young Lord in October 1970. The protest ended with a second occupation
of the FSUMC building.[24] She was struck, however, by the differences in
political culture that were on display, seemingly generational in nature. She
lightheartedly recalled the Young Lords' use of profanity and said, "I walked
on the sidewalk . . . in the company of an old Nationalist who couldn't take
it either." In a low-stakes microcosm of her approach to tactics not aligned
with her own principles, she simply moved to the side without letting
her support for the cause—and the Puerto Rican activists on its front
lines—waver.

By the time Feliciano asked her to serve on his defense committee, Reynolds had a rapport with some Young Lords. Those interactions increased significantly as they collaborated on the challenging case. Feliciano was not widely known among leftist activist circles in New York, so Reynolds and the defense committee took advantage of the expanded possibilities for coalition building in 1970s New York to help make his defense a cause célèbre among the Left. The Young Lords Party (YLP)—along with the Puerto Rican Socialist Party (PSP), El Comité, and the Puerto Rican Student Union (PRSU)—sent representatives to CFDC planning meetings.[25] Although mostly crushed by the US government, a weakened Nationalist Party also managed to send representatives regularly. Other activist groups, such as I Wor Kuen, the Black Panthers, Youth Against War and Fascism, and the Catholic Peace Fellowship, also expressed support for Feliciano.[26]

The coalition proved effective. As *New York Post* columnist José Torres explained to readers in 1973, "Feliciano has become a symbol of political struggle for Puerto Ricans both here and in Puerto Rico. . . . Today, in every protest, picket line or even in Puerto Rican parades in different cities throughout the US, his picture is prominently displayed with placards saying: 'Free Carlos Feliciano.'"[27] Reynolds participated in many of these protests (see figure 8.1).

In defending Feliciano, Reynolds and the other CFDC officers worked hard to create an organizational structure that aspired to promote coalition work with minimal conflict among supporters in spite of ideological and sometimes personal differences. Specifically, the four CFDC officers each eschewed affiliation with any Puerto Rican organization, with the exception of the Nationalist Party.[28] Her commitment to coalition-building across difference was an outgrowth of her years of experience developing her unique approach to solidarity. Though the Young Lords Party, the Puerto Rican Socialist Party, El Comité, and the Puerto Rican Student Union sent representatives to CFDC planning meetings, Reynolds and the other officers held ultimate veto power over planning decisions in order to thwart any affiliated group effort to steer CFDC resources toward partisan goals.[29]

As Feliciano awaited trial in the fall of 1971, Reynolds joined a class action lawsuit with Feliciano and several Puerto Rican organizations. The case was strategically situated squarely within this broader context of government suppression of the radical Left, and it included plaintiffs from diverse sectors of the Left. The suit asserted that the district attorneys had fabricated criminal charges against Feliciano with the aim to "harass, intimidate and deter" Puerto Ricans and their allies from expressing their belief

FIGURE 8.1 A 1971 march in Manhattan's lower East Side calling for Carlos Feliciano's release on bail. Reynolds is visible just behind the sign on the right. Walking next to her (with the bowler hat) is Jacinto Rivera Pérez of the Nationalist Party. The march ended at St. Mark's Church in-the-Bowery where planning meetings for the Carlos Feliciano Defense Committee took place. Source: Ruth M. Reynolds Papers. RMRe_b37_f06_0002. Archives of the Puerto Rican Diaspora, Center for Puerto Rican Studies, Hunter College, CUNY. Courtesy of Máximo Rafael Colón.

in independence for Puerto Rico. Reynolds was among the "allies"—one of the non–Puerto Rican plaintiffs representing "US citizens and residents favoring Puerto Rico's independence."[30] Mexican American and African American plaintiffs also asserted that Feliciano's prosecution would have a chilling effect not only on their ability to express solidarity with the Puerto Rican movement but also to advocate on behalf of their own rights.[31]

Within this broader ecosystem of suppression, Reynolds specifically suspected that the US and commonwealth governments were setting the stage with Feliciano's prosecution to suppress other independence voices. As Reynolds contended in one of the CFDC's first mailings in September 1970, Feliciano's arrest was "the first public action in an attempt to establish a false but judicial link between the bombings of public buildings in New York City and the bombings of Yankee-owned businesses in Puerto Rico, between

MIRA and the Nationalist Party of Puerto Rico." All of these links were in service, she believed, of tying the activists to Cuba. Once such a link was established through Feliciano's conviction, Reynolds asserted, "The government will feel confident to proceed at will against Puerto Rican Nationalists both in the United States and in Puerto Rico, incarcerating whomsoever it wishes on false charges of bombing or conspiring to bomb public and private buildings."[32]

When it came to the issue of repression, Reynolds brought with her first-hand knowledge about the lengths to which the government would go to quiet its opponents. Reynolds's suspicions that the government had used radiation on Albizu Campos fueled her conviction that the government had framed Feliciano. For a time in 1951, Feliciano had been incarcerated with Albizu Campos, making Feliciano one of the few living witnesses to the suspected abuse. "It is therefore to the advantage of the United States government to have him imprisoned for a long period of time," Reynolds explained to Carlos Feliciano Defense Committee supporters, "and to have his credibility destroyed by conviction for a very serious crime."[33]

When a judge's dismissal of the suit denied the defense committee remedy in federal court, Reynolds and her defense committee colleagues continued to make the case through grassroots outreach. During its five-year existence, the CFDC held fundraisers, conducted petition and letter-writing campaigns, and organized demonstrations that emphasized shared struggle in the United States and Puerto Rico. One fundraiser was attended by actress Rita Moreno, whose Oscar for *West Side Story* catapulted her to national fame, as well as activist-actor Ossie Davis and activist-lawyer Florence Kennedy.[34] The MPI, the Puerto Rican Student Union, and the Young Lords were among the multiple groups visible at CFDC-initiated rallies.[35] As flyers read at one such rally in the Bronx, "To free Carlos, free all political prisoners and show that we will not allow the violence of repression in our streets, we will march."[36]

When evidence of police misconduct led to Feliciano's acquittal in June 1972, Reynolds was relieved. But the reprieve was short-lived. Despite the Bronx County acquittal, New York County put Feliciano on trial. The Manhattan court found him guilty for possession of explosive substances and sentenced him to four years in prison.[37] Updating CFDC supporters about the new trial in the fall of 1973, Reynolds had emphasized that the committee was "more convinced than ever" that Feliciano was the victim of a coordinated political "frame-up."[38] Following the conviction, Reynolds and García called for a letter-writing campaign directed at the appeal judges that emphasized the plot to discredit Feliciano's testimony with regard to Albizu Campos. The letters also highlighted that evidence of police misconduct was excluded from the New York County trial.[39] Feliciano, however, remained in prison.

Despite such ongoing failures, support for his release did not flag. Reynolds was in attendance at the 1974 rally at Madison Square Garden of 20,000 people expressing support for Puerto Rico's independence. Speakers included statements in support of Feliciano's case.[40] The Puerto Rican Socialist Party (PSP), a Marxist independence group based in Puerto Rico, was the engine behind both the mass rally in 1974 and the US-based permanent solidarity committee that emerged from it—the Puerto Rican Solidarity Committee (PRSC).[41]

In the end, Reynolds's work with the CFDC came to a close before Feliciano was released. In May 1975, Reynolds and García sent a letter to supporters of the defense committee announcing that they were closing their offices. All the legal appeals they'd made to "defeat the conspiracy" (Feliciano's indictment) had failed, and Feliciano himself requested the shutdown. It was a discouraging moment after such a sustained and broad-based effort on his behalf.

Nevertheless, Attorney William Kunstler continued to work on the case, aiming for Feliciano's early release after exhausting the appeals process.[42] Kunstler was already widely known for representing the Chicago Eight defendants on charges related to the 1968 protests of the Democratic National Convention. Meanwhile, while defending Feliciano, Kunstler was also working with defendants connected to the Attica Prison riot and the American Indian Movement's occupation of Wounded Knee.[43] It was a sign of the times. And, at last, Kunstler made headway in the Feliciano case when he succeeded with the argument that sentencing had overlooked credit for the time Feliciano served when he could not afford bail.[44] On July 9, 1975, Feliciano regained his freedom.

Meanwhile, there were complexities behind the scenes that made this a good moment for Reynolds to shift her focus elsewhere. As she wrote a colleague, "You probably know that Carlos Feliciano lost his head and came under the influence of the Prairie Fire crowd, which is a most violent offshoot of the Students for a Democratic Society." She was referring to a sector of the white Left in the United States and its members' turn to revolutionary violence. This offshoot's "bombing divisions," she continued, "known as Weathermen Underground, had to go underground and their strongest elements are still there." Unfortunately, she wrote, "Carlos became better acquainted with some of them in prison, and came under their influence."[45] Presumably wary of the Weathermen's "bring the war home" solidarity politics, she felt it a good moment to regroup after the closure of the CFDC.[46] For Reynolds, this meant focusing on freeing "The Five."

Free the Five

Reynolds did not even stop to celebrate the victory of Feliciano's release, nor did she nurse her disappointment over his turn toward the Weathermen. Instead, she focused on lobbying for the release of remaining Nationalist Party prisoners. As a participant in these efforts, Reynolds continued to negotiate her approach to solidarity with the diverse sectors of the much-expanded independence movement that included both international pressure for the release of the prisoners and a broad coalition of activists in the United States, with especially pivotal actors and organizations located in Chicago and New York.[47] Reynolds contributed in the ways that she could and that were consistent with her pacifist principles from her home base in New York. Within a few years, this mobilization of diverse groups and actors helped to secure the freedom of the five Nationalists who were still incarcerated for their participation in the 1950 Truman assassination attempt and the 1954 shooting at the Capitol: Oscar Collazo, Lolita Lebrón, Irvin Flores Rodríguez, Rafael Cancel Miranda, and Andrés Figueroa Cordero. These five became a cause célèbre for Puerto Rico activists.

In 1977, Reynolds worked with the Puerto Rican Solidarity Committee to take advantage of the Carter administration's critical look at US foreign policy.[48] Public opposition at the beginning of the decade to US intervention in Vietnam, combined with the 1976 Senate report revealing that the CIA had plotted the assassination of foreign leaders, made Carter's presidential campaign promise of a US foreign policy centered on human rights appealing to many voters.[49] In 1977, Carter's human rights rhetoric continued in the Oval Office, and the PRSC flagged the new administration's outlook as an opening. As the PRSC's 1977 "National Workplan" noted, "The statements that Carter has made on human rights and political prisoners in the context of his appeal to the public to be recognized as a defender of the rights of the discriminated against, the downtrodden, etc. can be taken advantage of and used as a lever to secure the release of the five." That same year, the PRSC established the US Committee to Free the Five Puerto Rican Nationalists (USCFF).[50]

Reynolds declined the PRSC's 1977 invitation to join its national board for familiar reasons. The PRSC was, in essence, a North American arm of the Marxist-oriented Puerto Rican Socialist Party (PSP). While she personally favored socialism, her radical solidarity demanded that she recognize and maintain her position as a non–Puerto Rican supporter of the archipelago's independence. It also demanded that she steer clear of telling Puerto Ricans how to run an independent Puerto Rico, which she believed a socialist or communist organization working for Puerto Rico's independence approached too closely. Nevertheless, recognizing the opening that Carter's human rights agenda provided, she worked with PRSC leadership on the USCFF.[51] As with the Feliciano case, she did this work as an individual because the APRI determined that its members could organize more effectively by affiliating individually with the multiple groups working to free Nationalist prisoners.[52]

Reflecting the inclusive perspective that was the hallmark of her approach to allyship, Reynolds refused to "take sides" among the different groups involved or require ideological adherence to any specific mode of activism among the groups represented. Prior to a mid-October 1977 PRSC event at the University of Pennsylvania, advertised as "The Role of North Americans in the Independence of Puerto Rico," Reynolds notified organizers that she planned to "speak in terms of what North Americans should do in general terms." Most visibly, she refused to take sides between two key groups, the Puerto Rican Solidarity Committee and the Committee for Puerto Rican Decolonization (CPRD), a group dedicated to using the United Nations to advance Puerto Rican independence. She maintained her neutrality even though she had closer ties to the latter group. She elaborated, "If I am urging North Americans to become involved in the struggle for Puerto Rico's independence, I can't be in the position of favoring the PRSC over the CPRD, nor of favoring the CPRD over the PRSC at a meeting sponsored by the latter." She clarified that her agnosticism was grounded in her conviction that "there is room for 500 organizations advocating independence for Puerto Rico, just as there were multiple organizations opposing the war in Vietnam, and each one can make its contribution."[53]

On December 22, 1977, Reynolds represented the US Committee to Free the Five Nationalist Prisoners (USCFF), on a delegation that visited the White House. Together, they asked President Carter for a Christmas pardon of the remaining Nationalist prisoners from the 1950s. The delegation also included leaders from Puerto Rico's Catholic, Protestant, and Episcopal churches, as well as representatives from the National Council of Churches (which had issued its own resolution calling for their release), the Hispanic Task Force of the United Methodist Church, and the American Friends

Service Committee. Also joining were attorney John (Juan) Passalacqua of the Comité Nacional Pro Libertad de los Presos Nacionalistas, and a delegate from the office of US representative Herman Badillo, a Caguas-born congressman representing the South Bronx.[54]

Meeting with two Carter aides, the delegates presented their appeals from different angles. Reynolds delivered the approximately 8,000 signatures of a USCFF petition and a promise to continue the petition campaign for as long as necessary. Religious leaders from Puerto Rico appealed to Carter's faith by invoking the Old Testament's Levitical concept of the Jubilee Year of offering liberty and the New Testament's Gospel of Luke recounting Jesus's declaration that he came "to preach deliverance to the captives." The American Friends Service Committee delegate emphasized that releasing the remaining prisoners would enhance Carter's credibility as a world leader of human rights.[55] The experience convinced Reynolds that continual and intensive pressure from multiple sectors across the United States would be required to successfully release the prisoners. She shared her perspective on how the event had been received with USCFF supporters: "We left with the feeling that the release of these prisoners is being considered but was not imminent."[56]

In a letter to USCFF supporters, Reynolds specifically called for increased pressure. She hoped for additional delegations to the White House and "intensive letter-writing and petition campaigns demonstrating to President Carter that the freedom of these prisoners is a serious human rights issue within his own country, and is gaining increasingly widespread support that cannot be ignored."[57] Writing letters was a solidarity strategy that Reynolds had employed for years—as an act of her faith and a means of political resistance. She never knew whether the recipients of her letters even read her correspondence. Still, in the most uncertain of times, she had disseminated her arguments in defense of the incarcerated and critiqued those who put them there one letter at a time. She encouraged those joining the struggle to do the same.

Two more years of lobbying resulted in victory. After serving more than a quarter century in prison, Collazo, Lebrón, Flores Rodríguez, and Cancel Miranda walked free on September 10, 1979, and went directly to Chicago to thank the community for their work since they had been pivotal to the campaign.[58] Their comrade Andrés Figueroa Cordero had been pardoned by Carter earlier because of his advanced cancer, but he died in Puerto Rico several months before he could witness his compatriots' release.[59] Collazo, Lebrón, Flores Rodríguez, and Cancel Miranda had previously refused to petition for clemency, yet Carter nonetheless commuted their sentences when confronted by a robust movement demanding their release, citing "human considerations."[60] Of course, there were other practical reasons, as well. Though the Carter administration denied any formal prisoner exchange with Cuba, Carter's clemency for the Puerto Rican prisoners paved the way for Fidel Castro to free several US citizens.[61]

After the release, Reynolds was in the crowd that met the four at the airport in New York, and she managed to gain entrance into the packed press conference at the United Nations. She stayed with them for long enough, she wrote a colleague, "to embrace each of the four before I had to go to work that night."[62] Indeed, in the midst of supporting herself as an assistant librarian and lobbying for the release of Nationalist Party prisoners, Reynolds was also once again lobbying the United Nations for Puerto Rico's independence—and her efforts there demanded her attention as well, notwithstanding her great relief at the release of The Four.

A few weeks after The Four's arrival in Puerto Rico, where they were given a hero's welcome, an interviewer queried Reynolds about how "the present reaction of Puerto Ricans to the freeing of the Nationalist Prisoners compare[d] to the situation between 1950 and 1954." She answered, "I don't believe that the sentiment in these two periods is that different. It's only in how it's expressed." To make her point, Reynolds juxtaposed the thousands who regularly gathered to hear Albizu Campos speak in Puerto Rico in the late 1940s, to the oppressive climate she encountered upon a visit there in 1954. She described how people she had known for years "walked straight ahead as though they didn't see you. Then they send word to you by night to apologize." The support was there in the 1950s, but its expression was suppressed. The overwhelmingly positive reception for the four Nationalists in 1979, she elaborated, "is an indication of the sentiment in Puerto Rico. And what I experienced in the January day in 1954 is an indication of how people behave when police repression is severe."[63] It was a statement that spoke to both the lost opportunity of the 1950s to make Puerto Rico a sovereign nation and an optimistic perspective on the possibility of the current moment to achieve the long-standing goal.

Decolonization at the United Nations

In the early 1970s, while advocating for the prisoners' release, Reynolds faced new opportunities to take up solidarity efforts at the United Nations. The United States' ability to keep the colonial case of Puerto Rico out of the

United Nations had begun to falter. Finally, after so many years, a large number of activists from different corners of the US Left joined Reynolds in undertaking solidarity work at the United Nations. The expanded activist networks that Reynolds connected with in the 1970s were a part of these regalvanized UN lobbying efforts. Some activists she had known for years; others were new acquaintances. And in this context, the staying power of her radical solidarity enabled her to bridge generations, buttressing the new strength in numbers and broad-based interest with long-standing knowledge and experience.

With the exception of Reynolds and Thelma Mielke, none of the North American solidarity activists in this new political environment of the 1970s had experienced firsthand the UN battles during the 1940s and 1950s, which had made the international organization such an unfriendly site for advancing Puerto Rico's independence. The United States had kept Puerto Rico off the radar of the United Nations ever since it had successfully petitioned to remove the archipelago from the United Nations' list of non-self-governing territories in 1953. The United States had pointed to the commonwealth status as a means of affirming its support of self-determination for Puerto Rico, but in reality, the United States had ensured that the archipelago remained within the orbit of its control without UN interference. After Puerto Rico was removed from the United Nations' list of non-self-governing territories, matters having to do with Puerto Rico at the United Nations had to go through US representatives, which effectively blocked efforts by nonaligned UN member-nations to reintroduce the colonial case of Puerto Rico in the international organization.

During the 1960s, Reynolds and other pro-independence advocates observed that a more receptive environment for independence work at the United Nations was taking shape, thanks to geopolitical changes. Because of the longevity of her work in this space, she was able to harness relationships of trust cultivated over many years and under the most difficult of circumstances toward tracking shifting alignments at the United Nations. And there had, indeed, been significant shifts. In 1950, the United Nations had evicted the Nationalist Party and its delegate, Mielke—an indication of just how unfriendly the United Nations had become as a site for challenging US colonialism in Puerto Rico. Then, after the 1959 revolution, Cuba—a former US ally at the United Nations—emerged as an outspoken critic of US colonialism and a strong advocate for Puerto Rico's independence at the United Nations.[64] In 1961, Cuba's revolutionary government had granted Reynolds's friends Laura Meneses de Albizu Campos and Nationalist Party leader Juan Juarbe Juarbe citizenship and made them members of its permanent UN delegation, enabling both to travel legally to the United States and take up residence in New York, despite the absence of diplomatic relations.[65] They met regularly in New York during Meneses de Albizu Campos's time there between 1961 and 1967. In one of her regular letters to Meneses in 1968 after Meneses de Albizu Campos's return to Cuba, Reynolds included a *New York Times* clipping about UN discussions related to Caribbean colonies. It exemplified one of the many subtle ways that these longtime colleagues supported each other and exchanged information in their distinct but lengthy struggles for an independent Puerto Rico.[66]

A geopolitical shift in UN membership made it possible for Reynolds and other independence activists to reengage the United Nations with more hope than they had experienced in several decades of hard work. The success of decolonization movements across Asia and Africa in the 1950s and 1960s meant that dozens of newly independent nations inducted into the United Nations demanded worldwide decolonization and helped to create the structures that might bring it about.[67] In 1960, the General Assembly issued its boldest anticolonial position in years with Resolution 1514 (XV), asserting that "immediate measures should be taken to transfer all power to the people" of territories "in trust and not autonomous, and in all other countries which have not won their independence."[68] After the enactment of Resolution 1514, Puerto Rican politicians, activists, and their allies attempted to put Puerto Rico on the agenda of the UN Committee on Decolonization. The MPI and then the PSP took the lead in these efforts, working closely with the Cuba mission at the United Nations to get the case of Puerto Rico before this new UN Committee on Decolonization.[69]

It was not until the early 1970s, however, that ongoing efforts by Puerto Rican politicians, activists, and their allies began to yield results. Because of the longevity of her solidarity efforts, Reynolds was well positioned to "ring the alarm" about the urgency and unprecedented nature of the moment for those expanding activist networks in the United States who were new to the struggle at the United Nations. And she did it in her characteristic way—by attempting to educate them. One way that Reynolds did so was by serving as director of the "United Nations Project" for the Committee for Puerto Rican Decolonization (CPRD), founded in 1973. In this role, she wrote up a fact sheet called "Puerto Rico at the United Nations." It traced the history between the United Nations' 1945 creation and the Committee on Decolonization's enactment of two resolutions between 1972 and 1973. These resolutions recognized "the inalienable right of the people of Puerto

Rico to self-determination and independence" and requested that the US government "refrain from taking any measures which might obstruct the full and free exercise by the people of their inalienable right to self-determination and independence." As Reynolds interpreted, the resolutions meant "that the Puerto Rican question will continue to be discussed in the international body, something [that] the United States in the past has been able to prevent from happening."[70] Drawing on decades of experience, she was determined for there to be a different outcome this time.

In 1977, Reynolds joined the lobby of the UN Committee on Decolonization to include Puerto Rico under the rubric of 1514. Among the US Left, the Puerto Rican Solidarity Committee spearheaded the US People's Delegation in 1977, a coalition of over thirty diverse US organizations. In his address to the UN Committee on Decolonization in August 1977, Robert Chrisman, a professor and publisher of the *Black Scholar* who represented the coalition, proclaimed that the massive 1974 Madison Square Garden rally had "heralded a new period for the solidarity movement in the US." Chrisman pointed to Reynolds and US congressman Vito Marcantonio as predecessors. He noted that during the 1930s and 1940s, Marcantonio "was one of the staunchest advocates of Puerto Rican independence."[71] He also noted Reynolds's leadership and the fact that she "served 19 months in a Puerto Rican jail in the early 1950s for her sympathy with the liberation struggle." As Chrisman asserted, "The tradition they have established grows today."[72]

Claimed as a predecessor by this expanded network, Reynolds still felt that there was a distinct contribution for her to make in this moment through her educational approach. She told Rafael Anglada, the PSP spokesperson at the United Nations, "[There] are things that I think should be said that I don't think that the PRSC or [Chrisman] the spokesman elected by the diverse groups that have been called here are going to say."[73] Experience had taught her that UN decisions were made on material presented the *previous* year. Thus, she prepared a brief that gathered together a history of US congressional deception that she had followed over many years.[74] She did so in her role as APRI secretary.

Reynolds prepared a twenty-two-page brief on behalf of the APRI and personally took it to each member and each delegation on the Committee on Decolonization. Over a decade later in 1986, she still considered her brief to be "the best statement that's been made that details the machinations of the United States government in regard to Puerto Rico from 1898 on."[75] Reynolds's brief—titled "Puerto Rico under the United States Flag: Self-Determination or Congressional Determination?"—focused on dishonest congressional maneuverings to deny the people of Puerto Rico their self-determination. She asserted the APRI's demand that Puerto Rico's independence was a *"prerequisite* for the exercise of self-determination," and she included a wealth of evidence that it had never exercised genuine self-determination under US control.[76]

The APRI, she wrote, had concluded from its extensive study of the situation that the US government had repeatedly "imped[ed] the exercise of true self-determination by the Puerto Rican people." Emphasizing the significance of this point, Reynolds explained, "During the past several years, discussion of the case of Puerto Rico in the United Nations and elsewhere has revolved around the issue of whether, as the United States Government alleges, Puerto Rico has already exercised full self-determination and freely chosen her present relationship to the United States, or whether complete independence from that country is a prerequisite to the exercise of true self-determination."[77]

Among the slew of examples that she offered, which dated as far back as 1898, Reynolds pointed to the most recent plebiscite in Puerto Rico in 1967, which she characterized as a "gauge of political sentiment in Puerto Rico." She complained that the US government and press "continue to ignore the 43% abstention and to proclaim that 60% of the Puerto Rican people voted in favor of the commonwealth." Reynolds also elaborated the multiple ways that Congress had used its unilateral power over Puerto Rico to delay the plebiscite for years, and then its legislative response to the results died in committee in 1976. However, just weeks earlier, the US representative to the United Nations under the new Carter administration had invoked the 1967 plebiscite as *proof* that US policy toward Puerto Rico was "based on complete acceptance of the right of the people of Puerto Rico to self-determination."[78] By offering this sort of critical context and background information, Reynolds encouraged both her fellow activists and new delegates to the United Nations to be wary of Congress's long-standing use of obfuscation.[79]

Whether her work the previous year had made a difference is not clear. But there was, indeed, a breakthrough the following year. In a 1978 resolution, the committee called for "a democratic process" utilizing "a mechanism freely chosen by the Puerto Rican people" to resolve the archipelago's status.[80] The resolution implied that previous mechanisms, most notably several US-sponsored votes on the archipelago's status, had not been truly representative.

In 1980, two years after the breakthrough resolution, Reynolds spoke directly to the Committee on Decolonization on behalf of the APRI to combat a new attempt by the United States to deflect international charges of colonialism. In August 1979, Congress passed a joint resolution reaffirming congressional support for the "right of political self-determination of the people of Puerto Rico." Despite its rights-based wording, however, the resolution was actually an attempt to prevent Puerto Ricans and their allies from reintroducing debate about Puerto Rico's sovereignty at the United Nations.

Reynolds ensured that her audience on the decolonization committee understood that the 1979 congressional resolution had no teeth, and she exposed the underhanded manner by which the United States continued to affirm its support for Puerto Rican self-determination while ensuring its continued subordination. Tellingly, Congress had recently rejected a request from the government of Puerto Rico for greater political authority. Reynolds reminded her audience of the massive repression on the archipelago in advance of the commonwealth vote, and how that vote passed with a minority of Puerto Rico's population, in part because so many people refused to participate in what they considered a sham event. Only 34 percent of the archipelago's inhabitants chose commonwealth status.

Indeed, Congress's intention in passing the 1979 resolution, according to Reynolds, was to make it appear that the US government's "decisions regarding Puerto Rico have been self-determined by" the people of Puerto Rico, without obligating Congress to take up any additional legislation on Puerto Rico. In other words, the resolution was an empty promise. Her proof: senators' quotes reassuring each other that the resolution did not bind Congress to further action. She read them aloud, further analyzing that the 1979 resolution was a congressional commitment to "Puerto Rico's right to self-*expression*" but "in no way at all" a commitment "to Puerto Rico's right to self-*determination*."[81]

For decades, US officials had managed to thwart debate in the United Nations about the colonial status of Puerto Rico. This time they did not succeed. The last-minute congressional resolution did not stop the UN Committee on Decolonization from adopting its own resolution criticizing US colonialism in Puerto Rico. The day after Reynolds and representatives from multiple other organizations testified, the Committee on Decolonization adopted a resolution urging the US government to "adopt all necessary measures for the full transfer of powers to the people of Puerto Rico" and to present a "plan for the decolonization of Puerto Rico." The United States, of course, rejected the UN committee's work as a "misrepresentation of the facts."[82]

It was the longevity of her activism that gave her this insight to make these cogent arguments about how the US government had over many years deflected UN charges of imperialism through empty resolutions and the outright repression of its oppositional voices. Reynolds had successfully used the international stage of the United Nations to offer a critical voice from within the United States that did not align with the official US government narrative. She was well aware that her testimony was among a chorus of voices—both Puerto Rican and North American—demanding the United Nations finally hold the United States accountable for its colonial regime in Puerto Rico.[83]

What she could not accomplish by pressuring her own government from within, she attempted to do by operating in the international arena of diplomacy. In this way, Reynolds carried Albizu Campos's strategic efforts to use the United Nations, her perspective as a political prisoner, and her insight as part of a community threatened by the US government into her lobbying work at the United Nations. Her commitment to solidarity activism as a North American activist put her in a position to help keep the question of Puerto Rico's independence alive in the arena of international politics in a way that enabled the Nationalist Party to meaningfully participate in the era of decolonization.

In this sense, a lot had changed in the forty years since she and Mielke first began lobbying the United Nations to take up the colonial case of Puerto Rico. However, fundamentally nothing had changed at the United Nations in relationship to the independence of Puerto Rico. As Reynolds noted in the mid-1980s, "Puerto Rico has been there from the beginning and nothing [has] happened, really. I mean, nothing's been achieved. A lot has happened, but nothing's been achieved for Puerto Rico, except statements."[84] At the same time, she wondered about her own legacy. By then, she had been diagnosed with cancer. "I don't believe my own life has been wasted," she concluded, "though tangible success is difficult to see."[85]

Radical solidarity was a long game, and she was still playing it. Guided by her belief in the power of truth, she noted that the United Nations' "committee on decolonization has said that Puerto Rico, like every other people in the world, they have a right." The United States might disagree, she maintained, "but they know their posture is wrong. And, they can't get away with it forever."[86] Reynolds continued to work for victory in her lifetime.

Conclusion

Looking back on her years of activism for an independent Puerto Rico in a 1985 interview, Ruth Reynolds mused, it "has been the hardest area. . . . People have been the least receptive and still are." "Sometimes I feel like a complete failure because I've been in this thing for forty-some years and so little dent has been made," Reynolds asserted. She asked rhetorically, "Should I have done this, should I have done that? Should I have trusted the Almighty to feed me instead of taking a crazy job?"[1]

While participating in this supremely difficult struggle over the course of nearly five decades, Reynolds crafted a powerful vision of radical solidarity and globally engaged justice. Recognizing the experiences and positionality of Puerto Ricans as colonial subjects, as well as her own positionality as a colonizing citizen, she became a leader in the Puerto Rican independence movement. Yet her unique vision of radical solidarity aimed to be transformative, never hegemonic. Reynolds did not premise her support upon independence-minded colleagues adhering to her political views or following certain strategies that she favored. Instead, she defined her role as amplifying the work of Puerto Ricans resisting US empire. And just as she viewed Puerto Ricans as agents of their own national destiny, she concentrated on her *own* agency in challenging the United States to live up to its democratic promise. A clear and consistent awareness of who she was and what she could bring to the struggle guided her throughout decades of struggle even as she traversed geographic distances and reached out to others with vastly different life experiences. As she put it later in her life, "My own posture is you stand up where you are and assert yourself."[2] Throughout her life, she maintained that her liberation and indeed the liberation of the United States were inseparable from the liberation of Puerto Rico.

Reynolds's lived experience of radical solidarity stands as an enduring model of allyship for political activists in the United States and beyond. She had to be willing to take risks and suffer the consequences of those risks, including giving up her own freedom, just as those with whom she claimed solidarity did. The costs were many, but so too were the rewards. Reynolds, as a result of her activism, encountered family disapproval, economic hardship, and imprisonment. But she also lived a life of purpose in community with people she loved and admired. Indeed, her wide circle of friends and allies enabled her to continue this work despite the difficulties.

For her entire life, Reynolds was steeped in community: the Harlem Ashram, the Fellowship of Reconciliation, the Peacemakers, Nationalist friends and colleagues, and fellow political prisoners. Although she witnessed and participated in some internecine debates and experienced ruptures with individuals, she also benefited from the staunch support of dear friends and allies. Some, like Albizu Campos, are well known. The majority, however, like Conrad Lynn, Thelma Mielke, Ralph Templin, Isabel Rosado Morales, and Laura Meneses de Albizu Campos, are less well known or have been largely erased from US history books.

On her journey from South Dakota to New York to Puerto Rico and back again, the most striking aspect of Reynolds's activism was her unwavering commitment, especially when it was so hard to see the "dents" of change. In her final decade, as she completed her work on the release of political prisoners and on decolonization for Puerto Rico at the United Nations, she also took on two other critical projects. The first was her involvement in the Vieques Support Network (VSN). Between 1979 and 1982, she became a founding member and participant in this group, which brought together Puerto Ricans and non–Puerto Ricans in the continental United States to support the "fisherman's war" on Puerto Rico's island municipality of Vieques. Reynolds's work with the VSN was an expression of her enduring solidarity activism in the multifront struggle against US colonialism. Since the 1940s, the United States had expropriated over three-quarters of this small island situated eight miles east of Puerto Rico's large island for US Navy operations. In 1978, Viequenses fishermen positioning their boats to stop navy warships sparked a broad-based grassroots movement in Vieques with widespread backing across Puerto Rico to oust the US Navy. The VSN mobilized to raise funds and to generate US and international pressure to bear on the US government and military to withdraw.[3]

To Reynolds, the anti-navy protests provided a glorious opportunity to sway more North Americans to the independence cause. Reynolds recognized that the government's abuses that fueled anti-navy protests set in stark relief the colonial relationship that independentistas denounced. She knew, moreover, that the anti-navy protests had brought together supporters from across the status question spectrum, not only independentistas. Thus, she hoped that Vieques might be a way to introduce, or reintroduce, North Americans to the status question in Puerto Rico. North Americans did not "have to stand for independence to get involved around Vieques." "But getting involved around the question of Vieques," she promised, "will open the eyes of a great many to the independence issue." For all these reasons, the grassroots struggle to oust the US Navy from Vieques, she told an interviewer in 1979, "may be setting the conditions for a future upsurge in the independence movement."[4]

Reynolds's other major project during her final decade involved preserving the history of the dramatic events that she had lived and witnessed. It took a revolution in academia for Reynolds's ideas to finally find a space there. In 1969, Puerto Rican and African American students occupied City University of New York (CUNY) buildings for two weeks, demanding the creation of Puerto Rican and Black Studies programs and admissions that more closely matched the demographic makeup of New York City. By 1973, the CUNY system claimed seventeen Puerto Rican Studies departments, and the Center for Puerto Rican Studies, which was created to support these departments, had begun acquiring research materials.[5]

This new generation of activist-scholars, working alongside pioneers in the field of Puerto Rican Studies, recognized the value of her counter-history of Puerto Rico under the US flag and of her own activism, as a non–Puerto Rican committed to the archipelago's independence and as a politically active woman in an era when men dominated politics. In 1985, Reynolds began meeting with Blanca Vázquez of the Center for Puerto Rican Studies for a set of oral history interviews. The interviews offered an opportunity for Reynolds to record what would be one of her final expressions of radical solidarity—detailing a history of repression and resistance that did not appear in US history books. Reflecting upon her cancer diagnosis, Reynolds explained to Vázquez that "Even before I became ill, I had come to the conclusion that the greatest, the best contribution I could make in the future . . . that the best contribution I could make is to put the material I have in proper archival order and deposit it somewhere where it would be used or be accessible." This goal pushed her to sift through decades of private correspondence and sustained her as she sat for hours and hours of interviews. It is "not for my personal pride, though that's involved also. But I do feel that my life has brought . . . me knowledge. Other people have had the same knowledge, not all of it from the same package." Referring to herself, Reynolds asserted, "But the package together is unique and is a contribution to the future."[6] That uniqueness included her role as a woman engaged in political activism across several decades of social and political change. On the topic of the burgeoning feminist movement, for instance, she reflected that though she was not involved, "I do feel that I have suffered economically because I am female. I do feel that I would have been listened to more on political issues if I had been male."[7]

Through these historical investigations, Vázquez uncovered a final gem: the existence of Reynolds's weighty manuscript on the 1948 University of Puerto Rico student strike.[8] Originally titled *Training for Treason*, Reynolds's analysis of US colonial power on the eve of the commonwealth had been denied an audience since 1950. The manuscript was among the items the police confiscated during her 1950 arrest in response to the Nationalist Party uprising. In 1989, at long last, the Center for Puerto Rican Studies published Reynolds's *Campus in Bondage: A 1948 Microcosm of Puerto Rico in Bondage*. Reynolds's enduring solidarity work was evident in the updated preface to her finally published book, where she insisted at the time of writing it in 1988, toward the end of her life, that "Puerto Rico is still in bondage."[9]

Reynolds died on December 2, 1989, not far from where she had been born in South Dakota. She never saw Puerto Ricans achieve independence. Nor did she live to see the intermediate victory she had been working on in her final years: it was not until 2003 that protesters and their allies finally forced the US Navy's withdrawal from significant territory in Vieques.[10] Still, in her last interview with Vázquez in 1986, Reynolds remained optimistic about her life's work: "Now, what about the future? I have no big answers." By then, she knew that it was very unlikely that she would see a sovereign Puerto Rico in her lifetime. But she looked to the past as a guide, explaining, "I feel that changes in history come at fortuitous moments."[11] Recalling a conversation with Laura Meneses de Albizu Campos, Reynolds explained, "Doña Laura said she would never have expected the freedom of Africa, but it came. It came." "India's freedom," she continued, "came at a time when Britannia could no longer rule the waves, but it would not have come at that time if there had not been the Indian National Congress, the movement of Gandhi, Nehru, and so on, and all the struggle that went into it."[12]

She remained hopeful for the future and committed to a radical vision of solidarity. She focused on what she held in common with those with whom she claimed allyship—a critique of US state violence and colonialism—rather than what separated them. She explained, "I'm an Albizuista. I was beside Don Pedro. Except on the issue of violence, I'm in complete agreement."[13]

· · · · · ·

In the spring of 2022, I returned to Puerto Rico for the first time since the twin disasters of Hurricane María and the COVID-19 pandemic. While there,

FIGURE C.1 A photo of the 1950 San Juan commemoration of the birth of José de Diego, the Puerto Rican politician who worked for Puerto Rico's independence from Spain and then from the United States.

I visited the Archivo General de Puerto Rico (AGPR). On previous trips, I had sifted through the vast government surveillance records of pro-independence figures held at this premier archive. I expected to find good images of Ruth Reynolds's activities, courtesy of FBI and insular police surveillance. One image stuck out.

Dated April 16, 1950, the photo was of Reynolds walking in a procession, a large Puerto Rican flag at the front. An insular police officer had circled Reynolds's image in blue ink and assigned the number one. Two others were similarly circled and had been assigned numbers. I flipped the image to find out who they were (see figures C.1 and C.2). The officer had neatly identified number two as Francisco Matos Paoli, the secretary-general of the Nationalist Party. His face obscured by the Puerto Rican flag, Nationalist Party president Pedro Albizu Campos was number three. By the time the photo was taken, Reynolds had already spent many months in Puerto Rico investigating state repression of the Nationalist Party. The sight of Reynolds walking with Albizu Campos, Matos Paoli, and many others struck me as a powerful

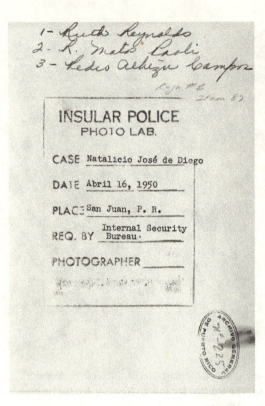

1- Ruth Reynolds
2- R. Matos Paoli
3- Pedro Albizu Campos

INSULAR POLICE
PHOTO LAB.

CASE Natalicio José de Diego

DATE Abril 16, 1950

PLACE San Juan, P. R.

REQ. BY Internal Security
Bureau.

PHOTOGRAPHER

FIGURE C.2 This image shows the text on the reverse side. Source: Archivo General de Puerto Rico, Archivo de fotografía, fondo: Departamento de Justicia (Tarea 90–29), serie: Documentos Nacionalistas "Conmemoración Natalicio de José De Diego, San Juan, 16 de abril de 1950." Fondo: Departamento de Justicia (Tarea 90–29), serie: Documentos Nacionalistas, item 87, fotografía número 2.

visual record of her radical solidarity—practicing pacifism, walking at the side of those with whom she claimed allyship, and experiencing unwanted government attention for mobilizing for the goals of a community of which she was not a part.

To my surprise, the curator of the AGPR's photographic archive was the granddaughter of Matos Paoli; María Rodríguez Matos had grown up hearing about Ruth Reynolds. She briefly alluded to the suffering inflicted upon her family because of their Nationalist affiliation. I already knew that a few months after the picture was taken, Matos Paoli was arrested and charged with violating the Gag Law, and was eventually sentenced to ten years in prison. Both Albizu Campos and Reynolds were likewise arrested and imprisoned. Wanting to learn more, I spoke with Rodríguez Matos again during my next trip to Puerto Rico as 2022 came to an end. We shared a bench in San Juan's Luis Muñoz Rivera Park, as Rodríguez Matos spoke to me about intergenerational trauma. Certainly, her Nationalist grandparents had suffered heavily. While Matos Paoli was imprisoned, his wife, her grandmother Isabel Freire de Matos (Isabelita) experienced "great economic precariousness" that of course also affected her mother Susana Isabel Matos Freire, and aunt María Soledad Freire (seven and five years old at the time of Matos Paoli's arrest).[14] The culture of fear that enveloped Puerto Rico, created by years of surveillance and the criminalization of independence, moreover, guaranteed economic and social precarity even after Matos Paoli's release. As Rodríguez Matos explained, "My mother and aunt's generation" experienced "constant hostility." "A glance or look of pity because they were the girls of Don Paco, of Isabelita" and many other acts of social marginalization, Rodríguez Matos explained, "marked them deeply." Rodríguez Matos did not suffer as did her grandparents' generation or her mother's, but her generation faced the challenge of processing the knowledge of that pain and injustice.[15]

Like Rodríguez Matos's family, many Puerto Ricans carry generations of trauma caused by government repression of pro-independence voices. Like Rodríguez Matos herself, some also carry the memory of Ruth Reynolds's commitment to the cause of independence. But both stories, of widespread repression and of Reynolds's life spent in radical solidarity with independentistas, are not well known beyond the archipelago. The determination of the US government to suppress independence voices for more than a century has obscured the reality of how and why the United States continues to rule "the oldest colony in the world."

In 2017, the response of even the most well-meaning and sympathetic US citizens who are not Puerto Rican to the devastation wrought by Hurricane María captured how this colonial history continues to be hidden. News reports made clear, in real-time, the trauma unfolding in Puerto Rico in 2017 in the wake of the Category 4 storm. The storm knocked out the archipelago's already fragile power grid, its water supply, and most emergency and health services, leaving millions in the dark without basic necessities for days and weeks on end. The heavy outmigration of Puerto Ricans to the continental United States in the years before the storm surged in the weeks and months after as people relocated to obtain basic services, medical care, education, and employment. By one estimate, about 160,000 made this journey in the first year after the storm.[16]

Generally, however, these news reports did not delve into the link between the catastrophic consequences of the storm and decades of US colonial policies that had made Puerto Rico vulnerable in the first place. Most immediately, even before the storm, the archipelago was suffering from more than a decade of massive debt and local austerity provoked in large part by the exodus of US corporations. Setting up shop in this US colony had become far less profitable after Congress's decision to phase out tax exemptions for US manufacturers operating in Puerto Rico went into full effect in 2006. The legacy of investor-friendly tax-exempt Puerto Rican bonds and predatory debt practices, as well as the fact that Puerto Rico was ineligible for federal bankruptcy and denied a federal "bailout," exacerbated the debt crisis. Subsequent austerity measures, imposed by a fiscal oversight board created by Congress in 2016, decimated public education, the power grid, and other essential infrastructure.[17] To many Americans, the image of President Donald Trump throwing paper towels at Puerto Ricans after the storm in 2017 captured a widespread callousness on his administration's part toward Puerto Ricans and the fate of the archipelago. Yet Puerto Rico's vulnerability to the storm, and its inability to address the destruction and suffering, was tied to a harvest of empire, the result of decades of extractive colonial policies imposed by both Democrats and Republicans in Washington, DC.[18]

Ironically, in an attempt to secure large-scale federal disaster relief, other US leaders and interested allies began to remind their fellow Americans that Puerto Ricans were US citizens too. Leading scholars and activists in Puerto Rico and beyond, however, have pointed out the limits of such "rhetorical incorporation" as a solidarity strategy.[19] These scholars and activists argue that Puerto Ricans do not need allies to affirm that they are Americans or that the archipelago is part of the United States. Instead, they need forms of solidarity that address the ugly by-products of colonialism starting with, according to one list, "debt cancellation, an end to the rule of the Federal Control Board, federal support for economic reconstruction, [and] a process of self-determination."[20] In other words, true solidarity demands grappling with the sources and consequences of US colonialism and a corresponding decolonized sovereignty.

At great personal sacrifice, Reynolds spent her life doing just that. In 2024, as the colonial relationship allows US investors to profit from displacing Puerto Ricans from their own homes and communities, and as increasing numbers of Puerto Ricans relocate to the continental United States, Reynolds's story and perspective remain as relevant as ever. Reynolds initially developed her solidarity politics in a unique moment through contact with a migrant and diasporic population that championed independence. Her story forces justice-oriented individuals to think not only about the future of Puerto Rico for Puerto Ricans but also what it means to take responsibility for US government–sanctioned injustice. She always believed that individuals could make a difference by asserting themselves where they stood. As she neared the end of her life, her faith in Puerto Rico's independence remained undiminished. As she asserted, "When it's going to coalesce, nobody knows. But it is our obligation wherever we are, whatever condition we are, and as long as we have life and breath, to continue to do our part and the rest is in the hands of history and of god."[21]

Acknowledgments

"Where is your mother from?" was a question that I frequently heard growing up. The answer was simple: Puerto Rico. Explaining that Puerto Rico was part of the United States—but also *not* part of the United States—was much harder. I have been thinking about this conundrum in one way or another for a long time. In this and many other ways, my mother is the inspiration for my ongoing exploration of the history of Puerto Rico and its relationship to the United States. I dedicate this book to her.

I am very grateful to the people and institutions who have made this book possible. Some of my first teachers of independentista history were women who made that history. I thank them for generously sharing their experiences and memories with me. Edda López Serrano welcomed me into her home for an interview at the earliest stages of my research and put me in contact with a generation of women independentistas who, in some cases, had been active since the 1930s. The opportunities to interview Alejita Firpi, Lydia Ramos, Isabel Rosado Morales, Adelaida Sambolín, Baldramina Sotero Cervoni, and Flavia Lugo de Marichal were experiences of a lifetime. They entrusted many stories to me that still need to be told to a larger audience. The powerful stories that Emilia Rodríguez Sotero relayed during several interviews continue to resonate with me. Yanina Moreno and Jimmie Moreno graciously facilitated several of these interviews by hosting a lunch at their home. I am also grateful to the members of Ruth Reynolds's family, including Jean Hirning, Robin Peterson, John Tysell, and James Tysell, who shared their warm recollections of her as well as personal collections. Despite the pain associated with her sister's arrest in Puerto Rico, Jean Hirning selflessly detailed her recollections of that difficult period in her family's life.

This book would not have been possible without Blanca Vázquez, who had the foresight to sit down with Ruth Reynolds and interview her for over a hundred hours toward the end of Reynolds's life. Nor would this book have happened without Olga Jiménez de Wagenheim, whose pioneering scholarship is a model of excellence, and who encouraged me to tell Reynolds's story at a critical juncture in my research on women's involvement in the struggle for Puerto Rico's independence. Since our first meeting in the archives, Olga's steadfast enthusiasm for my research has meant a great deal to me.

I have benefited from the expertise of numerous librarians, archivists, and colleagues. The assistance of archivist extraordinaire Magalis Cintrón Butler during my first challenging trip (amid the flooding of Hurricane Irene) to the Centro de Investigaciones Históricas de la Universidad de Puerto Rico, Río Piedras (CIH-UPR) and in the years since has always made it a pleasure to work in the CIH-UPR archives.

CIH-UPR director Marcial Ocasio Meléndez provided a unique opportunity to present my work to a large Spanish-speaking audience by including me in the CIH-UPR's excellent speaker series. Josué Caamaño-Dones accelerated my research timeline by introducing me to digital FBI files. Research trips to Puerto Rico were also made efficient by the expert assistance of Jeanmary Lugo González at the University of Puerto Rico's Colección Puertorriqueña; María Isabel Rodríguez Matos at the Archivo General de Puerto Rico; and Julio E. Quirós Alcalá and Carlos J. Vélez Mercado at the Archivo Históric de la Fundación Luis Muñoz Marín. Aníbal Arocho, Alberto Hernández-Banuchi, Pedro Juan Hernández, Yosenex Orengo, and Lindsay Wittwer helped me navigate the Center for Puerto Rican Studies at Hunter College's rich collections during my many visits there. Thank you to Daniel Goldstein and David Michalski for their guidance on UC Davis Library resources. I also gratefully acknowledge the assistance of archivists and staff at Boston University's Howard Gotlieb Archival Research Center, Princeton University Library's Department of Special Collections, the Swarthmore College Peace Collection, and the United Methodist Church Archives and History Center at Drew University.

This book has also benefited from the research assistance of Katharine Cortes, Griselda Jarquin Wille, Jordan Lahoun, José Ragas, Patricia Palma, Alyssa Kerikemeier, Melanie Peinado, Emmanuel Puig Chaparro, Joshua Kopin, and Liz Laurence. I sincerely thank each of them for their wonderful help.

Several grants and fellowships funded research trips and afforded me time to write. These included the Center for Puerto Rican Studies Historical Preservation and Research, several Small Grants in Aid of Research from UC Davis, the UC President's Faculty Research Fellowship in the Humanities, and the UC Davis Humanities Institute Faculty Research Fellowship.

A wonderful community of scholars and friends helped me get to the finish line. I am especially indebted to Ellen Hartigan-O'Connor, Rachel Jean-Baptiste, and Lorena Oropeza for critical engagement in my work. Each read multiple drafts of the book, helped me think through ideas during numerous conversations, and constantly reminded me how fun it is to have brilliant and kind friends. Corrie Decker has been a steadfast source of clear-headed advice, intellectual camaraderie, and warm friendship. José Juan Pérez Meléndez has taught me a great deal about Puerto Rico and the diaspora. The amazing Elena Abbott helped me get clarity on key arguments and added wind to my sails in the final stages of writing. Michelle Beckett and Kate Epstein offered wonderful feedback. Special thanks are also due to colleagues Ali Anooshahr, Eileen Boris, Joan Cadden, Howard Chiang, Edward Dickinson, Ellen DuBois, Sandra Eder, Stacy Farenthold, Juan Giusti Codero, A. Katie Harris, Kyu Hyun Kim, Chris Lesser, Susette Minn, Kimberly Nettles-Barcelón, Rebecca Jo Plant, Katherine Marino, Marian Schlotterbeck, Sudipta Sen, John Smolenski, Allison Sneider, Daniel Stolzenberg, Kathy Stuart, Julie Sze, Baki Tezcan, Cecilia Tsu, Grace Wang, and Judy Tzu-Chun Wu.

There are several other people who have sustained me during my many years at work on this book. Susan Beren and Rodrigo Pizarro helped me to defray the costs of research trips to New York by welcoming me into their home. I am also grateful for the support of mentors, birth family, and friends, including Sibia Naí Botello,

Angélica Feldt, Carmen García, Martha Gonzalez, Allison Hertog, Judy Loewe, Dalia Magaña, Regina Miesch, Megan Mock, and John Swain. Sylvia and Laurence Kaminsky helped with childcare and much more during research trips and periods of concentrated writing. I regret very much that I am not able to share the final product with Laurence.

I feel very fortunate to have connected with Debbie Gershenowitz at the University of North Carolina Press. Debbie was enthusiastic about the book from our first meeting and has been an amazing editor to work with. Among the many ways that Debbie has championed this project was finding fabulous readers. I sincerely thank Marisol LeBrón and Margaret Power for their intellectual investment in helping me make this a better book than it would have been without their feedback. Both read the manuscript twice, offered insightful feedback, and significantly deepened my thinking about when and why political solidarities take root and develop. I also want to acknowledge JessieAnne D'Amico, Lindsay Starr, and Thomas Bendenbaugh, who expertly guided me through the publication process.

I end my acknowledgments by returning to family. My mom not only sparked my desire to understand the history of Puerto Rico; she also became my travel partner during multiple research trips there. We have spent many hours discussing Puerto Rico, US colonialism, and Reynolds. We began these travels shortly after my dear father, Richard Stephen Materson, died. He would have *loved* to hear about our adventures. I am grateful to my brother Larry Materson for always cheering me on in my research and writing. My husband, Phil Kaminsky, has been a constant source of warmth, encouragement, and humor during the many twists and turns of this project. Our son, Joshua, was an infant when I received page proofs for my first book. And now, as this book goes out into the world, he is a teenager. During my years at work on this book, Josh has patiently endured my many absences due to professional obligations. Even so, I hope I have been a fraction of the parent to him as my parents were to me. Thank you to Phil and Josh for enriching my world beyond measure.

Notes

Abbreviations in the Notes

ACLU Records
    American Civil Liberties Union Records, Public Policy Papers,
    Department of Special Collections, Princeton University Library,
    Princeton, New Jersey
CIH   Centro de Investigaciones Históricas, Universidad de Puerto Rico,
    Recinto de Río Piedras, Puerto Rico
Fellowship Records
    Fellowship of Reconciliation (US) Records, Swarthmore College Peace
    Collection, Swarthmore, Pennsylvania
PAC   Pedro Albizu Campos
PNPR   Partido Nacionalista de Puerto Rico
RR Papers
    Ruth M. Reynolds Papers, Archives of the Puerto Rican Diaspora, Centro
    de Estudios Puertorriqueños, Hunter College, CUNY, New York
Templin Papers
    Ralph T. Templin Papers, United Methodist Church Archives—General
    Commission on Archives and History of the United Methodist Church
    (GCAH), Madison, New Jersey

Introduction

1. "The Case of Ruth M. Reynolds," series I, box 1, folder 1, RR Papers.

2. "The Case of Ruth Reynolds," series I, box 1, folder 1, RR Papers.

3. "Visit to Puerto Rico: A Report . . . October 6, 1951," Puerto Rico: (6) Peacemaker Actions folder, Templin Papers.

4. Stoler, "Tense and Tender Ties," 833; Kaplan, "'Left Alone with America,'" 3–21.

5. Jiménez de Wagenheim, *Puerto Rico's Revolt for Independence*, xiii, 5, 82, 113–16; Monge, *Puerto Rico*, 9–10; Meléndez, *Patria*, 21; Ayala and Bernabe, *Puerto Rico in the American Century*, 23–24.

6. Ayala and Bernabe, *Puerto Rico in the American Century*, 14.

7. Ponsa, "When Statehood Was Autonomy," 4.

8. Kennedy, *Decolonization*, 47–48, 53.

9. Ayala and Bolívar, *Battleship Vieques*, 1–5, 21–22.

10. Ayala and Barnabe, *Puerto Rico in the American Century*, 148–53.

11. Truman, "Statement by the President"; The Assistant Secretary of State for Congressional Relations (Jack K. McFall) to the Director, Bureau of the Budget

(Frederick Lawton), *Foreign Relations of the United States, 1952–1954*, United Nations Affairs, vol. 3, ed. Ralph R. Goodwin, document 901, accessed May 15, 2019, https://history.state.gov/historicaldocuments/frus1952-54v03/d901.

12. Dudziak, *Cold War Civil Rights*; Borstelmann, *Cold War and the Color Line*; Mollin, *Radical Pacifism in Cold War America*; Gore, Theoharis, and Woodard, *Want to Start a Revolution*; McDuffie, *Sojourning for Freedom*; Castledine, *Cold War Progressives*; Donohue, *Liberty and Justice for All?*

13. Ruth Reynolds interview by Blanca Vázquez, June 21, 1985, tape 5, series IX, box 45, folder 2, RR Papers. This is how Reynolds described her mother in particular.

14. "Julio Pinto Gandía," *Claridad*, July 2, 2008.

15. At the time, few US tourists traveled to the largely agricultural archipelago that was in the midst of industrializing, preferring instead to spend their dollars in casinos and luxury hotels in Cuba. Some North American wartime conscientious objectors also made Puerto Rico their temporary home in the 1940s. Merrill, *Negotiating Paradise*, 181–83, 194; Hinojosa, *Latino Mennonites*.

16. Report to the ALPRI, 1945, series III, box 14, folders 1–2, RR Papers.

17. Von Eschen, *Race against Empire*; Meriwether, *Proudly We Can Be Africans*; Gaines, *American Africans in Ghana*; Gore, *Radicalism at the Crossroads*; Plummer, *Rising Wind*.

18. Slate, *Colored Cosmopolitanism*; Horne, *End of Empires*.

19. This policy mandated alliances with antifascist groups, even noncommunist ones.

20. Power, "Friends and Comrades," 106–9, 111–14, 117–18.

21. Until his death in 1954, Vito Marcantonio was the other notable exception here. He used his position as a US congressman representing East Harlem to advance the cause of Puerto Rico's independence. See chapter 3 for further discussion of Marcantonio.

22. Well into the late twentieth century, US historians viewed their nation as exceptional with regard to the imperial ambitions of Western nations. Winks, "American Struggle with 'Imperialism,'" 143–77; Tyrrell, "American Exceptionalism," 1031–55.

23. May, *Homeward Bound*.

24. Materson, "Gender, Generation"; Mollin, *Radical Pacifism in Modern America*, 28.

25. Weigand, *Red Feminism*, 5; McDuffie, *Sojourning for Freedom*, 127, 155, 173.

26. May, *Homeward Bound*.

27. Newman, *White Women's Rights*; Santiago-Valles, "'Higher Womanhood,'" 47–73; Sneider, *Suffragists in an Imperial Age*; Jacobs, *White Mother*.

28. Bosque-Pérez, "Political Persecution," 13–47, 15–24.

29. Ruth Reynolds interview by Blanca Vázquez, August 15, 1985, tape 26, series IX, box 45, folder 7, RR Papers.

30. For a history of the origins of the term, see Scholz's *Political Solidarity*, 6–9; Arto Laitinen, "Solidarity," *Oxford Research Encyclopedia of Politics*, https://doi.org/10.1093/acrefore/9780190228637.013.2013.

31. The philosopher Sally Scholz defines political solidarity as "a moral relation that marks a social movement wherein individuals have committed to positive duties in response to perceived injustice." Scholz, *Political Solidarity*, 6.

32. Reynolds, *Campus in Bondage*, 5.

33. Lynn, *There Is a Fountain*, 132.

34. Ruth Reynolds to Helen [Tysell], June 21, 1951, series II, box 9, folder 3, RR Papers.

35. Ruth Reynolds, "On Confrontations," series III, box 16, folder 1, RR Papers.

Chapter 1

1. Ostler, *Lakotas and the Black Hills*, 3, 25–27.

2. Ostler, *Lakotas and the Black Hills*, 5–13.

3. Ostler, *Lakotas and the Black Hills*, xvii, 3, 11–13, 19, 23–24, 34.

4. Ostler, *Lakotas and the Black Hills*, xv, 28–29, 34–38, 68.

5. Wolfe, "Settler Colonialism"; Glen, "Settler Colonialism as Structure," 52–72.

6. "Dear Friends," series 1, box 1, folder 1, RR Papers; "Allaben Genealogical Chart," series I, box 1, folder 5, RR Papers; Handwritten notes on "Springfield Families," series I, box 1, folder 5, RR Papers; Sikes, *Richard Sikes and His Descendants*, 17; Brooks, *Timothy Brooks of Massachusetts*, 7–8. Some of these early ancestors may have been of Scottish descent as well.

7. Bureau of the Census, *United States Manuscript Census*, Caldwell County, Kentucky, 1870; Bureau of the Census, *United States Manuscript Census*, Butler County, Nebraska, 1880; Bureau of the Census, *United States Manuscript Census*, Lawrence County, South Dakota, 1900; Ruth Reynolds interview by Blanca Vázquez, June 11, 1985, tape 1, series IX, box 45, folder 1, RR Papers. According to family oral history, Reynolds's great-grandfather James Stewart arrived in the United States from Ireland in the 1850s, making him the last direct relative to immigrate to the United States. There are, indeed, several men listed on ship manifests from the late 1840s and early 1850s who fit James Stewart's description.

8. Ostler, *Lakotas and the Black Hills*, 80–88, 94.

9. Ostler, *Lakotas and the Black Hills*, 68–70, 87–88, 91–99.

10. Ostler, *Lakotas and the Black Hills*, 98–101; Ostler, *Plains Sioux and US Colonialism*. Crazy Horse also rejected the "agreement" but eventually surrendered in May 1877. Ostler, *Lakotas and the Black Hills*, 102–3.

11. Ruth Reynolds interview by Blanca Vázquez, June 11, 1985, tape 1.

12. "Allaben Genealogical Chart," series I, box 1, folder 5, RR Papers.

13. Mitchell, *Nuggets to Neutrinos*, 342.

14. Ruth Reynolds interview by Blanca Vázquez, June 11, 1985, tape 1.

15. Ruth Reynolds interview by Blanca Vázquez, June 11, 1985, tape 1.

16. "Allaben Genealogical Chart," series I, box 1, folder 5, RR Papers; Ruth Reynolds interview by Blanca Vázquez, June 11, 1985, tape 1.

17. Thompson, *New South Dakota History*, 306; Schell, *History of South Dakota*, 381–82.

18. Ruth Reynolds interview by Blanca Vázquez, June 11, 1985, tape 1.

19. *South Dakota Marriages, 1905–1949*, Ancestry database online, accessed June 3, 2024, https://www.ancestry.com/sharing/15876603?mark=7b22746f6b656e223a2238 322f506c3541684d344a534b454f5072774c6a466e4a46742f6478316a50574d 664634622f524c7434493d222c22746f6b656e5f76657273696f6e223a225632227d; Thompson, *New South Dakota History*, 307; Parker, *Deadwood*, 211–12; Mitchell, *Nuggets to Neutrinos*, 341–42; Oropeza, "Women, Gender."

20. Ruth Reynolds interview by Blanca Vázquez, June 11, 1985, tape 1.

21. Ruth Reynolds interview by Blanca Vázquez, June 11, 1985, tape 1.

22. Britz, "Deadwood's Days of '76," 52–53, 59–61.

23. Kasson, *Buffalo Bill's Wild West*, 5, 269.

24. Schuler, "Patriotic Pageantry," 355; Julin, *Marvelous Hundred Square Miles*, 81; Weinberg, *Real Rosebud*, 35.

25. "Coolidge Made Great Chief of the Oglala Sioux," *Chicago Daily Tribune*, August 5, 1927: 1; "Coolidge Becomes Chief of the Sioux," *New York Times*, August 5, 1927: 1, 3; Julin, *Marvelous Hundred Square Miles*, 81; Weinberg, *Real Rosebud*, 35.

26. "Coolidge Becomes Chief of the Sioux," 3.

27. Yellow Robe, "My Boyhood Days," 50; "Chief Yellow Robe, Sioux Educator, Dies," *New York Times*, April 8, 1930, 24.

28. "Chief Yellow Robe, Sioux Educator, Dies," 24; Yellow Robe, "My Boyhood Days," 53.

29. Weinberg, *Real Rosebud*, 22–24, 26–29, 38; Moses, *Wild West Shows*, 6; Yellow Robe, "Menace of the Wild West Show," 224–25; Kasson, *Buffalo Bill's Wild West*, 164.

30. Ruth Reynolds interview by Blanca Vázquez, June 11, 1985, tape 1.

31. Porter, *Native American Freemasonry*, 16, 22, 24–26, 48–49.

32. Ruth Reynolds interview by Blanca Vázquez, June 11, 1985, tape 1.

33. Ruth Reynolds interview by Blanca Vázquez, June 11, 1985, tape 1.

34. Ritterhouse, *Growing Up Jim Crow*, 2, 6–7, 20, 112, 115, 128–29, 134.

35. Ruth Reynolds interview by Blanca Vázquez, September 25, 1985, tape 48, series IX, box 46, folder 4; Ruth Reynolds interview by Blanca Vázquez, June 11, 1985, tape 1.

36. Mollin, *Radical Pacifism in Modern America*, 10.

37. Ruth Reynolds interview by Blanca Vázquez, September 25, 1985, tape 48; Schildgen, "How Race Mattered," 228–29; King, "West Looks East," 306.

38. Ruth Reynolds interview by Blanca Vázquez, September 25, 1985, tape 48.

39. Schell, *History of South Dakota*, 277–97; Lee, *New Deal for South Dakota*, x.

40. Solomon, *In the Company*, 148; Ruth Reynolds interview by Blanca Vázquez, June 11, 1985, tape 2, series IX, box 45, folder 1, RR Papers.

41. Ruth Reynolds interview by Blanca Vázquez, June 11, 1985, tape 3, series IX, box 45, folder 1, RR Papers.

42. Ruth Reynolds interview by Blanca Vázquez, June 11, 1985, tapes 2 and 3.

43. Hoover and Alexander, *From Idea to Institution*, 181, 188.

44. This relationship was governed through the Dakota Conference of Methodist ministers. Hoover and Alexander, *From Idea to Institution*, 186; Ruth Reynolds interview by Blanca Vázquez, June 11, 1985, tape 2.

45. Ruth Reynolds interview by Blanca Vázquez, June 11, 1985, tape 3.
46. Ruth Reynolds interview by Blanca Vázquez, June 11, 1985, tape 3.
47. May, *Homeward Bound*, 49–50.
48. Scharf, *To Work and to Wed*, 66, 85.
49. Ruth Reynolds interview by Blanca Vázquez, June 11, 1985, tape 3.
50. Ruth Reynolds interview by Blanca Vázquez, June 11, 1985, tape 3.
51. Mitchell, *Nuggets to Neutrinos*, 429, 464.
52. Biolsi, *Deadliest Enemies*, 20; Ostler, *Lakotas and the Black Hills*, 63.
53. Ostler, *Lakotas and the Black Hills*, 98–102.
54. Biolsi, *Deadliest Enemies*, 20.
55. Biolsi, *Deadliest Enemies*, 21.
56. Ostler, *Plains Sioux*, 50; Ostler, *Lakotas and the Black Hills*, 98–101.
57. Biolsi, *Deadliest Enemies*, 20–23.
58. Biolsi, *Organizing the Lakota*, 23–24.
59. Biolsi, *Organizing the Lakota*, 116–17.
60. Biolsi, *Organizing the Lakota*, 24–26.
61. Ruth Reynolds interview by Blanca Vázquez, June 11, 1985, tape 3.
62. Ruth Reynolds interview by Blanca Vázquez, June 11, 1985, tape 3.
63. Ruth Reynolds interview by Blanca Vázquez, June 21, 1985, tape 4, series IX, box 45, folder 2, RR Papers.
64. Ruth Reynolds interview by Blanca Vázquez, June 21, 1985, tape 4.
65. Mollin, *Radical Pacifism in Modern America*, 11–13; Cohen, *When the Old Left Was Young*, 80.
66. Cohen, *When the Old Left Was Young*, 80, 91–94.
67. Cohen, *When the Old Left Was Young*, 88–89.
68. "Holmes, Muste to Speak," *Daily Northwestern*, November 1, 1940, 3. The *Daily Northwestern* includes multiple announcements of Muste visits to the campus and the larger Evanston communities during the 1930s and 1940s.
69. Appelbaum, *Kingdom to Commune*, 186.
70. Miller, *How Shall They Hear*, 369–72, 401–7, 421, 446. He chaired the FOR's Midwest office during the late 1930s and early 1940s.
71. Ruth Reynolds interview by Blanca Vázquez, June 21, 1985, tape 4.
72. "Dear Friends: Here Is an Outline of My Life," series I, box 1, folder 1, RR Papers.
73. Danielson, *American Gandhi*, 9, 211, 218.
74. Office of Public Opinion Research, OPOR Poll # 1941-809: War Survey, Question 3, USOPOR.41-809.Q04KT, Office of Public Opinion Research (Cornell University, Ithaca, NY: Roper Center for Public Opinion Research, 1941), dataset, https://doi.org/10.25940/ROPER-31095288; Gallup Organization, Gallup Poll # 1941-0245: World War II/Employment/Congressional Election/Movies, Question 13, USGALLUP.41-245.QKT04, Gallup Organization (Ithaca, NY: Roper Center for Public Opinion Research, 1941), dataset, https://doi.org/10.25940/ROPER-31087228.
75. Ruth Reynolds interview by Blanca Vázquez, June 21, 1985, tape 4.

Chapter 2

1. "Release upon Receipt, January 26, 1944," Free India Campaigns folder, Templin Papers. January 26 is the day that the Indian National Congress demanded complete independence from Britain and independence activists simultaneously embarked on their civil disobedience campaign against British rule.

2. Danielson, *American Gandhi*, 203, 222.

3. Ruth Reynolds interview by Blanca Vázquez, June 21, 1985, tape 5, series IX, box 45, folder 2, RR Papers.

4. Ruth Reynolds interview by Blanca Vázquez, June 21, 1985, tape 6, series IX, box 45, folder 2, RR Papers; "Your honor, this case . . . ," undated document, Free India Campaigns folder, Templin Papers; "9 Held in Picketing British Consulate," newspaper clipping, *New York World Telegram*, January 27, 1944, Free India Campaigns folder, Templin Papers.

5. Ruth Reynolds interview by Blanca Vázquez, June 21, 1985, tape 5.

6. Ruth Reynolds interview by Blanca Vázquez, June 21, 1985, tape 4, series IX, box 45, folder 2, RR Papers; "Proposed Summer Ashram Training Course," Harlem Ashram, 1941–1945, box DG 013, section II, subseries A-3, 13, SCPC-DG-013, Fellowship Records.

7. Danielson, *American Gandhi*, 222; Slate, *Colored Cosmopolitanism*, 210.

8. Slate, *Colored Cosmopolitanism*, 208; D'Emilio, *Lost Prophet*, 53; Ruth Reynolds interview by Blanca Vázquez, June 21, 1985, tape 4; Danielson, *American Gandhi*, 222.

9. "2 US Clergymen Join Gandhi in Fast; Jailed for Picketing British Embassy," newspaper clipping, February 24, 1943, Free India Campaigns folder, Templin Papers; Slate, *Colored Cosmopolitanism*, 208.

10. "Our Weekly Chat," *Christian Advocate*, March 4, 1943, Free India Campaigns folder, Templin Papers; "Pacifists Join Gandhi in Protest Fast," *Christian Century*, March 10, 1943, Free India Campaigns folder, Templin Papers; Gordon, "Mahatma Gandhi's Dialogues with Americans," 337, 339.

11. Ruth Reynolds interview by Blanca Vázquez, June 26, 1985, tape 7, series IX, box 45, folder 3, RR Papers; Bryant, "Non-Hindu Ashrams," 60; Singh, *Jesus the Sadguru and His Discipleship*, 130.

12. Parekh, *Gandhi*, 68.

13. Parekh, *Gandhi*, 66–70.

14. "Templin Jailed in Washington for Picketing British Embassy," *Ramapo Valley Independent*, February 25, 1943, Free India Campaigns folder, Templin Papers; "Methodists v. Viceroy," *Time* 35, no. 17 (April 1940): 46; "Non-Political Missions," *Time* 36, no. 22 (November 1940): 22, 26.

15. Danielson, *American Gandhi*, 208–9.

16. Ruth Reynolds interview by Blanca Vázquez, June 21, 1985, tape 4; Farmer, *Lay Bare the Heart*, 93, 149–50; Danielson, *American Gandhi*, 204–5, 208–9. Ashram participants learned to align Gandhian-inspired direct action and "suffering love" with the Christian faith that they practiced through careful readings of FOR executive director A. J. Muste's 1940 book, *Non-violence in an Aggressive World*.

17. Bennett, *Radical Pacifism*, 94–95; "2 In Occoquan Break Fast with Gandhi," *Washington Post*, March 4, 1943: B14; "Indian Leader's Release Sought," newspaper clipping, no date, Free India Campaigns folder, Templin Papers.

18. Mollin, *Radical Pacifism in Modern America*, 10, 21–22.

19. Gilmore, *Defying Dixie*, 342–44; Karen Cook Bell, "Gender, Civil Rights, and the Case of Odell Waller," *Black Perspectives* (blog), February 26, 2018, www.aaihs .org/gender-civil-rights-and-the-case-of-odell-waller/.

20. Though the letter is undated, Reynolds wrote it while visiting Boston in August 1942. Letter from Ruth Reynolds to Mother Waller, [no date], series II, box 9, folder 1, RR Papers.

21. Ruth Reynolds interview by Blanca Vázquez, June 21, 1985, tape 5; Slate, *Colored Cosmopolitanism*, 209; Baldwin and Dekar, *In an Inescapable Network*, 114; Ruth Reynolds interview by Blanca Vázquez, June 26, 1985, tape 7.

22. Meier and Rudwick, *CORE*, 4–7; Danielson, *American Gandhi*, 225; Farmer, *Lay Bare the Heart*, 150, 152–53.

23. Ruth Reynolds interview by Blanca Vázquez, June 21, 1985, tape 5.

24. Letter from Ruth Reynolds to Folks, December 7, 1943, series II, box 9, folder 1, RR Papers.

25. Farmer, *Lay Bare the Heart*, 150, 152–53, 195–204.

26. Sánchez Korrol, *From Colonia to Community*, 58.

27. Sánchez Korrol, *From Colonia to Community*, 11–15, 17–34, 44–45; Thomas, *Puerto Rican Citizen*, 30; Ayala, *American Sugar Kingdom*, 221–27; Whalen, "Colonialism, Citizenship," 3.

28. Ruth Reynolds, "Ruth Reynolds Remembers 1950: North-Americans Must Act to Free Puerto Rico," Puerto Rico, Si! Factsheets on the colonial domination of Puerto Rico, prepared by the Committee for Puerto Rican Decolonization, Puerto Rico: (1) About folder, Templin Papers.

29. Soto Fontánez, *Misión a la puerta*, 52; del Moral, *Negotiating Empire*, 8, 19, 36, 49–50, 56.

30. Cotto Reyes was also among those Puerto Ricans for whom US possession of the archipelago resulted in religious conversion. With US possession, Protestant missionaries, including those representing the American Baptist Home Missionary Society, poured into Puerto Rico to proselytize the overwhelmingly Catholic population. Barnes, "Porto Rico and Paradise," 414–32; Riggs, *Baptists in Puerto Rico*.

31. Ayala and Bernabe, *Puerto Rico in the American Century*, 96, 104, 110–12.

32. Sánchez Korrol, *From Colonia to Community*, 31–32.

33. Soto Fontánez, *Misión a la puerta*, 50–56; Dunlap, *From Abyssinian to Zion*.

34. Hoffnung-Garskof, *Racial Migrations*; Meléndez, *Patria*.

35. Thomas, *Puerto Rican Citizen*, 116–19, 133–35.

36. Thomas, *Puerto Rican Citizen*, 96–97, 131; Vega, *Memoirs of Bernardo Vega*, 201–2.

37. Ruth Reynolds, "Ruth Reynolds Remembers 1950"; "Dear Fellowship Friend," Harlem Ashram, 1941–1945, box DG 013, section II, subseries A-3, 13, SCPC-DG-013, Fellowship Records.

38. Ruth Reynolds interview by Blanca Vázquez, June 21, 1985, tape 5.

39. Ruth Reynolds, "Ruth Reynolds Remembers 1950."

40. Ruth Reynolds interview by Blanca Vázquez, June 21, 1985, tape 5.

41. Ruth Reynolds interview by Blanca Vázquez, June 21, 1985, tape 5.

42. "Release upon Receipt, January 26, 1944," Free India Campaigns folder, Templin Papers; "Indian Independence Day Celebration," Free India Campaigns folder, Templin Papers; Roy, *Beyond Belief*, 70; Ruth Reynolds interview by Blanca Vázquez, June 21, 1985, tape 6.

43. Underline and capitalization are in the original. "Statement of Protesting Groups," Free India Campaigns folder, Templin Papers.

44. Roosevelt Annual Message to Congress, January 6, 1941; "Statement of Protesting Groups," Free India Campaigns folder, Templin Papers.

45. "Statement of Protesting Groups," Free India Campaigns folder, Templin Papers.

46. "Statement of Protesting Groups," Templin Papers.

47. "Statement of Protesting Groups," Templin Papers.

48. "Five women and four men . . . ," newspaper clipping, *PM*, January 27, 1944, Free India Campaigns folder, Templin Papers; Ruth Reynolds interview by Blanca Vázquez, June 21, 1985, tapes 5 and 6.

49. Rosado, *Pedro Albizu Campos*, 39.

50. Igartua, *Communities of Soul*, 54.

51. Santiago-Valles, "Our Race Today," 109–11; Benjamín Torres, "Símbolo de la América irredenta," *Suplemento de Claridad*, September 17, 1972.

52. Laura Meneses de Albizu Campos, "Cómo conocí a Albizu Campos," Colección Benjamín Torres, Serie Carpetas de Recortes, CIH, box 11, folder 1, item 89.

53. Established in 1904, the Union Party had included members favoring independence, autonomy, and statehood. Ayala and Bernabe, *Puerto Rico in the American Century*, 53, 59; Wagenheim and Jiménez de Wagenheim, *Puerto Ricans*, 142; Rosado, *Pedro Albizu Campos*, 111–16.

54. Meneses de Albizu Campos, "Comó conocí a Albizu Campos." For a discussion of these efforts, see chapter 4 of Power's *Solidarity across the Americas*.

55. Igartua, *Communities of Soul*, 53–54.

56. In particular, Stevens-Arroyo explores how Irish Catholics in Boston likely introduced Albizu Campos to the nineteenth-century Catalan Catholic theologian Jaime Balmes. Stevens-Arroyo, "Catholic Worldview."

57. Rosado, *Pedro Albizu Campos*, 70–72.

58. Stevens-Arroyo, "Catholic Worldview," 66–68; Newsinger, "James Connolly."

59. Sugarcane workers invited Albizu Campos to lead their strike. Rosado, *Pedro Albizu Campos*, 210–17.

60. For a discussion about opposition within the Nationalist Party to its militarization, as well as evidence of collaboration between such dissident Nationalist Party members and the government in a smear campaign and an assassination plot against Alibzu Campos in 1935, see Rosado, *Pedro Albizu Campos*, 216–32.

61. Power, *Solidarity across the Americas*, 4.

62. Stevens-Arroyo, "Catholic Worldview," 67–68; Rosado, *Pedro Albizu Campos,* 239–46.

63. Rafael Cancel Miranda, "Julio Pinto Gandía," *Claridad,* July 2, 2008, www .claridadpuertorico.com/content.html?news=1EF2A579D872C4519E61CA0928 3542DE; Rosado, *Pedro Albizu Campos,* 239–60. The specific charges against Albizu Campos were seditious conspiracy, recruiting to form an army against the United States, and conspiracy to commit offenses against the United States.

64. Ribes Tovar, *Albizu Campos;* "Puerto Rican Nationalist Prisoners: Symbols of Courage-Victims of Repression," factsheets on the colonial domination of Puerto Rico, prepared by the Committee for Puerto Rican Decolonization, Puerto Rico: (1) About folder, Templin Papers.

65. Ruth Reynolds interview by Blanca Vázquez, July 11 and July 15, 1985, tape 11, series IX, box 45, folder 3, RR Papers.

66. Pinto Gandía was born in 1908 in Manatí in northern Puerto Rico. Cancel Miranda, "Julio Pinto Gandía," *Claridad,* July 2, 2008; Elizabeth Dorna Cortés, "Presentación del libro: ¿Quién mató a Pinto Gandía?," *Claridad,* December 13, 2011; Ruth Reynolds interview by Blanca Vázquez, June 21, 1985, tape 5.

67. Pinto Gandía also served as a lawyer for Nationalist leaders Juan Antonio Corretjer, Clemente Soto Vélez, and Erasmo Velásquez. Cancel Miranda, "Julio Pinto Gandía," *Claridad,* July 2, 2008.

68. Ruth Reynolds interview by Blanca Vázquez, June 21, 1985, tape 5; Cancel Miranda, "Julio Pinto Gandía," *Claridad,* July 2, 2008.

69. Paralitici, "Imprisonment and Colonial Domination, 1898–1958," 73.

70. Marisa Rosado, "El nacionalismo puertorriqueño: de 1930 a 1954," *Claridad,* September 21, 2010.

71. Tovar, *Albizu Campos,* 91.

72. Mollin, *Radical Pacifism in Modern America,* 15–16, 17, 18–21.

73. Mollin, *Radical Pacifism in Modern America,* 16–18. Mollin does not specifi- cally discuss alliances with Nationalist Party prisoners but rather points to the alliances that radical pacifist men in prison crafted with "tough" working-class inmates as part of a strategy for rejecting slurs of effeminacy. Mollin, *Radical Paci- fism in Modern America,* 16–18.

74. Reynolds, "Ruth Reynolds Remembers 1950," 7; Ruth Reynolds interview by Blanca Vázquez, June 21, 1985, tape 5; "Biographical Data on Ruth Reynolds," series I, box 1, folder 1, RR Papers.

75. Ruth Reynolds interview by Blanca Vázquez, June 21, 1985, tape 6.

76. Ruth Reynolds interview by Blanca Vázquez, June 21, 1985, tape 5; Jay Holmes Smith to Comrade, January 15, 1944, Free India Campaigns folder, Templin Papers.

77. Ruth Reynolds interview by Blanca Vázquez, June 21, 1985, tape 5.

78. Jay Holmes Smith to Comrade, January 15, 1944.

79. Jay Holmes Smith, "Gandhi of Puerto Rico," 186–87.

80. Jay Holmes Smith to Comrade, January 15, 1944.

81. Ruth Reynolds interview by Blanca Vázquez, July 11 and July 15, 1985, tape 11.

82. Ruth Reynolds interview by Blanca Vázquez, June 26, 1985, tape 7.

83. Ruth Reynolds interview by Blanca Vázquez, June 21, 1985, tape 5; Ruth Reynolds interview by Blanca Vázquez, June 26, 1985, tape 7.

84. Chowdhury and Philipose, "Introduction," 12; Cohen, "Spirit of Solidarity." Though Chowdhury and Philipose's volume develops this concept in the context of alliances among women, this concept is applicable to Reynolds's political alliance with both Albizu Campos and other Nationalist leaders.

85. Ruth Reynolds interview by Blanca Vázquez, July 11 and July 15, 1985, tape 11.

86. Ruth Reynolds interview by Blanca Vázquez, July 22, 1985, tape 17, series IX, box 45, folder 5, RR Papers.

87. Ruth Reynolds interview by Blanca Vázquez, July 22, 1985, tape 17.

88. Ruth Reynolds interview by Blanca Vázquez, July 22, 1985, tape 17.

89. Ruth Reynolds interview by Blanca Vázquez, July 22, 1985, tape 17.

90. Ruth Reynolds interview by Blanca Vázquez, June 26, 1985, tape 7.

Chapter 3

1. "Additional Testimony of the American League for Puerto Rico's Independence on the Tydings Bill, US Senate, April 26, 1945," series IV, box 18, folder 2, RR Papers.

2. Ruth Reynolds interview by Blanca Vázquez, July 22, 1985, tape 8, series IX, box 45, folder 3, RR Papers.

3. Form letter from Roger N. Baldwin et al., October 7, 1944, series IV, box 18, folder 2, RR Papers. In addition to Reynolds, the list of signatories on this were the following: Roger N. Baldwin, J. Henry Carpenter, Elsie Elfenbein, A. Philip Randolph, George Schuyler, Jay Holmes Smith, Ashley Trotten, Oswald Garrison Villard, and Richard Walsh.

4. "Autonomy Is Asked in Puerto Rico Vote," *New York Times*, February 11, 1943, 6; *A Bill to Amend the Organic Act of Puerto Rico*, US Government Printing Office, 1943.

5. Anderson, *Party Politics in Puerto Rico*, 56; Bhana, *United States and the Development*, 70.

6. Anderson, *Eyes off the Prize*, 35–36, 38.

7. This initial meeting likely took place on Tuesday, October 3, 1944. Form Letter from Roger N. Baldwin et al., October 7, 1944.

8. According to Reynolds, Baldwin suggested that the group begin by contributing to Grace Tugwell's (the wife of Rexford Guy Tugwell, Puerto Rico's governor between 1941 and 1946) program distributing milk among Puerto Rico's poor children. Ruth Reynolds interview by Blanca Vázquez, July 22, 1985, tape 8; Minutes of Meeting on Puerto Rico, October 17, 1944, series IV, box 18, folder 2, RR Papers, "Morris Milgram, 81; Built Interracial Housing," *New York Times*, June 26, 1997, www.nytimes.com/1997/06/26/us/morris-milgram-81-built-interracial-housing.html?_r=0. Also see Kutulas, *American Civil Liberties Union*, 92–93, 111.

9. Walker, *In Defense of American Liberties*, 156–57. See chapter 4 of Kutulas, *American Civil Liberties Union*, for a discussion of the ACLU's tepid response to Japanese incarceration.

10. Power, *Solidarity across the Americas*, 136–44.

11. Walker, *In Defense of American Liberties*, 29, 51–52, 68.

12. Meyer, *Vito Marcantonio*, 56, 152, 154–56.

13. Kutulas, *American Civil Liberties Union*, 65–67, 72–73, 75, 79, 81; Lamont, *Trial of Elizabeth Gurley Flynn*, 8; Walker, *In Defense of American Liberties*, 128; Gregory, *Norman Thomas*, 176, 178.

14. Ruth Reynolds interview by Blanca Vázquez, July 22, 1985, tape 8.

15. Jay Holmes Smith and Ruth M. Reynolds to President of the United States, September 5, 1945, series IV, box 18, folder 6, RR Papers.

16. Ruth Reynolds interview by Blanca Vázquez, July 22, 1985, tape 8.

17. United States of America, Bureau of the Census, *Sixteenth Census of the United States, 1940*, Washington, DC: National Archives and Records Administration, *Rochester, Monroe, New York*; Roll: *T627_2842*; Page: *62A*; Enumeration District: *65–27*, Ancestry.com (Provo, UT: Ancestry.com Operations, 2012).

18. Shaffer, "Women and International Relations," 151–53.

19. Minutes of Meeting on Puerto Rico, October 17, 1944.

20. Ruth Reynolds interview by Blanca Vázquez, July 22, 1985, tape 8.

21. Ruth Reynolds interview by Blanca Vázquez, July 22, 1985, tape 8.

22. Centro de Investigaciones Históricas (CIH), Colección Material Audiovisual: CDs / DVDs, Federal Bureau of Investigation, Carpetas de Organizaciones e Individuos Independentistas, serie: Pedro Albizu Campos (PAC), subserie: 1–30, caja 1, número 17, subserie 3.

23. CIH, Colección Material Audiovisual: PAC, subserie: 1–30, caja 1, número 17, subserie 4.

24. Ruth Reynolds interview by Blanca Vázquez, July 22, 1985, tape 8.

25. Jay Holmes Smith and Ruth M. Reynolds to President of the United States, September 5, 1945, series IV, box 18, folder 6, RR Papers; Materson, "African American Women's Global Journeys."

26. Ruth Reynolds interview by Blanca Vázquez, July 22, 1985, tape 8.

27. Ayala and Bolívar, *Battleship Vieques*, 21, 24–25.

28. He had also introduced bills in 1936 and 1943. Anderson, *Party Politics in Puerto Rico*, 56; Trías Monge, *Puerto Rico*, 108.

29. Kramer, *Blood of Government*, 412; Johnson, "Anti-Imperialism," 103.

30. Kramer, *Blood of Government*, 412–13.

31. Johnson, "Anti-Imperialism," 104.

32. Johnson, "Anti-Imperialism," 103–5. Seeking to pursue US reform in the Caribbean, this was the strategic approach of US policymaker Ernest Gruening, who sought to implement a cross-national reform agenda in the Caribbean that included the United States. Johnson, "Anti-Imperialism," 95.

33. Anderson, *Party Politics in Puerto Rico*, 56.

34. For a discussion of Vito Marcantonio's many actions in support of Puerto Rico's independence and his defense work with Albizu Campos, see Meyer, "Pedro Albizu Campos."

35. Testimony of the American League for Puerto Rico's Independence on the Tydings Bill, US Senate, March 7, 1945, series IV, box 18, folder 2, RR Papers.

36. *Hearings before the Committee on Territories and Insular Affairs,* US Senate, 79th Cong., 1st sess. on S.227, Part 1, March 5, 6, 7, and 8, 1945 (Washington, DC: US Government Printing Office, 1945), 87–90.

37. Anderson, *Party Politics in Puerto Rico,* 56–58.

38. *Hearings before the Committee on Territories and Insular Affairs,* Part 1, 340.

39. *Hearings before the Committee on Territories and Insular Affairs,* Part 1, 83–87.

40. *Hearings before the Committee on Territories and Insular Affairs,* Part 1, 90–91.

41. *Hearings before the Committee on Territories and Insular Affairs,* Part 1, 15.

42. Kennedy, *Decolonization.*

43. *Oxford Research Encyclopedia of Latin American History,* ed. William Beezley (Oxford: Oxford University Press, 2018), s.v. "The Good Neighbor Policy."

44. Ruth Reynolds interview by Blanca Vázquez, July 11, 1985, tape 10, series IX, box 45, folder 3, RR Papers; Sherwood, "India," 422.

45. Alger, "Emerging Roles of NGO's," 93.

46. Anderson, *Eyes off the Prize,* 35–36, 38.

47. Anderson, *Eyes off the Prize,* 38–40.

48. Ruth Reynolds interview by Blanca Vázquez, July 11, 1985, tape 10.

49. *Independence for Puerto Rico, Hearings before the Committee on Territories and Insular Affairs,* US Senate, 79th Cong., 1st sess. on S.227, Part 2, April 23, 24, 26, 27, May 1 and 8, 1945 (Washington, DC: US Government Printing Office, 1945), 228–29.

50. *Independence for Puerto Rico,* Part 2, 228–29.

51. *Independence for Puerto Rico,* Part 2, 228.

52. *Independence for Puerto Rico,* Part 2, 228.

53. "Additional Testimony of the American League for Puerto Rico's Independence on the Tydings Bill, US Senate, April 26, 1945," series IV, box 18, folder 2, RR Papers.

54. Meléndez, *Puerto Rico's Statehood Movement,* 1–3, 37–40, 48–51, 57–65, 69–72.

55. *Independence for Puerto Rico,* Part 2, 158, 171–72.

56. *Independence for Puerto Rico,* Part 2, 167–68.

57. *Independence for Puerto Rico,* Part 2, 218.

58. *Independence for Puerto Rico,* Part 2, 158, 163–64.

59. *Independence for Puerto Rico,* Part 2, 172, 217.

60. *Hearings before the Committee on Territories and Insular Affairs,* Part 1, 326–27; Fisher, *Tribute to Women Lawyers Worldwide;* Rivera, "Esas mujeres desvergonzadas."

61. *Independence for Puerto Rico,* Part 2, 144.

62. Maldonado, *Luis Muñoz-Marín,* 108–58.

63. Ayala and Bernabe, *Puerto Rico in the American Century,* 136.

64. Maldonado, *Luis Muñoz Marín,* 11, 30, 99; Meléndez, *Puerto Rico's Statehood Movement,* 59; Ayala and Bernabe, *Puerto Rico in the American Century,* 136, 144.

65. Findlay, *We Are Left,* 48.

66. Anderson, *Party Politics in Puerto Rico,* 57; Trías Monge, *Puerto Rico,* 108; *Hearings before the Committee on Territories and Insular Affairs,* Part 1, 15.

67. Ayala and Bernabe, *Puerto Rico in the American Century,* 150. As Ayala and Bernabe explain, he had begun grappling with these ideas "after he studied the

conditions under which the Philippines were to be granted independence and after conversations with U.S. Tariff Commission economist Benjamin Dorfman."

68. Anderson, *Party Politics in Puerto Rico*, 52–59.

69. *Independence for Puerto Rico*, Part 2, 374.

70. *Independence for Puerto Rico*, Part 2, 378.

71. *Independence for Puerto Rico*, Part 2, 373–91.

72. See chapter 2.

73. Maldonado, *Luis Muñoz Marín*, 11.

74. Report to the American League for Puerto Rico's Independence, 1945, series III, box 14, folders 1–2, RR Papers.

75. Ruth Reynolds interview by Blanca Vázquez, June 26 and July 11, 1985, tape 9, series IX, box 45, folder 3, RR Papers.

76. Ruth Reynolds interview by Blanca Vázquez, June 26 and July 11, 1985, tape 9.

77. Anderson, *Party Politics in Puerto Rico*, 58, 61. The bill's hyphenated name derived from the PPD elected resident commissioner Jesús T. Piñero, who introduced the bill in the House of Representatives. Trías Monge, *Puerto Rico*, 107–8.

78. Trías Monge, *Puerto Rico*, 107–9.

79. "For Immediate Release," July 21, 1945, series IV, box 18, folder 2, RR Papers.

80. "In the United Nations: The American League for Puerto Rico's Independence vs. The United States of America," series IV, box 18, folder 2, RR Papers.

81. Trías Monge, *Puerto Rico*, 109.

82. Anderson, *Party Politics in Puerto Rico*, 59–60.

83. Ruth Reynolds interview by Blanca Vázquez, July 11 and July 15, 1985, tape 11, series IX, box 45, folder 3, RR Papers.

84. Form letter, series IV, box 18, folder 5, RR Papers.

85. Ruth Reynolds interview by Blanca Vázquez, July 11 and July 15, 1985, tape 11; Ruth Reynolds interview by Blanca Vázquez, July 29, 1985, tape 22, series IX, box 45, folder 6, RR Papers. Very likely this was Maurice R. Davie, a sociology professor at Yale at the time, who published a study on this subject based on questionnaires.

86. Ruth Reynolds interview by Blanca Vázquez, July 29, 1985, tape 22; Report to the American League for Puerto Rico's Independence, 1945.

Chapter 4

1. Report to the American League for Puerto Rico's Independence, 1945, series III, box 14, folders 1–2, chap. 12, p. 4, RR Papers.

2. Maldonado, *Luis Muñoz Marín*, 15; Ayala and Bernabe, *Puerto Rico in the American Century*, 97; Interview with Don Luis Muñoz Marín, President of the Popular Party, November 1, 1945, series III, box 16, folder 6, RR Papers.

3. After two trips to his office, a letter, and the queries of "prominent Populares friends," Reynolds finally gained a sitting with Muñoz Marín following a strategic conversation with insular auditor Rafael J. Cordero. Report to the ALPRI, chap. 12, pp. 2–3, RR Papers.

4. Report to the ALPRI, chap. 12, p. 6, RR Papers.

5. Report to the ALPRI, chap. 12, p. 10, RR Papers.

6. Report to the ALPRI, chap. 12, p. 25, RR Papers.

7. Report to the ALPRI, chap. 11, p. 1, RR Papers.

8. Ruth Reynolds interview by Blanca Vázquez, August 26, 1985, tape 32, series IX, box 45, folder 9, RR Papers. These comments about the depth of her expertise about Puerto Rico arose amid a discussion about her testimony before Congress in 1947.

9. See chapter 2 for a discussion about the dissident friendships between Nationalists and pacifists in New York. Chowdhury and Philipose, "Introduction."

10. Ruth Reynolds interview by Blanca Vázquez, July 29, 1985, tape 22, series IX, box 45, folder 6, RR Papers.

11. Report to the ALPRI, chap. 11, p. 2, RR Papers.

12. Ruth Reynolds interview by Blanca Vázquez, July 29, 1985, tape 22.

13. Blanca Vázquez, interview by author, New York, NY, August 21, 2013.

14. Ruth Reynolds interview by Blanca Vázquez, May 29, 1986, tape 111, series IX, box 47, folder 10. Reynolds was aware that Albizu Campos had a child out of wedlock in 1932.

15. Ruth Reynolds interview by Blanca Vázquez, July 17, 1985, tape 15, series IX, box 45, folder 4, RR Papers. This advice stemmed from the events connected to Albizu Campos's decision to expel Nationalist Party secretary general Juan Antonio Corretjer from the Nationalist Party in 1943. Corretjer had a relationship with and eventually married Consuelo Lee Tapia de Lamb. At the time that the relationship began, Consuelo was married to CPUSA leader Leonard Lamb. Albizu Campos was concerned that the relationship would negatively affect ties between the Nationalist Party and the CPUSA. Power, "Political and Transnational Ménage á Trois"; Power, "Friends and Comrades," 120–21.

16. Eliseo Combas Guerra, "En torno a la Fortaleza," *El Mundo*, October 10, 1945, 6; José Arnaldo Meyners, "Ruth Reynolds en plan de saber la verdad sobre Isla," *El Mundo*, October 16, 1945, 5; Teófilo Maldonado, "Lo que yo se," *El Mundo*, November 4, 1945, 6.

17. Dietz, *Economic History of Puerto Rico*, 182. Reynolds incorrectly recorded four seats among these three parties in her manuscript.

18. Report to the ALPRI, chap. 13, RR Papers.

19. Ruth Reynolds to Helen, June 21, 1951, series II, box 9, folder 3, RR Papers.

20. Report to the ALPRI, chap. 11, pp. 3–4, RR Papers.

21. Report to the ALPRI, chap. 13, p. 4.

22. Interview with Bolívar Pagán, President, Socialist Party, October 24, 1945, series III, box 16, folder 5, RR Papers.

23. Report to the ALPRI, chap. 13, pp. 7–8, RR Papers.

24. Interview with Juan Ángel Tió, Banker, San Germán, November 13, 1945, series III, box 16, folder 6, RR Papers.

25. Interview with Senator [Santiago] Palmer, San Germán, November 13, 1945, series III, box 16, folder 6, RR Papers; Figueroa, *La gran enciclopedia de Puerto Rico*,

305; Interview with Elpidio H. Rivera, October 13, 1945, series III, box 16, folder 5, RR Papers.

26. Interview with Andr[é]s Grillasca, Mayor of Ponce, November 16, 1945, series III, box 16, folder 6, RR Papers.

27. Interview with Barreto Rivera, Mayor of Mayagüez, November 14, 1945, series III, box 16, folder 6, RR Papers; Interview with Mr. Nelson Colberg, Mayor of Cabo Rojo, November 11, 1945, series III, box 16, folder 6, RR Papers.

28. Interview with Castro [Rafael Castro Grau], Mayor of Lares and the President of the CBT in Lares and a coffee-grower in Lares, December 1, 1945, series III, box 16, folder 6, RR Papers; Interview with one of the members appointed by the Government to Conference for Insurance against Hurricanes, Treasurer of the Coffee Growers' Association, December 2, 1945, series III, box 16, folder 6, RR Papers.

29. Interview with Roberto Garcia, Tobacco Dealer, Utuado, December 5, 1945, series III, box 16, folder 6, RR Papers.

30. Interview with Héctor Graciani, Secretary of the C. G. T., series III, box 16, folder 5, RR Papers.

31. Report to the ALPRI, chap. 1, p. 9, RR Papers.

32. Talk with Rafael Dueno, Manager of San Francisco Farms, October 16, 1945, series III, box 16, folder 5, RR Papers; Interview with Andr[é]s Grillasca, Mayor of Ponce, November 16, 1945; Talk with Mrs. Carmen Alvarado, October 17, 1945, series III, box 16, folder 5, RR Papers.

33. Interview with Mario Frau Colon, November 13, 1945, series III, box 15, folder 6, RR Papers.

34. He was a founding member of the United Front for the Establishment of the Republic of Puerto Rico in 1935.

35. Interview with Juan Enrique Soltero Peralta, November 9, 1945, series III, box 16, folder 6, RR Papers.

36. Report to the ALPRI, chap. 12, pp. 22–23, RR Papers.

37. See previous chapter. Talk with Rafael Dueno, Manager of San Francisco Farms, October 16, 1945; Interview with Andr[é]s Grillasca, Mayor of Ponce, November 16, 1945.

38. Report to the ALPRI, chap. 13, p. 28, RR Papers.

39. Dasenbrock, To the Beat, 95–98, 124; Wittner, Rebels against War, 70–72; Lillian and Bob Pope to Wally Nelson, November 19, 1951, Puerto Rico: (6) Peacemaker Actions folder, Templin Papers. These Civilian Public Service camps were heavily peopled by members of the Quaker, Mennonite, Brethren Mennonite, and Brethren Churches, who had traveled to Puerto Rico to either run or serve in them, often accompanied by family members.

40. Report to the ALPRI, chap. 13, p. 28, RR Papers.

41. Report to the ALPRI, chap. 13, p. 28, RR Papers.

42. Report to the ALPRI, chap. 13, p. 29, RR Papers.

43. Report to the ALPRI, chap. 4, p. 4, RR Papers.

44. Interview with Héctor Graciani, Secretary of the C. G. T.

45. Interview with Don Julio de Santiago, President-Interino of the Nationalist Party of Puerto Rico, December 14, 1945, series III, box 15, folder 6, RR Papers; Paralitici, "Imprisonment and Colonial Domination," 76.

46. Report to the ALPRI, chap. 13, p. 24, RR Papers.

47. During her interview with Warden Julián Antonio Alvarado of the Insular Penitentiary at Río Piedras, Reynolds requested to also interview the five incarcerated Nationalists. Alvarado (an independentista and the husband of CPI leader Carmen Rivera de Alvarado) agreed and served as an interpreter for the interview. Interview with Warden Alvarado, October 10, 1945, series III, box 16, folder 6, RR Papers; Talk with Mrs. Carmen Alvarado, October 17, 1945, series III, box 16, folder 5, RR Papers.

48. Paralitici, "Imprisonment and Colonial Domination," 74; Rodríguez Beruff, *Strategy as Politics*, 163–64.

49. Report to the ALPRI, chap. 13, p. 27, RR Papers.

50. Report to the ALPRI, chap. 13, pp. 27–28, RR Papers.

51. Paralitici, "Imprisonment and Colonial Domination," 74.

52. Quoted in Maldonado, *Luis Muñoz Marín*, 245.

53. Report to the ALPRI, chap. 12, p. 10, RR Papers. Emphasis added by author.

54. Report to the ALPRI, chap. 2, p. 7, RR Papers.

55. Report to the ALPRI, chap. 2, p. 7, RR Papers.

56. Report to the ALPRI, chap. 4, pp. 9–10, RR Papers.

57. Report to the ALPRI, chap. 4, p. 1, RR Papers.

58. Report to the ALPRI, chap. 6, pp. 1–2, RR Papers.

59. "Muñoz Marín dirige un manifesto a los puertorriqueños," *El Mundo*, June 25, 1936, 1, 5; Report to the ALPRI, chap. 6, pp. 8–9, 12, RR Papers.

60. Report to the ALPRI, chap. 6, p. 9, RR Papers. Reynolds, whose Spanish skills were still rudimentary, likely lifted the manifesto's English translation from the US Congressional Record. During his March 1945 congressional testimony, CPI president Gilberto Concepción de Gracia had entered the manifesto into the record to use Muñoz Marín's own words against his shifting status politics. *Hearings before the Committee on Territories and Insular Affairs*, US Senate, 79th Cong., 1st sess. on S.227, Part 1, March 5, 6, 7, and 8, 1945 (Washington, DC: US Government Printing Office, 1945), 31–41.

61. Report to the ALPRI, chap. 6, p. 13, RR Papers.

62. Report to the ALPRI, chap. 6, pp. 2–3, RR Papers.

63. Report to the ALPRI, chap. 12, pp. 15, 23, RR Papers.

64. Report to the ALPRI, chap. 12, pp. 15–17, RR Papers.

65. Report to the ALPRI, chap. 12, p. 23, RR Papers.

66. Report to the ALPRI, chap. 12, pp. 11–14, RR Papers.

67. Report to the ALPRI, chap. 12, p. 10, RR Papers.

68. Janeway, "Wartime Quartet"; Velázques, *Rexford G. Tugwell*.

69. Report to the ALPRI, chap. 12, pp. 18–19, RR Papers.

70. Report to the ALPRI, chap. 12, pp. 18–19, RR Papers.

71. CIH, Colección Material Audiovisual: Partido Nacionalista de Puerto Rico (PNPR), subserie: 1–52, caja 1, número 19-A, subserie 7.

72. Bosque-Pérez and Morera, *Carpetas y persecución política en Puerto Rico*, 40.

73. CIH, Colección Material Audiovisual: PAC, subserie: 1–30, caja 1, número 17, subserie 5.

74. Ruth Reynolds to Helen, June 21, 1951; Ruth Reynolds interview by Blanca Vázquez, August 26, 1985, tape 31; "In the United Nations: The American League for Puerto Rico's Independence vs. The United States of America," series IV, box 18, folder 2, RR Papers; Albizu Campos, "Memorandum on Non-Self-Governing Territories and the United Nations, November 17, 1947," in *Pedro Albizu Campos: Escritos*, 362–63.

75. Ruth Reynolds interview by Blanca Vázquez, August 26, 1985, tape 31, series IX, box 45, folder 9, RR Papers.

Chapter 5

1. Reynolds, *Campus in Bondage*, 248.

2. Reynolds, *Campus in Bondage*, 248.

3. Reynolds, *Campus in Bondage*, 248; Ruth Reynolds interview by Blanca Vázquez, September 5, 1985, tape 37, series IX, box 45, folder 11, RR Papers.

4. "Anuncian para el lunes vista sobre la UPR," clipping in carpeta, series X, box 48, folder 4, RR Papers.

5. Reynolds, *Campus in Bondage*, 248–49.

6. "Memorandum al jefe de la policía insular," carpeta, series X, box 48, folder 4, RR Papers.

7. Bosque-Pérez, "Political Persecution," 13–15.

8. Bosque-Pérez, "Carpetas y persecución política en Puerto Rico," 40.

9. *El Imparcial*, December 17, 1947, quoted in Seijo Bruno, *La insurrección nacionalista*, 39.

10. CIH, Colección Material Audiovisual: PAC, subserie: 1–30, caja 1, número 17, subserie 5; Rosado, *Pedro Albizu Campos*, 308–9.

11. Seijo Bruno, *La insurrección nacionalista*, 35–39; Acosta Lespier, *La Mordaza*, 46–47, 55–56.

12. *El Imparcial*, December 17, 1947, quoted in Seijo Bruno, *La insurrección nacionalista*, 39; Ayala Casás and Bolívar Fresneda, "The Cold War and the Second Expropriations," 10–35.

13. Acosta Lespier, *La Mordaza*, 57–58.

14. Seijo Bruno, *La insurrección nacionalista*, 39.

15. Bosque-Pérez, "Carpetas y persecución política en Puerto Rico," 55.

16. Navarro Rivera, *Universidad de Puerto Rico*, 54, 67–68.

17. Reynolds, *Campus in Bondage*, 9–10.

18. Reynolds, *Campus in Bondage*, 44; Rodríguez Castro, "La década de los cuarenta," 148.

19. Ayala and Bernabe, *Puerto Rico in the American Century*, 202–4.

20. Navarro Rivera, *Universidad de Puerto Rico*, 101–2, 114; Reynolds, *Campus in Bondage*, 95.

21. Reynolds, *Campus in Bondage*, 34, 42; Navarro Rivera, *Universidad de Puerto Rico*, 120. These students were José Gil de Lamadrid, Jorge Luis Landing, and Juan Mari Brás. Reynolds, *Campus in Bondage*, 59, 67–71, 80–82.

22. Reynolds, *Campus in Bondage*, 98; Ruth Reynolds to Mr. President, July 25, 1952, series II, box 9, folder 3, RR Papers.

23. Reynolds, *Campus in Bondage*, 104; Navarro Rivera, *Universidad de Puerto Rico*, 121–30.

24. Reynolds, *Campus in Bondage*, 105–9, 128–29.

25. Reynolds, *Campus in Bondage*, 130–52.

26. Reynolds, *Campus in Bondage*, 152–54; Acosta Lespier, *La Mordaza*, 70.

27. Reynolds, *Campus in Bondage*, 161, 166–69, 203.

28. Acosta Lespier, *La Mordaza*, 75–86, 92–93; Belknap, *Cold War Political Justice*, 22–27, 41–45.

29. Acosta Lespier, *La Mordaza*, 75–83, 88–99.

30. As quoted by Acosta Lespier, *La Mordaza*, 84.

31. Acosta Lespier, *La Mordaza*, 75–83, 92–93.

32. Seijo Bruno, *La insurrección nacionalista*.

33. Ruth Reynolds to Mr. President, July 25, 1952.

34. Reynolds, *Campus in Bondage*, 235–37; Ruth Reynolds to Mr. President, July 25, 1952.

35. Ruth Reynolds interview by Blanca Vázquez, September 5, 1985, tape 37.

36. Acosta Lespier, *La Mordaza*, 126.

37. Ruth Reynolds to Harry Truman, May 22, 1948; Ruth Reynolds to Jesus Piñero, May 22, 1948, series II, box 9, folder 2, RR Papers.

38. Ruth Reynolds to Clifford Forster, May 16, 1948, series II, box 9, folder 2, RR Papers.

39. Ruth Reynolds to Clifford Forster, May 16, 1948.

40. *Election of Governor, Hearings before the Subcommittee on Territorial and Insular Possessions of the Committee on Public Lands House of Representatives, Eightieth Congress First Session on H.R. 3309, A Bill to Amend the Organic Act of Puerto Rico, May 19, 1947, Printed for use of the Committee on Public Lands*, Committee Hearing No. 13 (Washington, DC: US Government Printing Office, 1947), 38, folder Puerto Rico: (1) About, Templin Papers.

41. Maldonado, *Luis Muñoz Marín*, 261.

42. Reynolds, *Campus in Bondage*, 203.

43. Full statement, June 7, 1948, signed by Arthur Garfield Hays, Roger N. Baldwin, and Clifford Forster, in Reynolds, *Campus in Bondage*, 209–11, 229–33; Acosta Lespier, *La Mordaza*, 125.

44. Ruth Reynolds interview by Blanca Vázquez, September 5, 1985, tape 37.

45. "Anuncian para el lunes vista sobre la UPR," clipping in carpeta, series X, box 48, folder 4, RR Papers.

46. In *Campus in Bondage*, Reynolds notes that her reception at the UPR Mayagüez was entirely different. As she detailed in the manuscript, "There I was received courteously by every member of the Administration whom I approached, and each person was willing to discuss the University crisis fully." Reynolds specu-

lated, "It must have resulted from a lack of thoroughness on Mr. Benítez' part. Evidently he did not foresee that we would go so far as to carry the investigation to Mayagüez, and consequently failed to instruct the Administration in Mayagüez to refuse to cooperate." Reynolds, *Campus in Bondage*, 255.

47. Reynolds, *Campus in Bondage*, 248–60.

48. Reynolds, *Campus in Bondage*, 1.

49. Reynolds, *Campus in Bondage*, 256.

50. Reynolds, *Campus in Bondage*, 259–60.

51. Ruth Reynolds interview by Blanca Vázquez, August 26, 1985, tape 31, series IX, box 45, folder 9, RR Papers; Reynolds, *Campus in Bondage*, 259–60.

52. Ruth Reynolds to Helen, June 21, 1951, box 9, folder 3. Reynolds was writing to her sister Helen from prison in 1951, explaining both the history of Puerto Rico and the various stages of her own involvement in the status politics of Puerto Rico.

53. Lillian and Bob Pope to Wally Nelson, November 19, 1951, Puerto Rico: (6) Peacemaker Actions folder, Templin Papers.

54. Lillian and Bob Pope to Wally Nelson, November 19, 1951, Templin Papers. Reynolds first met the Popes in 1948 at a demonstration against compulsory military service in Puerto Rico that the couple organized. Ruth Reynolds interview by Blanca Vázquez, September 5, 1985, tape 38, series IX, box 45, folder 12, RR Papers.

55. Lillian and Bob Pope to Wally Nelson, November 19, 1951.

56. Ruth Reynolds, "Several months ago . . . March 6, 1961," series III, box 12, folder 2, RR Papers.

57. Ruth Reynolds interview by Blanca Vázquez, September 5, 1985, tape 38.

58. Meneses Albizu-Campos, *Una vida de amor y sacrificio*, 24–28. Ruth Reynolds interview by Blanca Vázquez, September 5, 1985, tape 37.

59. "Actividades de Ruth Reynolds" and "Record relacionado con Ruth Reynolds," carpeta, series X, box 48, folder 4, RR Papers.

60. Seijo Bruno, *La insurrección nacionalista*, 77.

61. Ruth Reynolds, "Several months ago . . . March 6, 1961."

62. Ruth Reynolds, "Several months ago . . . March 6, 1961."

63. Ruth Reynolds, "Several months ago . . . March 6, 1961."

64. CIH, Colección Material Audiovisual: PAC, subserie: 1–30, caja 1, número 17, subserie 9, subserie 12.

65. Ruth Reynolds, "Several months ago . . . March 6, 1961."

66. Reynolds, Burgos, López, and Mejías took a *público* after Burgos's car was damaged. Seijo Bruno, *La insurrección nacionalista*, 79.

67. Seijo Bruno, *La insurrección nacionalista*, 78–79.

68. Seijo Bruno, *La insurrección nacionalista*, 79–81.

69. Maldonado, *Luis Muñoz Marín*, 301.

70. "Actividades de Ruth Reynolds" and "Record relacionado con Ruth Reynolds."

71. Reynolds, *Campus in Bondage*, 47.

72. Reynolds, *Campus in Bondage*, 165–66.

73. Reynolds, *Campus in Bondage*, 286–87.

74. Reynolds, *Campus in Bondage*, 102.

75. Hunt, *David Dellinger*, 86–94.

76. Rosado, *Pedro Albizu Campos*, 327; CIH, Colección Material Audiovisual: PNPR, subserie: 1–52, caja 1, número 19-A, subserie 10.

77. Ruth Reynolds to Felix Benítez Rexach, September 21, 1950, series IV, box 18, folder 7, RR Papers.

78. Ruth Reynolds to David Dellinger, September 11, 1950, series IV, box 18, folder 7, RR Papers.

Chapter 6

1. In May 1951, Albizu Campos first went public with details of his subjection to radiation poisoning at La Princesa. Rosado, *Pedro Albizu Campos*, 374–86.

2. Ruth Reynolds, "Memorandum on Experiences Phenomenal, Mostly in the Princesa Hotel," series III, box 16, folder 1, RR Papers.

3. For a discussion of the compromises that Muñoz Marín and his advisers made to negotiate Law 600 through Congress, see Maldonado, *Luis Muñoz Marín*, 290–98.

4. Public Law 81–600, *United States Statutes at Large*, 319–20.

5. Senate Committee on Interior and Insular Affairs on Public Law 81–600, *Providing for the Organization*, 3; House of Representatives Committee on Public Lands, *Providing for the Organization*, 3–4.

6. As he had since 1932, Albizu Campos rejected Nationalist participation in any elections under US rule.

7. Pedro Albizu Campos, speech in Lares, September 23, 1950, Paredón Records, P-2501; quoted in Seijo Bruno, *La insurrección nacionalista*, 43.

8. Seijo Bruno, *La insurrección nacionalista*, 339; from Harold J. Lidin, "Participants Describe the 1950 Uprising," *San Juan Star*, Sunday Magazine, December 10, 1989.

9. Seijo Bruno asserts that Albizu Campos had to have given the date and time of October 30 at noon for the start of the revolution after the arrests in Santurce. Seijo Bruno, *La insurrección nacionalista*, 80, 83.

10. Seijo Bruno, *La insurrección nacionalista*, 93–94.

11. Seijo Bruno, *La insurrección nacionalista*, 173.

12. Seijo Bruno, *La insurrección nacionalista*, 127, 131–34, 147, 150, 152–53, 157, 159, 182.

13. Seijo Bruno, *La insurrección nacionalista*, 147–58.

14. Seijo Bruno, *La insurrección nacionalista*, 91–98, 101, 114–16.

15. Canales, *La constitución es la revolución*, 3, 9–10, 24, 25–49; Seijo Bruno, *La insurrección nacionalista*, 127, 131–34.

16. Seijo Bruno, *La insurrección nacionalista*, 169–73.

17. Seijo Bruno, *La insurrección nacionalista*, 181–82.

18. Collazo, *Memorias de un patriota encarcelado*, 302–9; Chalmers M. Roberts and Alfred E. Lewis, "Plotters Felled by Blazing Guns at Blair House; Third Man Held: Police Slay Assassin at Truman's Door," *Washington Post*, November 2, 1950; "Assassins: At Blair House," *New York Times*, November 5, 1950, 1E, 2E.

19. "Arrestos en masa en la isla," *El Imparcial*, November 3, 1950, 3, 30.

20. "Arrestan miembros PIP toda la isla," *El Imparcial,* November 5, 1950, 2, 35; Anderson, *Party Politics in Puerto Rico,* 108.

21. Seijo Bruno, *La insurrección nacionalista,* 210, 225–30.

22. Pagán, *Historia de los partidos políticos puertorriqueños,* 300. This percentage is based on the 1950 census that reported a population of 1,035, 205 aged twenty and older. The voting age, however, was twenty-one, making the percentage only approximate. *Census of Population: 1950,* vol. 2, *Characteristics of the Population,* pts. 51–54 (Territories and Possessions) (US Bureau of the Census), pt. 53. Puerto Rico, 27.

23. Paul P. Kennedy, "Registration Peak Set in Puerto Rico: Unexpected Totals Counted as Observers Say Revolt Was Prematurely Sprung Links to Truman Assassination," *New York Times,* November 6, 1950, 20.

24. Teofilo Maldonado, "Inscripciones contestan A 'gangsterismo': Muñoz," *El Imparcial,* November 7, 1950, 6, 31.

25. These figures are based on calculations using the 1950 census figure of 1,035,205 adults aged twenty and over and a total population of 2,210,703. The adult population over the age of twenty in 1950 closely correlates with the number of adults eligible to vote, but not exactly. I used these census figures to place the following figures: of the 779,695 who had registered, 508,185 actually cast a ballot—with 75.6 percent of those voting in favor of Public Law 600—on June 4, 1951. Pagán, *Historia de los partidos políticos puertorriqueños,* 300; *Census of Population: 1950,* vol. 2, *Characteristics of the Population,* pts. 51–54 (Territories and Possessions) (US Bureau of the Census), pt. 53. Puerto Rico, 27.

26. "Puerto Rico Referendum Scored," *New York Times,* June 9, 1951, 4.

27. Acosta Lespier, *La Mordaza,* 177; Pagán, *Historia de los partidos políticos puertorriqueños,* 305.

28. See chapter 5 for a discussion of Reynolds's detention during these preemptive waves.

29. For Immediate Release, November 6, 1950, series IV, box 18, folder 3, RR Papers.

30. Jay Holmes Smith to whom it may concern, February 19, 1951, series IV, box 18, folder 3, RR Papers. A draft of a form letter prepared by Smith suggests that he faced questions about whether the group had violated the organization's bylaws by excluding officers. In the letter, Smith explained that the meeting had gathered "all of the officers who could be gotten together upon fairly short notice" and that "all of our efforts to communicate with Miss Reynolds prior to our action were to no avail, since she was apparently being held *incommunicado.*"

31. Ruth Reynolds interview by Blanca Vázquez, August 26, 1985, tape 32, series IX, box 45, folder 9, RR Papers.

32. Reynolds to mother and father, November 13, 1950, Private family collection shared with author.

33. Jean Hirning interview by author, Richmond, California, March 28, 2014.

34. The full list of RRDC officers included Thelma Mielke, chairman; Julius Eichel, treasurer; Sidney Aberman, David Dellinger, Rachel DuBois, Francis Hall,

Robert Ludlow, Conrad Lynn, Ruth Miller, A. J. Muste, James Peck, Irving Ravin, and Catharine Raymond.

35. Acosta Lespier, *La Mordaza*, 170, 175; Conrad J. Lynn to Herbert Monte Levy, August 4, 1951, Puerto Rico v. Reynolds, Ruth, MC001-02-04, box 1641, folder 3, ACLU Records.

36. Ruth Reynolds Defense Committee flyer, no date, "Dear Friend: The case of Ruth Reynolds is at a very critical stage . . . ," series IV, box 24, folder 4, RR Papers. This is clearly pretrial. It mentions Muste's June 27 visit with Reynolds, so it likely was sent out in July.

37. Lynn, *There Is a Fountain*, 87.

38. Lynn, *There Is a Fountain*, 128.

39. Lynn, *There Is a Fountain*, 87, 91.

40. Lynn, *There Is a Fountain*, 42–44, 68–69; Garry Pierre-Pierre, "Conrad J. Lynn, a Veteran Civil Rights Lawyer, Is Dead at 84," *New York Times*, November 18, 1995.

41. Lynn, *There Is a Fountain*, 108–13.

42. Lynn, *There Is a Fountain*, 116.

43. May, *Homeward Bound*; Findlay, *We Are Left*, 49, 76–89.

44. Lynn, *There Is a Fountain*, 128.

45. Julius Eichel to the Gano Group, April 8, 1951, series IV, box 24, folder 4, RR Papers.

46. Ruth Reynolds Defense Committee flyer, "Dear Friend: The case of Ruth Reynolds is at a very critical stage."

47. The Gano Group to Ruth Reynolds Defense Committee, April 3, 1952, series IV, box 24, folder 4, RR Papers; James Peck, "Not Like in Cicero," *Crisis* 58, no. 10 (December 1951): 653–56, 696; Mollin, *Radical Pacifism in Modern America*, 66–67.

48. Wittner, *Rebels against War*, 156–58; Danielson, "'It Is a Day of Judgment,'" 228–29.

49. The Gano Group to Ruth Reynolds Defense Committee, April 3, 1952, series IV, box 24, folder 4, RR Papers.

50. The Gano Group to Ruth Reynolds Defense Committee, April 3, 1952.

51. As editor of *The Peacemaker*, Lloyd Danzeisen presumably wrote this statement and decided upon its inclusion in the Peacemakers' main organ.

52. "Confidence in Reynolds," June 22, 1951 (vol. 3, no. 2): 3, *The Peacemaker* (1948–1953) folder, Templin Papers.

53. Dorothy A. Hickie, "Questions Ruth Reynolds Defense," *The Peacemaker*, June 22, 1951 (vol. 3, no. 2): 3, *The Peacemaker* (1948–1953) folder, Templin Papers; Marion Bromley, "Letters: What about the Rest of Us?," *The Peacemaker*, July 7, 1951 (vol. 3, no. 3): 4–5, file *The Peacemaker* (1948–1953) folder, Templin Papers.

54. Other Nationalists on trial, including Albizu Campos, proceeded with jury trials. I do not have further insight into their decision to waive a jury trial. Indictment. The People of Puerto Rico v. Ruth M. Reynolds, Rafael Burgos Fuentes, Eduardo López Vázquez, and José Mejías Flores, Criminal Appeal No. 15456, Puerto Rico

v. Reynolds, Ruth, MC001-02-04, box 1641, folder 4, ACLU Records; John E. Tysell, M.D. to Francis Heisler, January 21, 1951, series IV, box 24, folder 4, RR Papers.

55. Acosta Lespier, *La Mordaza*, 177; "Caso contra Ruth M. Reynolds," September 17, 1951, carpeta, series X, box 48, folder 4, RR Papers. Jury selection began on August 20, 1951.

56. Acosta Lespier, *La Mordaza*, 170–77.

57. Herbert Monte Levy to Morris L. Ernst, Conrad K. Fraenkel, Arthur Garfield Hays, and Raymond L. Wise, Puerto Rico v. Reynolds, Ruth, MC001-02-04, box 1641, folder 3, ACLU Records.

58. Minutes, Free Speech Committee, May 22, 1952, Puerto Rico v. Reynolds, Ruth, MC001-02-04, box 1641, folder 3, ACLU Records. The following is a shortened excerpt of Albizu Campos's speech leading up to his administering the oath: "I accept the office of President of the Party, but before I do, I want to tell you a few things. I accuse the Nationalists of Puerto Rico, you, right here, of being indifferent toward the liberating movement. You are not doing anything. The liberating movement can expect nothing of the patriots if these are not ready to sacrifice their lives and part with their fortunes. I must announce that the National Treasure is depleted. . . . It cannot be expected that the enemies of independence will contribute that money. It is not 3 or 4 thousand dollars that the liberating movement needs. I cannot continue occupying this office and incurring personal obligations. You, yourselves, are the ones who have placed this burden on me. I ask you to help me rid myself of it. . . . He who is not ready to cooperate and continues with such little shame, I am going to dismiss from the party. It is best that they go right now."

59. Lynn, *There Is a Fountain*, 127.

60. Indictment, Puerto Rico v. Reynolds, Ruth, MC001-02-04, box 1641, folder 3, ACLU Records; "The Case of Ruth M. Reynolds," series I, box 1, folder 1, RR Papers.

61. "Visit to Puerto Rico: A Report . . . October 6, 1951," Puerto Rico (6): Peacemaker Actions folder, Templin Papers.

62. "Visit to Puerto Rico: A Report . . . October 6, 1951."

63. In the report, the delegation described its contacts with other North American pacifists in Puerto Rico as such: "Besides the Methodist Mission project in Vieques, we visited four other community projects which are under mission boards in the U.S.: Yuquiyu, La Plata, Castaner, and El Guacio. A number of pacifists from the states are living in these communities. We also saw teachers, professors, ministers, government workers who are pacifists from the States." "Visit to Puerto Rico: A Report . . . October 6, 1951."

64. "Visit to Puerto Rico: A Report . . . October 6, 1951."

65. Acosta Lespier, *La Mordaza*, 170–74. Albizu Campos's trial took place between July 30 and August 17, 1951. He was sentenced on August 28. Acosta Lespier, *La Mordaza*, 170–77.

66. Lynn, *There Is a Fountain*, 132.

67. "Visit to Puerto Rico: A Report . . . October 6, 1951"; "Caso contra Ruth M. Reynolds," September 17, 1951, carpeta, series X, box 48, folder 4, RR Papers; Lynn, *There Is a Fountain*, 132.

68. "Visit to Puerto Rico: A Report . . . October 6, 1951." This is Bromley, Nelson, and Templin's account of what Reynolds said.

69. Conrad Lynn to Mrs. Harry Reynolds, September 11, 1951, Private family collection.

70. "Visit to Puerto Rico: A Report . . . October 6, 1951."

71. Ruth Reynolds interview by Blanca Vázquez, October 3 and 7, 1985, tape 56, series IX, box 46, folder 6, RR Papers; Reynolds, "Memorandum on Experiences Phenomenal."

72. Reynolds, "Memorandum on Experiences Phenomenal."

73. Reynolds, "Memorandum on Experiences Phenomenal."

74. Reynolds, "Memorandum on Experiences Phenomenal."

75. Reynolds, "Memorandum on Experiences Phenomenal."

76. "Memorandum [1954]," series V, box 31, folder 3, RR Papers.

77. Reynolds, "Memorandum on Experiences Phenomenal."

78. McCoy, *Question of Torture*, 7–8.

79. Welsome, *Plutonium Files.*

80. Briggs, *Reproducing Empire*, 9, 135–41.

81. Reynolds, "Memorandum on Experiences Phenomenal."

82. "Visit to Puerto Rico: A Report . . . October 6, 1951."

83. Belknap, *Cold War Political Justice.*

84. A. J. Muste, "Report on Visit to Ruth Reynolds in Puerto Rico," July 10, 1951, Puerto Rico v. Reynolds, Ruth, MC001-02-04, box 1641, folder 3, ACLU Records.

85. Conrad J. Lynn to Herbert M. Levy, August 4, 1951, Puerto Rico v. Reynolds, Ruth, MC001-02-04, box 1641, folder 3, ACLU Records.

86. Herbert Monte Levy to Roger N. Baldwin, August 8, 1951, Puerto Rico v. Reynolds, Ruth, MC001-02-04, box 1641, folder 3, ACLU Records.

87. Belknap, *Cold War Political Justice.*

88. Herbert Monte Levy to Roger N. Baldwin, August 8, 1951.

89. Conrad J. Lynn to Herbert M. Levy, August 21, 1951, Puerto Rico v. Reynolds, Ruth, MC001-02-04, box 1641, folder 3, ACLU Records.

90. During the trial, Conrad Lynn informed ACLU leadership: "The Bar [in Puerto Rico] seems to be jubilant that the test is being made here." Lynn to Levy, August 21, 1951, Puerto Rico v. Reynolds, Ruth, MC001-02-04, box 1641, folder 3, ACLU Records.

91. Lynn, *There Is a Fountain*, 131.

92. Lynn, *There Is a Fountain*, 131. These quotes are from Lynn's recollections of his arguments that he discusses in his autobiography. The two free speech Supreme Court cases from which Lynn drew these quotes were *Gitlow v. New York* (1925) and *Terminiello v. City of Chicago* (1949).

93. "Visit to Puerto Rico: A Report . . . October 6, 1951"; "Caso contra Ruth M. Reynolds," September 17, 1951, carpeta, series X, box 48, folder 4, RR Papers; Lynn, *There Is a Fountain*, 132.

94. Lynn, *There Is a Fountain*, 132.

95. "Visit to Puerto Rico: A Report . . . October 6, 1951."

96. "Visit to Puerto Rico: A Report . . . October 6, 1951."

97. Lynn to Mrs. Harry Reynolds, September 11, 1951. Family private collection.

98. Jasanoff, *Biological Mind*; DeVeaux, "Trauma of the Incarceration Experience"; Liebling and Maruna, *Effects of Imprisonment*; Calvo and Gutiérrez-García, "Cognition and Stress," 139–44; Iffland and Neuner, "Trauma and Memory," 161–67.

99. Report to the ALPRI, 1945, chap. 13, p. 27, series III, box 14, folders 1–2, RR Papers.

100. Isabel Rosado Morales, interview by author, October 6, 2010, Ceiba, Puerto Rico; Cruz Lamoutte, "Introducción," 9; Rosado Morales, *Mis testimonios*, 30, 47.

101. Jiménez de Wagenheim, *Nationalist Heroines*, 166, 203–10; Ruth Reynolds interview by Blanca Vázquez, September 18, 1985, tape 47B, series IX, box 46, folder 3, RR Papers.

102. Ruth Reynolds to Dr. Read, April 5, 1962, series II, box 10, folder 1, RR Papers.

103. Jiménez de Wagenheim, *Nationalist Heroines*, 91–104, 293–94; Seijo Bruno, *La insurrección nacionalista*, 115–17. Leonides Díaz Díaz's formal schooling ended in the third grade.

104. The 1920 census lists the then twenty-year-old Leonides Díaz Díaz (and her entire family) as "mulatto." 1920 US Census, Factor, Arecibo, Puerto Rico; Roll: T625_2046; p. 22B; Enumeration District: 192; 1920 US Census Place, Chupacallos, Ceiba, Puerto Rico; Roll: T625_2051; p. 4B; Enumeration District: 1023; 1935 US Census, Santurce, San Juan, Puerto Rico; Roll: 68; p. 10A; Enumeration District: 8–22.

105. Isabel Rosado Morales, interview by author, October 6, 2010; Miñi Seijo Bruno, "Isabel Rosado: Ejemplo de valor y sacrificio," *Claridad en rojo*, June 8–14, 1979, 2; Ayala and Bernabe, *Puerto Rico in the American Century*, 116.

106. Jiménez de Wagenheim, *Nationalist Heroines*, 107, 185, 204.

107. Seijo Bruno, *La insurrección nacionalista*, 215.

108. Jiménez de Wagenheim, *Nationalist Heroines*, 91–104, 293–94; Seijo Bruno, *La insurrección nacionalista*, 115–17, 130.

109. Jiménez de Wagenheim, *Nationalist Heroines*, 203–10.

110. "Padre de Olga Viscal acusa a La Reynolds," *El Imparcial*, September 5, 1941, 3.

111. Power, "Women, Gender," 132–33.

112. As quoted by Jiménez de Wagenheim, *Nationalist Heroines*, 109. Carmen María Pérez González interviewed by Olga Jiménez de Wagenheim on April 21, 1998.

113. "Discurso pronunciado por Pedro Albizu Campos en Utuado, Puerto Rico, el día 23 de febrero de 1950," fondo: Departamento de Justicia, serie: Documentos Nacionalistas, tarea 90-29, caja 21, item 16b, Archivo General de Puerto Rico, San Juan; "Discurso pronunciado por Pedro Albizu Campos en Ponce, P.R. el día 21 de marzo de 1950," fondo: Departamento de Justicia, tarea 90-29, serie: Documentos Nacionalistas, caja 21, item 16c, Archivo General de Puerto Rico, San Juan.

114. As quoted by Jiménez de Wagenheim, *Nationalist Heroines*, 108, 300.

115. Roy-Féquière et al., *Puerto Rico*, 534; Sánchez Huertas, "Algunas ideas tentativas del pensamiento social cristiano en Albizu Campos," 139, 153.

116. Jiménez de Wagenheim, *Nationalist Heroines*, 91–104, 293–94; Seijo Bruno, *La insurrección nacionalista*, 115–17.

117. Lynn, *There Is a Fountain*, 129; "The Case of Ruth M. Reynolds," series I, box 1, folder 1, RR Papers.

118. The arraignment took place on January 3, 1951. "Case of Ruth M. Reynolds."

119. Jiménez de Wagenheim, *Nationalist Heroines*, 105–14.

120. Jiménez de Wagenheim, *Nationalist Heroines*, 203–10.

121. For most of this period, Reynolds and Viscal Garriga shared a calabozo. By contrast, Monserrate del Valle del Toro, Juanita Ojeda Maldonado, and Leonides Díaz Díaz were housed among the Arecibo District Jail's general population. Ruth Reynolds interview by Blanca Vázquez, September 18, 1985, tape 47C, series IX, box 46, folder 3, RR Papers.

122. Ruth Reynolds interview by Blanca Vázquez, September 18, 1985, tape 47B; Ruth Reynolds interview by Blanca Vázquez, October 1, 1985, tape 51, series IX, box 46, folder 5, RR Papers; "Case of Ruth M. Reynolds."

123. Ruth Reynolds interview by Blanca Vázquez, October 3 and 7, 1985, tape 56; Ruth Reynolds interview by Blanca Vázquez, October 7, 1985, tape 57, series IX, box 46, folder 6, RR Papers.

124. Ruth Reynolds interview by Blanca Vázquez , September 18, 1985, tape 47B.

125. Reynolds, "Memorandum on Experiences Phenomenal."

126. Ruth Reynolds interview by Blanca Vázquez, September 18, 1985, tape 47C.

127. Ruth Reynolds interview by Blanca Vázquez, October 7, 1985, tape 57.

128. The papers of Muñoz Marín's office contain multiple letters from Reynolds's supporters protesting her treatment as well as correspondence among Muñoz Marín's office, the Department of Justice in Puerto Rico, and prison administration about addressing the situation. Fondo: Oficina del Gobernador, tarea 96-20, caja 2236, Archivo General de Puerto Rico, San Juan.

129. Ruth Reynolds interview by Blanca Vázquez, October 7, 1985, tape 57.

130. Inmates purchased or relied on family to deliver other necessities. Ruth Reynolds interview, tape 51, series IX, box 46, folder 5, RR Papers; Rosado Morales, *Mis testimonios*, 35.

131. Rosado Morales, *Mis testimonios*, 35.

132. Rosado Morales, *Mis testimonios*, 35.

133. Ruth Reynolds interview by Blanca Vázquez, October 7, 1985, tape 58, series IX, box 46, folder 6, RR Papers.

134. Seijo Bruno, "Isabel Rosado," 3.

135. Ruth Reynolds interview by Blanca Vázquez, October 24, 1985, tape 59, series IX, box 46, folder 7, RR Papers. According to a secret police memorandum in Reynolds's carpeta, bail was set on March 5, 1952. "Memorandum al comdte. negociado seg. interna," carpeta, series X, box 48, folder 4, RR Papers.

136. The three were Félix Rodríguez of Caguas, who owned a furniture store; Ramón M. Vicente of Santurce; and Santiago Ruíz of Ciales, who owned a department store. Their bail was set at $10,000, but they were required to pay $20,000 because they did not post cash. An Internal Security memo noted that both Rodríguez and Vicente had individual carpetas (#6624 and #4517) and that at least one employee of Ruíz's store had an individual carpeta. "Memorandum para el comandante del negociado de seguridad interna," June 23, 1952, carpeta, series X, box 48, folder 4, RR Papers; Ruth Reynolds interview by Blanca Vázquez, October 24, 1985, tape 59.

137. Ruth Reynolds interview by Blanca Vázquez, October 24, 1985, tape 59.

138. "Memorandum al comandante del negociado de seguridad interna," July 11, 1952, carpeta, series X, box 48, folder 4, RR Papers. According to a memo in her carpeta, Reynolds departed on July 10, 1952.

139. Ruth Reynolds to Conrad Lynn, June 22, 1952, box 31, file R. Reynolds Appeal, Conrad Lynn Papers, Howard Gotlieb Archival Center, Boston University.

140. Acosta Lespier, *La Mordaza*, 195.

141. Jiménez de Wagenheim, *Nationalist Heroines*, 213; Acosta Lespier, *La Mordaza*, 195–206.

142. Ruth Reynolds interview by Blanca Vázquez, October 3 and 7, 1985, tape 56.

143. Monserrate del Valle del Toro's husband was sentenced to more than 480 years for his role in the uprising in Arecibo. She suffered nearly two years of separation from her two young daughters as she awaited trial for the Gag Law violations for which she was eventually acquitted. Jiménez de Wagenheim, *Nationalist Heroines*, 91–104, 293–94; Seijo Bruno, *La insurrección nacionalista*, 115–17.

144. They were tried together with two others: Alvaro Rivera Walker and Juan José Muñoz Matos. Jiménez de Wagenheim, *Nationalist Heroines*, 91–104, 114–15, 191–92, 293–94; Acosta Lespier, *La Mordaza*, 203–204; Seijo Bruno, *La insurrección nacionalista*, 115–17.

145. According to Reynolds, Torresola Roura and Pérez González also passed their accounts of mistreatment in prison onto Hernández Vallé during the meeting. Ruth Reynolds interview by Blanca Vázquez, October 7, 1985, tape 58. For more on the accounts of Torresola Roura, Pérez González, and Albizu Campos, see "Testimonio de Doris Torresola, 29 de agosto de 1953," folder 8561.4, num 3, Colección Pedro Aponte Vázquez y Judith Ortiz Roldán, Archivo Histórico de la Fundación Luis Muñoz Marín; "Memorandum [1954]," series V, box 31, folder 3, RR Papers; Partido Nacionalista de Puerto Rico, Secretaría de Relaciones Exteriores, *Tortura de los presos políticos en Puerto Rico: Denuncia elevada a la Organización de los Estadas Americanos*, Cuba, 1952; and Marín Torres, *Eran ellos.*

Chapter 7

1. Ruth Reynolds interview by Blanca Vázquez, November 27, 1985, tape 69, series IX, box 46, folder 10, RR Papers.

2. The four Nationalists' intentions are discussed in "Creen tiroteo se reflejará acto Caracas," *El Mundo*, March 3, 1954: 7; and James F. Cunningham, "Finalidad era se tratara independencia en Caracas," *El Mundo*, March 3, 1954, 11.

3. Jiménez de Wagenheim, *Nationalist Heroines*, 242, 246–47, 250–51, 256–59.

4. Ruth Reynolds interview by Blanca Vázquez, November 27, 1985, tape 69.

5. Ruth Reynolds interview by Blanca Vázquez, November 27, 1985, tape 69.

6. Ruth M. Reynolds, Americans for Puerto Rico's Independence, For Immediate Release, May 6, 1964, series IV, box 19, folder 2, RR Papers.

7. Benjamin Bradlee, "Collazo Guilty of Blair House Murder; Death Is Mandatory," *Washington Post*, March 8, 1951, 1.

8. Ruth Reynolds to Mr. President, July 25, 1952, series II, box 9, folder 3, RR Papers.

9. Jiménez de Wagenheim, *Nationalist Heroines*, 219, 228, 230.

10. The other five who picked her up at the airport were Rosa Collazo, Conrad Lynn, Yolanda Moreno Lynn, Ralph Templin, and Charles Wellman. Ruth Reynolds to Juanito et al., July 26, 1952, series II, box 9, folder 3, RR Papers.

11. Jiménez de Wagenheim, *Nationalist Heroines*, 230–32.

12. Ruth Reynolds to Mr. President, July 25, 1952.

13. Ruth Reynolds to Mr. President, July 25, 1952.

14. Ruth Reynolds to Mr. President, July 25, 1952.

15. Anthony Leviero, "Assassin Spared by Truman in Gesture to Puerto Rico," *New York Times*, July 25, 1952, 1, 5; "Today Puerto Rico Is a Colony," *New York Times*, July 25, 1953, 5.

16. The Assistant Secretary of State for Congressional Relations (Jack K. McFall) to the Director, Bureau of the Budget (Frederick Lawton), *Foreign Relations of the United States, 1952–1954*, United Nations Affairs, vol. 3, ed. Ralph R. Goodwin, document 901, https://history.state.gov/historicaldocuments/frus1952-54v03/d901 (accessed May 15, 2019).

17. Ruth Reynolds interview by Blanca Vázquez, October 28, 1985, tape 62, series IX, box 46, folder 8, RR Papers.

18. Thomas, *Puerto Rican Citizen*, 151–52.

19. See chapters 2 and 6 for further discussion.

20. Press Release, Committee for the Organization of Americans for Puerto Rico's Independence, July 25, 1952, series IV, box 19, folder 1, RR Papers.

21. Press Release, Committee for the Organization of Americans for Puerto Rico's Independence.

22. Ruth Reynolds interview by Blanca Vázquez, October 28, 1985, tape 62.

23. Thelma Mielke to H. E. Lester B. Pearson, October 30, 1952, series V, box 27, folder 2, RR Papers. Mielke became the Nationalist Party's official UN observer on January 9, 1947. The United Nations permitted nongovernmental organizations to send representatives. The Nationalist Party applied for and obtained permission to name an observer. In taking up this work, Mielke continued a role that she had initiated at the international conference to form the United Nations that took place in San Francisco in 1945. See chapter 2 for a discussion of Mielke's involvement at the 1945 conference. Ruth Reynolds interview by Blanca Vázquez, July 11, 1986, tape 10, series IX, box 45, folder 3, RR Papers.

24. Mazower, *No Enchanted Palace*; Pearson, "Defending Empire."

25. "In the United Nations: The American League for Puerto Rico's Independence vs. The United States of America," series IV, box 18, folder 2, RR Papers.

26. Ruth Reynolds to Helen, June 21, 1951, series II, box 9, folder 3, RR Papers; Ruth Reynolds interview by Blanca Vázquez, August 26, 1985, tape 31, series IX, box 45, folder 9, RR Papers; "Memorandum on Non-Self-Governing Territories and the United Nations, November 17, 1947," 362–63.

27. Thelma Mielke to Trygve Lie, October 31, 1950, series V, box 27, folder 2, RR Papers.

28. Chief, Section for Non-Governmental Organizations to Thelma Mielke, November 6, 1950, series V, box 27, folder 2, RR Papers; Ruth Reynolds interview by

Blanca Vázquez, October 28 and November 20, 1985, tape 63, series IX, box 46, folder 8, RR Papers.

29. Plummer, *Rising Wind*, 239.

30. *Government of Puerto Rico and the United States Government, Submitted by the Organizing Committee of Americans for Puerto Rico's Independence to the United Nations Committee on Information from Non-Self-Governing Territories*, September 15, 1952, series IV, box 19, folder 1, RR Papers.

31. Why Puerto Rico Can Not Be Removed from Classification as a Non-Self-Governing Territory by the United Nations, September 23, 1952, series IV, box 19, folder 1, RR Papers.

32. García Muñoz, "Puerto Rico and the United States," 26–27.

33. Julio Pinto Gandía to H. S. Loomes, [1953], series V, box 27, folder 2, RR Papers.

34. Julio Pinto Gandía to H. S. Loomes, [1953].

35. Thelma Mielke to H. E. Lester B. Pearson, October 30, 1952, series V, box 27, folder 2, RR Papers.

36. Julio Pinto Gandía to H. S. Loomes, [1953].

37. Rosa Collazo, her two daughters Lydia and Iris Collazo, Lolita Lebrón, and four other Nationalist Party women identified themselves as the Women's Committee for the Release of the Political Prisoners of Puerto Rico (Comité Femenino Pro-Libertad de los Presos Políticos). "Damas del Comité Femenino Pro-Presos Políticos de Puerto Rico arrestadas frente a las Naciones Unidas," *Puerto Rico en Marcha*, September–October 1953, fondo: Departamento de Justicia, serie: Documentos Nacionalistas, tarea 90-29, caja 9, item 30, Archivo General de Puerto Rico, San Juan; Kathleen McLaughlin, "India Disputes U.S. over Puerto Rico," *New York Times*, September 1, 1953, 7; "11 Who Picketed U.N. Are Found Disorderly," *New York Times*, September 22, 1953, 10.

38. Letter to Guy, no date, series V, box 27, folder 2, RR Papers.

39. Letter to Guy, no date.

40. García Muñoz, "Puerto Rico," 48.

41. Letter to Guy, no date.

42. Letter to Guy, no date.

43. Ruth Reynolds interview by Blanca Vázquez, October 28 and November 20, 1985, tape 63.

44. Ruth Reynolds to A. J. Muste, July 12, 1953, series II, box 9, folder 4, RR Papers.

45. Ruth Reynolds to Henry Babcock, October 28, 1953, series II, box 9, folder 4, RR Papers.

46. "Memorandum," [1954], series V, box 31, folder 3, RR Papers. The press release appeared in *El Imparcial* in February 1952.

47. "Memorandum," [1954], series V, box 31, folder 3; Thelma Mielke, "Addendum to Report of February 12, 1954," series V, box 31, folder 3, RR Papers.

48. Ruth Reynolds to Dr. Buttrick, February 15, 1954, series II, box 9, folder 4, RR Papers; Ruth Reynolds to Victor Patschkiss, February 18, 1954, series II, box 9, folder 4, RR Papers.

49. The other members of the committee were Sidney Aberman of the War Resisters League, David Dellinger of the Libertarian Press, and Harold Wurp of the Contemporary Press. Sidney Aberman, Davie Dellinger, Ruth Reynolds, Harold Wurp to Franklin Miller, February 17, 1954, series II, box 9, folder 4, RR Papers.

50. Moore, *Disrupting Science*, 54, 56; Ruth Reynolds interview by Blanca Vázquez, November 27, 1985, tape 69.

51. Ruth M. Reynolds, Americans for Puerto Rico's Independence, For Immediate Release, May 6, 1964, series IV, box 19, folder 2, RR Papers.

52. "Refuerzan policía en Harlem," *El Mundo*, March 3, 1954, 1, 12; "Vigilan en Chicago a hermano de nacionalista Lolita Lebrón," *El Mundo*, March 4, 1954, 1, 16; "Policía arresta a cinco; Busca a Gonzalo Lebrón," *El Mundo*, March 6, 1954, 1, 21; "Arrestan Chicago otros 8 boricuas," *El Mundo*, March 6, 1954, 1; Juan Martínez Chapel, "Arrestan 29 nacionalistas," *El Mundo*, March 6, 1954, 1, 16; "Arrestan líderes nacionalistas en Ponce," *El Mundo*, March 8, 1954, 14.

53. "Policía Cuba vigila pasos sra. Albizu," *El Mundo*, March 4, 1954, 1, 16; "Arrestan siete nacionalistsas; cinco en Chicago y dos en Cuba," *El Imparcial*, March 5, 1954, 3.

54. "Police Alerted for Local Clues," *New York Times*, March 2, 1954; Peter Kihss, "Puerto Rico Hunt Turns up 3 More," Special to the *New York Times*, March 9, 1954, 21; "91 Puerto Ricans Rounded Up Here," *New York Times*, March 9, 1954, 1.

55. Ruth Reynolds interview by Blanca Vázquez, January 24, 1986, tape 73, series IX, box 46, folder 11, RR Papers.

56. Ruth Reynolds interview by Blanca Vázquez, January 29, 1986, tape 74, series IX, box 46, folder 12; A. J. Muste to Dear Friends, December 18, 1954, Puerto Rico v. Reynolds, Ruth, MC001-02-04, box 1641, folder 4, ACLU Records. The full list of RRDC officers included Thelma Mielke, chairman; Carl Colodne, secretary; Julius Eichel, treasurer. The remaining members of the RRDC were Sidney Aberman, Ernest Bromley, Rachel Davis DuBois, Francis Hall, Murray Kempton, Robert Ludow, Conrad Lynn, Wallace Nelson, James Peck, Irving Ravin, Catherine Raymond, Ralph Templin, Noah Walter, Roger O'Neill, and Walter Longstreth. Ruth Reynolds Defense Committee, "Ruth Reynolds Opposes," series I, box 1, folder 1, RR Papers.

57. As Reynolds further explained, "A. J. and others felt that there was no way at all that people could be appealed to, except on the basis of fair play, fair trial. It was the only thing that people would respond to. He was right, they were right." Ruth Reynolds interview by Blanca Vázquez, January 29, 1986, tape 74.

58. A. J. Muste to David Dellinger, March 23, 1954, series IV, box 20, folder 5, RR Papers.

59. Ruth Reynolds interview by Blanca Vázquez, November 27, 1985, tape 69.

60. Ruth Reynolds interview by Blanca Vázquez, January 29, 1986, tape 74.

61. Ruth Reynolds interview by Blanca Vázquez, January 24, 1986, tape 73.

62. *Report of John Edgar Hoover, Director Federal Bureau of Investigation United States Department of Justice*, Fiscal Year 1955, 20.

63. Ruth Reynolds interview by Blanca Vázquez, January 29, 1986, tape 74.

64. Rodríguez-Morazzani, "Political Cultures," 2.

65. Power, *Solidarity across the Americas*, 184.

66. The historian Margaret Power asserts that into the 1950s, "CPUSA leadership offered camaraderie, as well as material and legal support, to Nationalist Party leadership." Power, "Seeing the U.S. Empire," 189–92.

67. Ruth Reynolds interview by Blanca Vázquez, January 29, 1986, tape 75, series IX, box 46, folder 12, RR Papers.

68. Ruth Reynolds interview by Blanca Vázquez, July 15 and 17, 1985, tape 14, series IX, box 45, folder 4, RR Papers.

69. A. J. Muste to Luis Muñoz Marín, May 5, 1954, series IV, box 20, folder 5, RR Papers.

70. A. J. Muste to Office of Superintendent of Prisons, May 5, 1954, series IV, box 20, folder 5, RR Papers.

71. "Puerto Ricans Get Maximum Terms," *New York Times*, July 9, 1954, 1; Jiménez de Wagenheim, *Nationalist Heroines*, 264.

72. The full list includes Rosa Collazo, Julio Pinto Gandía, Juan Francisco Ortíz Medina, José A. Otero Otero, Juan Bernardo Lebrón, Carmelo Álvarez Román, Jorge Luis Jiménez, Armando Díaz Matos, and Manual Rabago Torres. "13 Puerto Ricans Get 6-Year Terms," *New York Times*, October 27, 1954, 12.

73. The People of Puerto Rico v. Ruth M. Reynolds et al., 1954, PRSC, Puerto Rico v. Reynolds, Ruth, MC001-02-04, box 1641, folder 4, ACLU Records.

74. Conrad Lynn to Herbert Monte Levy, November 27, 1954, Puerto Rico v. Reynolds, Ruth, MC001-02-04, box 1641, folder 4, ACLU Records.

75. The case was People v. Burgos, 75 P.R. December 535 (1953). Malavet, *America's Colony*, 186, 197.

76. A. J. Muste to Dear Friends, December 18, 1954, ACLU Records.

77. Acosta Lespier, *La Mordaza*, 237–52.

78. "We cross Puerto Rico on foot on a mission of peace and good will," Puerto Rico: (6) Peacemaker Actions, 125 3-4-1, 12, Templin Papers.

79. Ruth Reynolds to Conrad Lynn, September 26, 1961, series II, box 10, folder 1, RR Papers.

80. "We Oppose Political Imprisonment of Puerto Rican Nationalists," [APRI document, 1963], series IV, box 19, folder 1, RR Papers.

81. Ruth Reynolds to Ana Celia, October 7, 1977, series II, box 11, folder 3, RR Papers; "Dear Friends: Here is an outline of my life . . . ," series I, box 1, folder 1, RR Papers; "Biographical Data on Ruth M. Reynolds," series I, box 1, folder 1, RR Papers.

82. In 1963, the other two were Susan Geller and Al Uhrie. In 1964, Seymore Eichel joined Reynolds and Miller. Edward W. Pearlstein to Dear Friend, November 19, 1963, series IV, box 19, folder 2, RR Papers. Rafael López Rosas, "Piquete damas pide acelerar caso Albizu ante el Supremo," *El Mundo*, August 21, 1964, 44; Untitled document, "If a robber . . . ," series IV, box 19, folder 2, RR Papers.

83. "We Oppose Political Imprisonment of Puerto Rican Nationalists," [APRI document, 1963], series IV, box 19, folder 1, RR Papers.

84. López Rosas, "Piquete damas"; Untitled document, "If a robber. . . ."

85. Ruth M. Reynolds, for Americans for Puerto Rico's Independence, For Immediate Release, series IV, box 19, folder 2, RR Papers.

86. Ruth Reynolds to Dear Friend, December 21, 1964, series IV, box 19, folder 3, RR Papers.

87. Ruth M. Reynolds, "100,000 Puerto Ricans Attend Campos Rites," *The Peacemaker*, [1965], series III, box 12, folder 2, RR Papers.

Chapter 8

1. In 1975, Lebrón had requested that Reynolds visit her. Lolita Lebrón to Ruth [Miller], November 8, 1975, series II, box 6, folder 7, RR Papers. In this correspondence, Reynolds called the lobbying group the United States Committee for the Release of the Five Nationalist Political Prisoners. It appears to be the same group despite this slight variation.

2. Ruth M. Reynolds to Lolita Lebrón, October 27, 1977, series II, box 11, folder 3, RR Papers.

3. Ruth M. Reynolds to Oscar Collazo, Leavenworth Penitentiary, October 27, 1977, series II, box 11, folder 3; Ruth M. Reynolds to Irving Flores Rodríguez, Federal Correctional Institution, October 27, 1977, series II, box 11, folder 3, RR Papers; Ruth M. Reynolds to Rafael Cancel Miranda, Federal Correctional Institution, Marion, Illinois, October 27, 1977, series II, box 11, folder 3, RR Papers.

4. Lolita Lebrón to Ruth Reynolds, October 29, 1977, series II, box 7, folder 2, RR Papers.

5. Rafael Cancel Miranda to Ruth M. Reynolds, November 8, 1977, series II, box 7, folder 2, RR Papers.

6. "30 in Puerto Rican Group Held in Liberty I. Protest," *New York Times*, October 26, 1977, 30.

7. J. T. Williford to Ruth M. Reynolds, December 9, 1977, series II, box 7, folder 2, RR Papers. A case manager at the US Penitentiary in Leavenworth, Kansas, also denied Reynolds's request to visit Flores Rodríguez and Collazo unless each man submitted a formal application to add her to a visiting list. J. G. Wickman to Ruth M. Reynolds, December 14, 1977, series II, box 7, folder 2, RR Papers.

8. J. T. Williford to Ruth M. Reynolds, January 13, 1978, series II, box 7, folder 3, RR Papers.

9. Carlos Feliciano et al. v. Frank Hogan and Burton B. Roberts, series IV, box 21, folder 3, RR Papers; Ruth Reynolds, "Carlos Feliciano: Forged Link between Bombings in New York and in Puerto Rico," September 1970, series IV, box 21, folder 2, RR Papers; Ruth Reynolds, "The Current Status of the Case of Carlos Feliciano," October 27, 1973, series IV, box 21, folder 2, RR Papers.

10. Ruth Reynolds, "Carlos Feliciano: Forged Link between Bombings in New York and in Puerto Rico," [September 1970], series IV, box 21, folder 2, RR Papers; Berger, *Struggle Within*, 30–31. The links between MIRA and Cuba were theoretically driven. During his youth in New York, MIRA's founder Filiberto Ojeda Ríos had been a member of M26, the Cuban nationalist organization that Fidel Castro founded to oust Cuba's US-backed dictator Fulgencio Batista.

11. Carlos Feliciano et al. v. Frank Hogan and Burton B. Roberts, series IV, box 21, folder 3, RR Papers.

12. Ruth Reynolds interview by Blanca Vázquez, May 13, 1986, tape 105, series IX, box 47, folder 9, RR Papers; Lacey Fosburgh, "St. Mark's: A Forum for City's Militants," *New York Times*, January 17, 1971, 76.

13. Ruth Reynolds interview by Blanca Vázquez, May 7, 1986, tape 104, series IX, box 47, folder 9, RR Papers.

14. "The Case of Carlos Feliciano: The Man, the Frame-up, the Nation," series IV, box 21, folder 2, RR Papers; Alfredo Lopez, "Puerto Rican Nationalist Faces New York Frame-Up," *The Militant*, December 25, 1970: 19; Ruth Reynolds interview by Blanca Vázquez, May 7, 1986, tape 104.

15. Ruth Reynolds interview by Blanca Vázquez, May 7, 1986, tape 104.

16. García-Colón, *Colonial Migrants*, 3–4.

17. Fernández, *Young Lords*, 3.

18. Ayala and Bernabe, *Puerto Rico in the American Century*, 197–200, 268–75.

19. Fernández, *Young Lords*, 379.

20. Fernández, *Young Lords*.

21. Ruth Reynolds interview by Blanca Vázquez, May 7, 1986, tape 104.

22. Fernández, *Young Lords*, 157, 163–67, 172–78.

23. "The Young Lords and Us," February 14, 1970, series II, box 12, folder 3, RR Papers.

24. "Young Lords and Us," February 14, 1970; Fernández, *Young Lords*, 319.

25. "The Case of Carlos Feliciano: The Man, the Frame-up, the Nation," series IV, box 21, folder 2, RR Papers.

26. "Committee Holds March: Activities to Be Stepped Up," series IV, box 21, folder 2, RR Papers.

27. José Torres, "Fabricated Case?," *New York Post*, June 30, 1973, series IV, box 21, folder 2, RR Papers.

28. David A. García and Ruth M. Reynolds to Carlos, April 26, 1975, series IV, box 20, folder 10, RR Papers.

29. "Case of Carlos Feliciano."

30. The other plaintiffs joining Reynolds were Seymour Eichel, Maurice Goldman, Ralph Templin, Elizabeth Aberman, Hedda Garza, Richard Garza, Edward Pearlstien, and Constance Webb. The full list of plaintiffs also included Antulio Parrilla-Bonilla, Hector Davila Alonso, Andres Marrero Cortes, Luis N. Rivera, José G. Marrero, Gilberto Gerena Valentín, David García, the Young Lords, the Puerto Rican Student Union, El Comité, the National Association of Puerto Rican Social Workers, El Centro Chicano, the Black Workers Congress, and the National Committee of Clergymen and Laymen for Liberation.

31. Carlos Feliciano et al. v. Frank Hogan and Burton B. Roberts, series IV, box 21, folder 3, RR Papers. Representatives from El Chicano Centro, the Black Workers Congress, and the National Committee of Clergymen and Laymen for Liberation joined as plaintiffs.

32. Ruth Reynolds, "Carlos Feliciano: Forged Link between Bombings in New York and in Puerto Rico," [September 1970], series IV, box 21, folder 2, RR Papers.

33. Ruth Reynolds, "Carlos Feliciano."

34. "We, the undersigned . . . ," series IV box 20, folder 8, RR Papers; An evening with Carlos Feliciano invitation, December 1971, series IV, box 21, folder 2, RR Papers.

35. "Libertad para Carlos Feliciano Ahora!," *Palante*, vol. 3, no. 4, March 5–19, 1971: 11; "Committee Holds March: Activities to Be Stepped Up," February 22, 1971, series IV, box 21, folder 2, RR Papers.

36. May 20 March and Demonstrate, [May 1972] flyer, series IV, box 21, folder 2, RR Papers.

37. José Torres, "Fabricated Case?," *New York Post*, June 30, 1973, series IV, box 21, folder 2, RR Papers; David A. García and Ruth Reynolds form letter, May 1, 1975, series IV, box 20, folder 10, RR Papers.

38. Ruth Reynolds, "The Current Status of the Case of Carlos Feliciano," October 27, 1973, series IV, box 21, folder 2.

39. David A. García and Ruth M. Reynolds to Dear Friend, October 6, 1974, series IV, box 21, no. 2, RR Papers; Sample Letter to Judges, series IV, box 21, folder 2, RR Papers.

40. Ronald Smothers, "Freedom Sought by Puerto Ricans," *New York Times*, March 3, 1975.

41. Starr, "'Hit Them Harder,'" 141.

42. David A. García and Ruth Reynolds form letter, May 1, 1975, series IV, box 20, folder 10, RR Papers.

43. Conrad Lynn had worked previously with Kunstler on the "Harlem Six." Lynn, *There Is a Fountain*, 3–33; Kunstler and Isenberg, *My Life*.

44. Marcia Chambers, "Judge Frees Man Convicted on a Bomb Charge," *New York Times*, July 10, 1975, 34.

45. Ruth Reynolds to Juan, January 9, 1978, series II, box 11, folder 4, RR Papers. The letter does not include the last name of the recipient, but it was likely either John (Juan) Passalacqua or Juan Juarbe Juarbe.

46. For a discussion of the Weathermen's turn to violence as a form of solidarity with colonized and racially minoritized groups, see Berger, *Outlaws of America*.

47. Within the United States, the lawyers representing the five and many leading organizers in the campaign were based in Chicago, where a large Puerto Rican community emerged after World War II. For more information on the Puerto Rican community in Chicago, see Lilia Fernández's *Brown in the Windy City*.

48. Reynolds declined the PRSC's 1977 invitation to join its national board, but she worked closely with its leadership on the USCFF. Rosa Borenstein to Friends, August 11, 1977, series IV, box 24, folder 2, RR Papers.

49. Ruth Reynolds interview by Blanca Vázquez, July 22, 1985, tape 8, series IX, box 45, folder 3, RR Papers; Schmitz and Walker, "Jimmy Carter," 113.

50. Rosa Borenstein to Friends, August 11, 1977, series IV, box 24, folder 2, RR Papers. The full list of groups participating at the organizing meeting included the Americans for Puerto Rico's Independence, Attica Committee to Free Dacajaweiah, El Comité, Irish Republican Clubs, National Alliance Against Racist and Political Repression, National Lawyers Guild, National Coalition for the Defense

of Political Prisoners, Puerto Rican Socialist Party, Puerto Rican Solidarity Committee, Queens Coalition for Peace and Justice, Seven Days Magazine, and Socialist Workers Party. "Puerto Rico Solidarity Committee National Workplan: June–December, 1977," series IV, box 24, folder 2, RR Papers.

51. Rosa Borenstein to Friends, August 11, 1977, series IV, box 24, folder 2, RR Papers.

52. Ruth Reynolds interview by Blanca Vázquez, May 7, 1986, tape 104.

53. Ruth Reynolds to Ana Celia, October 7, 1977, series II, box 11, folder 3, RR Papers.

54. Ruth M. Reynolds to Dear Friend, [1977 or 1978], series II, box 11, folder 3, RR Papers; "Report of the Ecumenical Visit to the White House on December 22, 1977, Seeking a Christmas Pardon for the Four Puerto Rican Nationalist Political Prisoners," series II, box 11, folder 4, RR Papers.

55. "Report of the Ecumenical Visit to the White House on December 22, 1977.

56. Ruth M. Reynolds to Dear Friend.

57. Ruth M. Reynolds to Dear Friend.

58. Tom Bryan, "Nacionalistas se disponen probar que 25 ó más años cárcel no fueron en vano," El Mundo, September 12, 1979, 18A.

59. "Pardoned Activist Dies in Puerto Rico, Andres Figueroa Cordero, 54, Was Jailed after House Shootings," New York Times, March 8, 1979, 21.

60. Nathaniel Sheppard, Jr., "4 Freed Puerto Rican Nationalists Vow to Continue Fight," New York Times, September 11, 1979, A16.

61. Steven R. Weisman, "Congressmen Seeking a Prisoner Exchange to Free Puerto Ricans," New York Times, March 25, 1979, 23; LeoGrande and Kornbluh, Back Channel to Cuba, 386.

62. Ruth M. Reynolds to Bob Horton, October 26, 1979, series II, box 11, folder 4, RR Papers. She was working part-time as an assistant librarian at the New York Psychoanalytic Institute. She had been working for the institute since beginning work there as a secretary to the librarian in 1956. "My Duties as Assistant Librarian of the Abraham A. Brill Library of the New York Psychoanalytic Institute," series I, box 1, folder 1, RR Papers.

63. "The following is the second part of an interview . . ." [1979], series IV, box 26, folder 3, RR Papers; Rafael Anglada López, "Miles reciben a los héroes," Claridad, September 14, 1979: 2.

64. Rivera and Duany, "Introduction," 7–8.

65. "Grupo APU envía cabel a Fidel," El Mundo, January 25, 1961, 21. The US government restricted them to an area of Manhattan. Ruth Reynolds interview by Blanca Vázquez, March 6, 1986, tape 91, series IX, box 47, folder 4, RR Papers.

66. Ruth Reynolds to Juan and Doña Laura, June 25, 1968, series II, box 10, folder 6, RR Papers. The clipping does not appear with the original letter but is the only New York Times article that matches the letter's description of the article. "The Proceedings in the UN," New York Times, June 25, 1968, 10.

67. Plummer, Rising Wind, 257, 289.

68. As cited by Linsley, "U.S.-Cuban Relations," 121.

69. Rivera and Duany, "Introduction," 7–8.

70. "Puerto Rico at the United Nations," CPRD flyer, series IV, box 20, folder 6, RR Papers.

71. Vito Marcantonio died in 1954 at the age of fifty-one. See chapter 3 for a discussion of Marcantonio's ties to Albizu Campos and Reynolds.

72. Robert Chrisman, "The Case for the Independence of Puerto Rico," *The Black Scholar*, October 1977: 53. Signers included the Puerto Rican Solidarity Committee, the Committee to End Sterilization Abuse, the US Committee for Puerto Rican Decolonization, the Labor Task Force for the National Organization of Women, the National Committee to Reopen the Rosenberg Case, the American Committee on Africa, the Native American Solidarity Committee, and the Third World Coalition of the American Friends' Service Committee.

73. Ruth Reynolds interview by Blanca Vázquez, May 7, 1986, tape 104.

74. In 1977, a financially strained and politically marginalized Nationalist Party credentialed Reynolds to represent them at the United Nations before its Committee on Decolonization. Given her penchant for working in solidarity with but independent from Puerto Rican groups, it is unlikely that she accepted the invitation.

75. Ruth Reynolds interview by Blanca Vázquez, May 7, 1986, tape 104.

76. Statement of Americans for Puerto Rico's Independence to the United Nations' Committee on Decolonization, August 19, 1980, series IV, box 19, RR Papers; emphasis added.

77. "Puerto Rico under the United States Flag: Self-Determination or Congressional Determination?" Presented to the United States Committee on Decolonization by Americans for Puerto Rico's Independence, August 1977, series IV, box 19, folder 5, RR Papers.

78. "Puerto Rico under the United States Flag."

79. By her account, Ricardo Alarcón, the head of the Cuba mission at the United Nations, indicated to her without going into details that her efforts had facilitated his efforts in 1977. Ruth Reynolds interview by Blanca Vázquez, May 7, 1986, tape 104.

80. Ana M. López and Gabriela Reardon, "Puerto Rico at the United Nations," *NACLA*, November 26, 2007, https://nacla.org/article/puerto-rico-united-nations.

81. Statement of Americans for Puerto Rico's Independence to the United Nations' Committee on Decolonization, August 19, 1980, series IV, box 19, RR Papers.

82. Pastor, "International Debate on Puerto Rico"; Collo, "Legislative History of Colonialism"; *United States Participation in the UN: Report by the President to the Congress for the Year 1979* (Washington, DC: US Government Printing Office, 1980), 247, 282–84, 303.

83. "The following is the second part of an interview . . ." [1979], series IV, box 26, folder 3, RR Papers.

84. Ruth Reynolds interview by Blanca Vázquez, November 25, 1985, tape 66, series IX, box 46, folder 9, RR Papers.

85. Ruth Reynolds interview by Blanca Vázquez, November 25, 1985, tape 66.

86. Ruth Reynolds interview by Blanca Vázquez, November 25, 1985, tape 66.

Conclusion

1. Ruth Reynolds interview by Blanca Vázquez, November 25, 1985, tape 66, series IX, box 46, folder 9, RR Papers.

2. Ruth Reynolds interview by Blanca Vázquez, August 26, 1985, tape 33, series IX, box 45, folder 9, RR Papers.

3. VSN informational flyer, series IV, box 26, folder 3, RR Papers.

4. "The following is the second part of an interview . . ." [1979], series IV, box 26, folder 3, RR Papers.

5. Pérez, "Two Reading Rooms"; Hernández, "Evolution"; Thomas and Lauria Santiago, *Rethinking the Struggle*, 104.

6. Ruth Reynolds interview by Blanca Vázquez, May 29, 1986, tape 112, series IX, box 47, folder 10, RR Papers.

7. Ruth Reynolds interview by Blanca Vázquez, August 26, 1985, tape 33.

8. Blanca Vázquez, interview by author, New York, August 21, 2013.

9. Reynolds, *Campus in Bondage*, xvi. It is worth noting that despite their disagreements about her activism, Reynolds devoted the book to her parents.

10. Amílcar Barreto, *Vieques*, 41–43; Bosque-Pérez and Colón Morera, "Introduction," 2–3.

11. Ruth Reynolds interview by Blanca Vázquez, May 29, 1986, tape 112.

12. Ruth Reynolds interview by Blanca Vázquez, May 29, 1986, tape 112.

13. Ruth Reynolds interview by Blanca Vázquez, May 29, 1986, tape 112.

14. María Rodríguez Matos, interview by author, San Juan, December 14, 2022.

15. María Rodríguez Matos, interview by author, San Juan, December 14, 2022.

16. Jennifer Hinojosa and Edwin Meléndez, "Puerto Rican Exodus: One Year since Hurricane Maria," *Centro Research Brief*, September 2018.

17. Klein, *Battle for Paradise*, 47–50; Bonilla and LeBrón, "Introduction," 5–7.

18. I borrow this terminology from Juan Gonzalez's *Harvest of Empire*.

19. Negrón-Muntaner, "Our Fellow Americans."

20. Rafael Bernabe and Manuel Rodríguez Banchs, "Solidarity without Erasure: Responding to Trump on Puerto Rico," *CounterPunch*, April 9, 2019, www.counter punch.org/2019/04/09/solidarity-without-erasure-responding-to-trump-on-puerto -rico/.

21. Ruth Reynolds interview by Blanca Vázquez, May 29, 1986, tape 112.

Bibliography

Archives and Manuscript Collections

Archives of the Puerto Rican Diaspora, Centro de Estudios Puertorriqueños,
    Hunter College, CUNY, New York
    Centro de Estudios Puertorriqueños/Center for Puerto Rican Studies Records
    Ruth M. Reynolds Papers
Archivo General de Puerto Rico, San Juan
    Departamento de Justicia, Documentos Nacionalistas 90–92
    Oficina del Gobernador
Archivo Histórico de la Fundación Luis Muñoz Marín, San Juan
    Colección Pedro Aponte Vázquez y Judith Ortiz Roldán
Centro de Investigaciones Históricas, Universidad de Puerto Rico, Río Piedras
    Colección Benjamín Torres
    Colección Material Audiovisual: CDs / DVDs, FBI, Carpetas de Organizaciones
        e Individuos Independentistas
        Partido Nacionalista de Puerto Rico
        Pedro Albizu Campos
Colección Puertorriqueña, Universidad de Puerto Rico, Río Piedras
    Colección Jaime Benítez
Department of Special Collections, Princeton University Library, New Jersey
    American Civil Liberties Union Records: Subgroup 2, Legal Case Files Series
Howard Gotlieb Archival Center, Boston University, Massachusetts
    Conrad Lynn Papers
Private family collection, Rapid City, South Dakota
Swarthmore College Peace Collection, Swarthmore College, Pennsylvania
    Fellowship of Reconciliation (U.S.) Records
    Marion Bromley and Ernest Bromley Papers
United Methodist Church Archives, General Commission on Archives and History,
    Madison, New Jersey
    Ralph T. Templin Papers

Oral History Interviews with Author

Hirning, Jean. Richmond, California, March 28, 2014.
Rodríguez Matos, María. San Juan, Puerto Rico, December 14, 2022.
Rosado Morales, Isabel. Ceiba, Puerto Rico, October 6, 2010.
Vázquez, Blanca. New York, New York, August 21, 2013.

Newspapers and Periodicals

Chicago Daily Tribune
Claridad (San Juan, Puerto Rico)
Crisis (New York)
Daily Northwestern (Evanston, Illinois)

El Imparcial (San Juan, Puerto Rico)
El Mundo (San Juan, Puerto Rico)
New York Times
Washington Post

US Government Documents

A Bill to Amend the Organic Act of Puerto Rico. Hearings before a Subcommittee on Territories and Insular Affairs, United States Senate, 78th Cong, 1st sess. on S. 1407 . . . November 16–26 and December 1, 1943. Washington, DC: US Government Printing Office, 1943.

Bureau of the Census, *United States Manuscript Census*
Butler County, Nebraska, 1880.
Caldwell County, Kentucky, 1870.
Chupacallos, Ceiba, Puerto Rico, 1920.
Factor, Arecibo, Puerto Rico, 1920.
Lawrence County, South Dakota, 1900.
Rochester, Monroe, New York, 1940.
Santurce, San Juan, Puerto Rico, 1935.

Franklin D. Roosevelt Annual Message to Congress, January 6, 1941; Records of the United States Senate; SEN 77A-H1; Record Group 46; National Archives. https://www.archives.gov/milestone-documents/president-franklin -roosevelts-annual-message-to-congress.

Hearings before the Committee on Territories and Insular Affairs, US Senate, 79th Cong., 1st sess. on S.227, Part 1, March 5, 6, 7, and 8, 1945. Washington, DC: US Government Printing Office, 1945.

House of Representatives Committee on Public Lands, Report No. 2275, June 19, 1950, *Providing for the Organization of a Constitutional Government by the People of Puerto Rico, 81st Cong., 2nd sess.* Washington, DC: US Government Printing Office, 1950, 3–4.

Independence for Puerto Rico, Hearings before the Committee on Territories and Insular Affairs, US Senate, 79th Cong., 1st sess. on S.227, Part 2, April 23, 24, 26, 27, May 1 and 8, 1945. Washington, DC: US Government Printing Office, 1945.

Public Law 81–600: Approved July 3, 1950. An Act to Provide for the Organization of a Constitutional Government by the People of Puerto Rico, 1950, *United States Statutes at Large, Containing the Laws and Concurrent Resolutions Enacted, 81st Cong., 2nd sess. Congress of the United States of America, 1950–1951, and Proclamations, Treaties, International Agreements Other Than Treaties, and Reorganization Plans, vol 64, Part 1: Public Laws and Reorganization Plans.* Washington, DC: US Government Printing Office, 1952, 319–20.

Senate Committee on Interior and Insular Affairs on Public Law 81–600, Report No. 1779, June 6, 1950, *Providing for the Organization of a Constitutional Government by the People of Puerto Rico, 81st Cong., 2nd sess.* Washington, DC: US Government Printing Office, 1950.

Books and Articles

Acosta Lespier, Ivonne. *La Mordaza (The Gag Law): The Attempt to Crush the Independence Movement in Puerto Rico, 1948–1957.* 5th ed. Río Piedras: Editorial Edil, 2018.

Albizu Campos, Pedro, Laura Albizu-Meneses, and Mario A. Rodríguez León. *Pedro Albizu Campos: Escritos.* Hato Rey, PR: Publicaciones Puertorriqueñas, 2007.

Alger, Chadwick. "The Emerging Roles of NGOs in the UN System: From Article 71 to a People's Millennium Assembly." *Global Governance* 8, no. 1 (2002): 93–117.

Amílcar Barreto, Antonio. *Vieques, the Navy, and Puerto Rican Politics.* Gainesville: University Press of Florida, 2022.

Anderson, Carol. *Eyes off the Prize: The United Nations and the African American Struggle for Human Rights, 1944–1955.* Cambridge: Cambridge University Press, 2003.

Anderson, Robert W. *Party Politics in Puerto Rico.* Stanford, CA: Stanford University Press, 1965.

Appelbaum, Patricia. *Kingdom to Commune: Protestant Pacifist Culture between World War I and the Vietnam Era.* Chapel Hill: University of North Carolina Press, 2009.

Araiza, Lauren. *To March for Others: The Black Freedom Struggle and the United Farm Workers.* Philadelphia: University of Pennsylvania Press, 2014.

Aran Gosnell, Patria. "The Puerto Ricans in New York City." PhD diss., New York University, 1945.

Ayala, César J. *American Sugar Kingdom: The Plantation Economy of the Spanish Caribbean, 1898–1834.* Chapel Hill: University of North Carolina Press, 1999.

Ayala, César J., and Rafael Bernabe. *Puerto Rico in the American Century: A History since 1898.* Chapel Hill: University of North Carolina Press, 2007.

Ayala, César J., and José L. Bolívar. *Battleship Vieques: Puerto Rico from World War II to the Korean War.* Princeton, NJ: Markus Wiener, 2011.

Ayala Casás, César, and José Bolívar Fresneda. "The Cold War and the Second Expropriations of the Navy in Vieques." *Centro Journal* 18, no 1 (2006): 10–35.

Baldwin, Lewis V., and Paul R. Dekar. *"In an Inescapable Network of Mutuality": Martin Luther King, Jr. and the Globalization of an Ethical Idea.* Eugene, OR: Cascade Books, 2013.

Barnes, L. Call. "Porto Rico and Paradise." *The Baptist Home Missionary Monthly* 30, no. 11 (November 1908): 414–32.

Barreto Velázquez, Norberto. *Rexford G. Tugwell: El ultimo de los tutores.* San Juan, PR: Ediciones Huracán, 2004.

Belknap, Michal R. *Cold War Political Justice: The Smith Act, the Communist Party, and American Civil Liberties.* Westport, CT: Greenwood, 1977.

Bennett, Scott H. *Radical Pacifism: The War Resister League and Gandhian Nonviolence in America, 1915–1963.* Syracuse, NY: Syracuse University Press, 2003.

Berger, Dan. *Outlaws of America: The Weather Underground and the Politics of Solidarity.* Oakland, CA: AK Press, 2006.

———. *The Struggle Within: Prisons, Political Prisoners, and Mass Movements in the United States.* Montreal: PM, 2014.

Bernabe, Rafael, and Manuel Rodríguez Banchs. "Solidarity without Erasure: Responding to Trump on Puerto Rico." *CounterPunch,* April 9, 2019.

Bhana, Surrendra. *The United States and the Development of the Puerto Rican Status Question, 1936–1968.* Lawrence: University Press of Kansas, 1975.

Biolsi, Thomas. *Deadliest Enemies: Law and the Making of Race Relations on and off Rosebud Reservation.* Berkeley: University of California Press, 2001.

———. *Organizing the Lakota: The Political Economy of the New Deal on the Pine Ridge and Rosebud Reservations.* Tucson: University of Arizona Press, 1998.

Bonilla, Yarimar, and Marisol LeBrón. "Introduction: Aftershocks of Disaster." In *Aftershocks of Disaster: Puerto Rico before and after the Storm,* edited by Yarimar Bonilla and Marisol LeBrón, 1–16. Chicago: Haymarket Books, 2019.

Borstelmann, Thomas. *The Cold War and the Color Line: American Race Relations in the Global Arena.* Cambridge, MA: Harvard University Press, 2003.

Bosque-Pérez, Ramón. "Carpetas y persecución política en Puerto Rico: La dimensión federal." In *Las carpetas: Persecución y derechos civiles en Puerto Rico (ensayos y documentos),* edited by Ramón Bosque-Peréz and José Javier Colón Morera, 37–90. Río Piedras: Centro para la Investigación y Promocíon de los Derechos Civiles, 1997.

———. "Political Persecution against Puerto Rican Anti-Colonial Activists in the Twentieth Century." In *Puerto Rico under Colonial Rule: Political Persecution and the Quest for Human Rights,* edited by Ramón Bosque-Pérez and José Javier Colón Morera, 13–48. Albany: State University of New York Press, 2006.

Bosque-Pérez, Ramón, and José Javier Colón Morera. "Introduction: Puerto Rico's Quest for Human Rights." In *Puerto Rico under Colonial Rule,* edited by Ramón Bosque-Pérez and José Javier Colón Morera, 1–12. Albany: State University of New York Press, 2006.

———, eds. *Carpetas y persecución política en Puerto Rico: La dimensión federal.* San Juan, PR: Centro para la Investigación y Promoción de los Derechos Civiles, 1997.

Briggs, Laura. *Reproducing Empire: Race, Sex, Science, and US Imperialism in Puerto Rico.* Oakland: University of California Press, 2002.

Britz, Kevin. "Deadwood's Days of '76: The Wild West Show as Community Celebration." *South Dakota History* 40, no. 1 (Spring 2010): 52–84.

Brooks, Robert Peacock. *Timothy Brooks of Massachusetts and His Descendants.* Pompton Lakes, NJ: Biblio, 1927.

Bryant, M. Darol. "Non-Hindu Ashrams." In *Encyclopedia of Community: From the Village to the Virtual World*, edited by David Levinson and Karen Christenson, 60. Vol. 2. Thousand Oaks, CA: Sage, 2003.

Calvo, M. G., and A. Gutiérrez-García. "Cognition and Stress." In *Stress: Concepts, Cognition, Emotion, and Behavior*, edited by George Fink, 139–44. Cambridge, MA: Academic Press, 2016. https://doi.org/10.1016/B978-0-12-800951-2.00016-9.

Canales, Blanca. *La Constitución es la revolución*. San Juan, PR: Congreso Nacional Hostosiano, 1997.

Castledine, Jacqueline. *Cold War Progressives: Women's Interracial Organizing for Peace and Freedom*. Urbana: University of Illinois Press, 2012.

Chenault, Lawrence R. *The Puerto Rican Migrant in New York City*. New York: Columbia University Press, 1938.

Chowdhury, Elora Halim, and Liz Philipose. "Introduction." In *Dissident Friendships: Feminism, Imperialism, and Transnational Solidarity*, edited by Elora Chowdhury and Liz Philipose, 1–8. Urbana: University of Illinois Press, 2016.

Cohen, Lauren. "A Spirit of Solidarity: Transatlantic Friendships among Early Twentieth-Century Female Peace Activists (Wilpfers)." In *Dissident Friendships: Feminism, Imperialism, and Transnational Solidarity*, edited by Elora Chowdhury and Liz Philipose, 203–20. Urbana: University of Illinois Press, 2016.

Cohen, Robert. *When the Old Left Was Young: Student Radicals and America's First Mass Student Movement, 1929–1941*. New York: Oxford University Press, 1993.

Collazo, Oscar. *Memorias de un patriota encarcelado*. San Juan, PR: Ediciones Callejón, 2014.

Collo, Martin J. "The Legislative History of Colonialism: Puerto Rico and the United States Congress, 1950–1990." *Journal of Third World Studies* 13, no. 1 (1996): 215–32.

Cruz Lamoutte, Ramón Luis. "Introducción." In *Mis testimonios*, by Isabel Rosado Morales. Caguas, PR: Biblioteca Albizu Campos, 2007.

Danielson, Leilah. *American Gandhi: A. J. Muste and the History of Radicalism in the Twentieth Century*. Philadelphia: University of Pennsylvania Press, 2014.

———. "'It Is a Day of Judgment': The Peacemakers, Religion, and Radicalism in Cold War America." *Religion and American Culture: A Journal of Interpretation* 18, no. 2 (Summer 2008): 228–29.

Dasenbrock, J. Henry. *To the Beat of a Different Drummer: A Decade in the Life of a World War II Conscientious Objector*. Winona, MN: Northland Press of Winona, 1989.

Del Moral, Solsiree. *Negotiating Empire: The Cultural Politics of Schools in Puerto Rico, 1898–1952*. Madison: University of Wisconsin Press, 2013.

D'Emilio, John. *Lost Prophet: The Life and Times of Bayard Rustin*. Chicago: University of Chicago Press, 2003.

DeVeaux, Mika'il. "The Trauma of the Incarceration Experience." *Harvard Civil Rights–Civil Liberties Law Review* 48, no. 1 (2013): 257–77.

Dietz, James L. *Economic History of Puerto Rico: Institutional Change and Capitalist Development*. Princeton, NJ: Princeton University Press, 1987.

Donohue, Kathleen, ed. *Liberty and Justice for All? Rethinking Politics in Cold War America*. Amherst: University of Massachusetts Press, 2012.

Dudziak, Mary. *Cold War Civil Rights: Race and the Image of American Democracy*. Princeton, NJ: Princeton University Press, 2000.

Dunlap, David. *From Abyssinian to Zion: A Guide to Manhattan's Houses of Worship*. New York: Columbia University Press, 2012.

Farmer, James. *Lay Bare the Heart: An Autobiography of the Civil Rights Movement*. Fort Worth: Texas Christian University Press, 1985.

Fernández, Johanna. *The Young Lords: A Radical History*. Chapel Hill: University of North Carolina Press, 2020.

Fernández, Lilia. *Brown in the Windy City: Mexicans and Puerto Ricans in Postwar Chicago*. Chicago: University of Chicago Press, 2012.

Figueroa, Javier. *La gran enciclopedia de Puerto Rico*, Tomo 14, *Diccionario histórico-biográfico*. Madrid: Ediciones R, 1976.

Findlay, Eileen J. Suárez. *Imposing Decency: The Politics of Sexuality and Race in Puerto Rico, 1870–1920*. Durham, NC: Duke University Press, 1999.

——. *We Are Left without a Father Here: Masculinity, Domesticity, and Migration in Post-War Puerto Rico*. Durham, NC: Duke University Press, 2014.

Fisher, Beatrice. *A Tribute to Women Lawyers Worldwide: FIDA, 1944–1994*. London: Createspace, 2015.

Friedman, Andrea. *Citizenship in Cold War America: The National Security State and the Possibilities of Dissent*. Amherst: University of Massachusetts Press, 2015.

——. "The Empire at Home: Radical Pacifism and Puerto Rico in the 1950s." In *A New Insurgency: The Port Huron Statement and Its Times*, edited by Howard Brick and Gregory Parker, 253–64. Ann Arber, MI: Michigan Publishing, 2015.

Gaines, Kevin. *American Africans in Ghana: Black Expatriates and the Civil Rights Era*. Chapel Hill: University of North Carolina Press, 2008.

García-Colón, Ismael. *Colonial Migrants at the Heart of Empire: Puerto Rican Workers on U.S. Farms*. Oakland: University of California Press, 2020.

García Muñoz, Humberto. "Puerto Rico and the United States: The United Nations Role, 1953–1975." *Revista Jurídica de la Universidad de Puerto Rico* 53, no. 1 (1984): 1–265.

Gilmore, Glenda Elizabeth. *Defying Dixie: The Radical Roots of Civil Rights, 1919–1950*. New York: W. W. Norton, 2008.

Glen, Evelyn Nakano. "Settler Colonialism as Structure: A Framework for Comparative Studies of U.S. Race and Gender Formation." *Sociology of Race and Ethnicity* 1, no. 1 (2015): 52–72. https://doi.org/10.1177/2332649214560440.

Gonzalez, Juan. *Harvest of Empire: A History of Latinos in America*, rev. ed. New York: Penguin, 2011.

Gordon, Leonard A. "Mahatma Gandhi's Dialogues with Americans." *Economic and Political Weekly* 37, no. 4 (2002): 337–52.

Gore, Dayo F. *Radicalism at the Crossroads: African American Women Activists during the Cold War*. New York: New York University Press, 2011.

Gore, Dayo F., Jeanne Theoharis, and Komozi Woodard, eds. *Want to Start a Revolution: Radical Women in the Black Freedom Struggle.* New York: New York University Press, 2009.

Gregory, Raymond F. *Norman Thomas: The Great Dissenter.* New York: Algora, 2008.

Hernández, Pedro Juan. "The Evolution of Centro's Archives of the Puerto Rican Diaspora, 1973–2012." *Latino(a) Research Review* 1–2 (2011–2012): 85–100.

Hinojosa, Felipe. *Latino Mennonites: Civil Rights, Faith, and Evangelical Culture.* Baltimore: Johns Hopkins University Press, 2014.

Hinojosa, Jennifer, and Edwin Meléndez. "Puerto Rican Exodus: One Year since Hurricane Maria." *Centro Research Brief,* September 2018.

Hoffnung-Garskof, Jesse. *Racial Migrations: New York City and the Revolutionary Politics of the Spanish Caribbean.* Princeton, NJ: Princeton University Press, 2019.

Holmes Smith, Jay. "The Gandhi of Puerto Rico." *Fellowship* 10, no. 11 (November 1944): 186–87.

Hoover, Herbert T., and Ruth Ann Alexander. *From Idea to Institution: Higher Education in South Dakota.* Freeman, SD: Pine Hill Press, 1989.

Horne, Gerald. *The End of Empires: African Americans and India.* Philadelphia: Temple University Press, 2008.

Hunt, Andrew E. *David Dellinger: The Life and Times of a Nonviolent Revolutionary.* New York: New York University Press, 2006.

Iffland, B., and F. Neuner. "Trauma and Memory." In *Stress: Concepts, Cognition, Emotion, and Behavior,* edited by George Fink, 161–67. Cambridge, MA: Academic Press, 2016. https://doi.org/10.1016/B978-0-12-800951-2.00019-4.

Igartua, José E. *Communities of Soul: A Short History of Religion in Puerto Rico.* Montreal: McGill-Queen's University Press, 2022.

Jacobs, Margaret D. *White Mother to a Dark Race: Settler Colonialism, Materialism, and the Removal of Indigenous Children in the American West and Australia, 1880–1940.* Lincoln: University of Nebraska Press, 2009.

Janeway, Michael. "The Wartime Quartet: Muñoz Marín, Tugwell, Ickes, and FDR." In *Island at War: Puerto Rico in the Crucible of the Second World War,* edited by Jorge Rodríguez Beruff and José L. Bolivar Fresneda, 82–110. Jackson: University Press of Mississippi, 2015.

Jasanoff, Alan. *The Biological Mind: How Brain, Body, and Environment Collaborate to Make Us Who We Are.* New York: Basic Books, 2018.

Jiménez, Mónica A. "Searching for Monse." *Radical History Review* 148 (2024): 30–48.

Jiménez de Wagenheim, Olga. *Nationalist Heroines: Puerto Rican Women History Forgot, 1930s–1950s.* Princeton, NJ: Markus Wiener, 2016.

———. *Puerto Rico's Revolt for Independence: El Grito de Lares.* Princeton, NJ: Markus Wiener, 1993.

Johnson, Robert David. "Anti-Imperialism and the Good Neighbor Policy: Ernst Gruening and Puerto Rican Affairs, 1934–1939." *Journal of Latin American Studies* 29, no. 1 (1997): 89–110.

Julin, Suzanne Barta. *A Marvelous Hundred Square Miles: Black Hills Tourism, 1880–1941*. Pierre: South Dakota State Historical Society Press, 2009.

Kaplan, Amy. "'Left Alone with America': The Absence of Empire in the Study of American Culture." In *Cultures of United States Imperialism*, edited by Amy Kaplan and Donald E. Pease, 3–21. Durham, NC: Duke University Press, 1993.

Kasson, Joy. *Buffalo Bill's Wild West: Celebrity, Memory, and Popular History*. New York: Hill and Wang, 2000.

Kennedy, Dane. *Decolonization: A Very Short History*. New York: Oxford University Press, 2016.

King, David P. "The West Looks East: The Influence of Toyohiko Kagawa on American Mainline Protestantism." *Church History* 80, no. 2 (June 2011): 302–20.

Klein, Naomi. *The Battle for Paradise: Puerto Rico Takes on the Disaster Capitalists*. Chicago: Haymarket, 2018.

Kramer, Paul A. *The Blood of Government: Race, Empire, the United States, and the Philippines*. Chapel Hill: University of North Carolina Press, 2006.

Kunstler, William Moses, and Sheila Isenberg. *My Life as a Radical Lawyer*. New York: Birch Lane, 1996.

Kutulas, Judy. *The American Civil Liberties Union and the Making of Modern Liberalism, 1930–1960*. Berkeley: University of California Press, 2014.

Lamont, Corliss. *The Trial of Elizabeth Gurley Flynn by the American Civil Liberties Union*. New York: Monthly Review Press, 1969.

Lee, R. Alton. *A New Deal for South Dakota: Drought, Depression, and Relief, 1920–1941*. Pierre: South Dakota Historical Society Press, 2016.

LeoGrande, William M., and Peter Kornbluh. *Back Channel to Cuba: The Hidden History of Negotiations between Washington and Havana*. Chapel Hill: University of North Carolina Press, 2014.

Liebling, Alison, and Shadd Maruna, eds. *The Effects of Imprisonment*. London: Willan, 2005.

Linsley, Austin. "U.S.-Cuban Relations: The Role of Puerto Rico." In *Cuba in the World*, edited by Cole Blasier and Carmelo Mesa-Lago, 119–30. Pittsburgh: University of Pittsburgh Press, 1979.

Luciano, David, and Gabriel Haslip-Viera. "Adjustment Challenges: Puerto Ricans in New York City, 1938–1945; The Writings of Patria Aran Gosnell, Lawrence Chenault, and Frances M. Donohue." *Centro Journal* 31, no. 1 (Spring 2019): 26–55.

Lynn, Conrad. *There Is a Fountain: The Autobiography of Conrad Lynn*. New York: Lawrence Hill Books, 1993.

Malavet, Pedro A. *America's Colony: The Political and Cultural Conflict between the United States and Puerto Rico*. New York: New York University Press, 2004.

Maldonado, A. W. *Luis Muñoz Marín: Puerto Rico's Democratic Revolution*. San Juan: La Editorial Universidad de Puerto Rico, 2006.

Marín Torres, Heriberto. *Eran ellos*. 3rd ed. Río Piedras, PR: Ediciones Ciba, 2000.

Materson, Lisa G. "African American Women's Global Journeys and the Construction of Cross-Ethnic Racial Identity." *Women's Studies International Forum* 21, no. 1 (January–February 2009): 35–42.

———. "Gender, Generation, and Women's Independence Organizing in Puerto Rico." *Radical History Review* 128 (2017): 121–46.

———. "Ruth Reynolds, Solidarity Activism, and the Struggle against US Colonialism in Puerto Rico. *Modern American History* 2, no. 2 (2019): 183–87.

May, Elaine Tyler. *Homeward Bound: American Families in the Cold War Era.* New York: Basic Books, 2008.

Mazower, Mark. *No Enchanted Palace: The End of Empire and the Ideological Origins of the United Nations.* Princeton, NJ: Princeton University Press, 2000.

McCoy, Alfred. *A Question of Torture: CIA Interrogation, from the Cold War to the War on Terror.* New York: Metropolitan Books, 2006.

McDuffie, Eric. *Sojourning for Freedom: Black Women, American Communism, and the Making of Black Left Feminism.* Durham, NC: Duke University Press, 2011.

Meier, August, and Elliot Rudwick. *CORE: A Study in the Civil Rights Movement, 1942–1968.* New York: Oxford University Press, 1973.

Meléndez, Edgardo. *Patria: Puerto Rican Revolutionary Exiles in Late Nineteenth Century New York.* New York: Centro, 2020.

———. *Puerto Rico's Statehood Movement.* New York: Greenwood, 1988.

Melendez, Miguel. *We Took to the Streets: Fighting for Latino Rights with the Young Lords.* New Brunswick, NJ: Rutgers University Press.

Meneses Albizu-Campos, Cristina, and Silvia Lora Gamarra. *Una vida de amor y sacrificio.* San Juan: Publicaciones Puertorriqueños, 2009.

Meriwether, James H. *Proudly We Can Be Africans: Black Americans and Africa, 1935–1961.* Chapel Hill: University of North Carolina Press, 2002.

Merrill, Dennis. *Negotiating Paradise: US Tourism and Empire in Twentieth-Century Latin America.* Chapel Hill: University of North Carolina Press, 2009.

Meyer, Gerald J. "Pedro Albizu Campos, Gilberto Concepción de Gracia, and Vito Marcantonio's Collaboration in the Cause of Puerto Rico's Independence." *Centro Journal* 23, no. 1 (Spring 2011): 87–123.

———. *Vito Marcantonio: Radical Politician, 1902–1954.* Albany: State University of New York Press, 1989.

Miller, Robert Moats. *How Shall They Hear without a Preacher? The Life of Ernest Fremont Tittle.* Chapel Hill: University of North Carolina Press, 1971.

Mitchell, Steven T. *Nuggets to Neutrinos: The Homestake Story.* Bloomington: Xlibris, 2011.

Mollin, Marian. *Radical Pacifism in Modern America: Egalitarianism and Protest.* Philadelphia: University of Pennsylvania Press, 2006.

Monge, José Trías. *Puerto Rico: The Trials of the Oldest Colony in the World.* New Haven, CT: Yale University Press, 1997.

Moore, Kelly. *Disrupting Science: Social Movements, American Scientists, and the Politics of the Military, 1945–1975.* Princeton, NJ: Princeton University Press, 2008.

Moses, L. G. *Wild West Shows and the Images of American Indians, 1893–1933.* Albuquerque: University of New Mexico Press, 1999.

Muñoz Marín, Luis. *Luis Muñoz Marín: Memorias, autobiografía pública, 1940–1952.* San Juan, PR: Fundación Luis Muñoz Marín, 2003.

Muste, A. J. *Non-violence in an Aggressive World*. New York: Fellowship, 1944.

Navarro Rivera, Pablo. *Universidad de Puerto Rico: De control político a crisis permanente, 1903–1952*. Río Piedras: Ediciones Huracán, 2000.

Negrón-Muntaner, Frances. "Our Fellow Americans: Why Calling Puerto Ricans 'Americans' Will Not Save Them." In *Aftershocks of Disaster: Puerto Rico before and after the Storm*, edited by Yarimar Bonilla and Marisol LeBrón, 113–23. Chicago: Haymarket Books, 2019.

Newman, Louise. *White Women's Rights: Racial Origins of Feminism in the United States*. New York: Oxford University Press, 1999.

Newsinger, John. "James Connolly and the Easter Rising." *Science & Society* 47, no. 2 (1983): 152–77. www.jstor.org/stable/40402480.

Oropeza, Lorena. "Women, Gender, Migration, and Modern US Imperialism." In *The Oxford Handbook of American Women's and Gender History*, edited by Ellen Hartigan-O'Connor and Lisa G. Materson, 87–108. New York: Oxford University Press, 2018.

Ostler, Jeffrey. *The Lakotas and the Black Hills: The Struggle for Sacred Ground*. New York: Viking Penguin, 2010.

———. *The Plains Sioux and US Colonialism from Lewis and Clark to Wounded Knee*. Cambridge: Cambridge University Press, 2004.

Pagán, Bolívar. *Historia de los partidos políticos puertorriqueños, 1898–1956*. San Juan, PR: Librería Campos, 1959.

Paralitici, José (Ché). "Imprisonment and Colonial Domination, 1898–1958." In *Puerto Rico under Colonial Rule*, edited by Ramón Bosque-Pérez and José Javier Colón Morera, 67–82. Albany: State University of New York Press, 2006.

Parekh, Bhikhu. *Gandhi: A Very Short Introduction*. New York: Oxford University Press, 1997.

Parker, Watson. *Deadwood: The Golden Years*. Lincoln: University of Nebraska Press, 1981.

Pastor, Robert. "The International Debate on Puerto Rico: The Costs of Being an Agenda-Taker." *International Organization* 38, no. 3 (1984): 575–95.

Pearson, Jessica Lynne. "Defending Empire at the United Nations: The Politics of International Colonial Oversight in the Era of Decolonisation." *Journal of Imperial and Commonwealth History* 45, no. 3 (2017): 525–49.

Pérez, Nélida. "Two Reading Rooms and the Librarian's Office: The Evolution of the Centro Library and Archives." *Centro Journal* 21, no. 2 (Fall 2009): 199–218.

Plummer, Brenda Gayle. *Rising Wind: Black Americans and U.S. Foreign Affairs, 1935–1960*. Chapel Hill: University of North Carolina Press, 1996.

Ponsa, Christina Duffy. "When Statehood Was Autonomy." In *Reconsidering the Insular Cases: The Past and Future of the American Empire*, edited by Gerald L. Neuman and Tomiko Brown-Nagin, 1–28. Cambridge, MA: Harvard University Press, 2015.

Porter, Joy. *Native American Freemasonry: Associationalism and Performance in America*. Lincoln: University of Nebraska Press, 2019.

Power, Margaret. "Friends and Comrades: Political and Personal Relationships between Members of the Communist Party USA and the Puerto Rican

Nationalist Party, 1930s–1940s." In *Making the Revolution: Histories of the Latin American Left*, edited by Kevin A. Young, 105–28. New York: Cambridge University Press, 2019.

———. "A Political and Transnational Ménage a Trois: The Communist Party USA, the Puerto Rican Communist Party, and the Puerto Rican Nationalist Party, 1934–1945." In *Transnational Communism across the Americas*, edited by Marc Becker, Margaret M. Power, Tony Wood, and Jacob A. Zumoff, 123–44. Urbana: University of Illinois Press, 2023.

———. "Seeing the U.S. Empire through the Eyes of Puerto Rican Nationalists Who Opposed It." *Modern American History* 2, no. 2 (2019): 189–92. https://doi.org /10.1017/mah.2019.18.

———. *Solidarity across the Americas: The Puerto Rican Nationalist Party and Anti-Imperialism.* Chapel Hill: University of North Carolina Press, 2023.

———. "Women, Gender, and the Puerto Rican Nationalist Party." In *Gendering Nationalism: Intersections of Nation, Gender and Sexuality*, edited by Jon Mulholland, Nicola Montagna, and Erin Sanders-McDonagh, 129–43. London: Palgrave Macmillan, 2018.

Reynolds, Ruth M. *Campus in Bondage: A 1948 Microcosm of Puerto Rico in Bondage.* New York: Centro de Estudios Puertorriqueños/Hunter College CUNY, 1989.

Riggs, George Alanson. *Baptists in Puerto Rico: Brief Historical Notes of Forty Years of Baptist Work, 1899–1939.* Ponce, PR: Puerto Rico Evangelico, 1939.

Ritterhouse, Jennifer. *Growing Up Jim Crow: How Black and White Southern Children Learned Race.* Chapel Hill: University of North Carolina Press, 2006.

Rivera, Carmen Haydée, and Jorge Duany. "Introduction: 'Two Wings of a Bird.'" In *Cuba and Puerto Rico: Transdisciplinary Approaches to History, Literature, and Culture*, edited by Carmen Haydée Rivera and Jorge Duany, 1–27. Gainesville: University of Florida Press, 2023.

Rivera Rivera, Luis Rafael. "Esas mujeres desvergonzadas: Ponencia." *Revista Jurídica de la Universidad Interamericana de Puerto Rico* 49, no. 17 (August– May 2014–2015): 17–23.

Rodríguez Beruff, Jorge. *Strategy as Politics: Puerto Rico on the Eve of the Second World War.* San Juan: La Editorial Universidad de Puerto Rico, 2007.

Rodríguez Castro, Malena. "La década de los cuarenta: De la torre a las calles." In *Frente a la torre: Ensayos del cetenario de la Universidad de Puerto Rico, 1903–2003*, 132–75. San Juan: Universidad de Puerto Rico, 2005.

Rodríguez-Morazzani, Roberto P. "Political Cultures of the Puerto Rican Left in the United States." In *The Puerto Rican Movement: Voices from the Diaspora*, edited by Andrés Torres and José E. Velázquez, 25–47. Philadelphia: Temple University Press, 1998.

Rosado, Marisa. *Pedro Albizu Campos: Las llamas de la aurora acercamiento a su biografía.* 5th ed. San Juan, PR: Ediciones Puerto, 2008.

Rosado Morales, Isabel. *Mis testimonios.* Caguas, PR: Biblioteca Albizu Campos, 2007.

Roy, Srirupa. *Beyond Belief: India and the Politics of Postcolonial Nationalism.* Durham, NC: Duke University Press, 2007.

Roy-Féquière, Magali, Arturo Dávila, María T. Vaquero de Ramírez, Margot Arce de Vázquez, and Matilde Albert Robatto. *Puerto Rico: Lengua, educación, reforma universitaria, política, cultura y religión.* San Juan: Editorial de la Universidad de Puerto Rico, 2001.

Sánchez Huertas, Ernesto. "Algunas ideas tentativas del pensamiento social cristiano en Albizu Campos." In *La nación puertorriqueña: Ensayos en torno a Pedro Albizu Campos,* edited by Juan Manuel Carrion, Teresa C. Garcia Ruiz, and Carlos Rodriguez Fraticelli, 139–60. San Juan: Editorial de la Universidad de Puerto Rico, 1993.

Sánchez Korrol, Virginia. *From Colonia to Community: The History of Puerto Ricans in New York City.* Berkeley: University of California Press, 1994.

Santiago-Valles, Kelvin. "'Higher Womanhood' among the 'Lower Races': Julia McNair Henry in Puerto Rico and the 'Burdens' of 1898." *Radical History Review* 73 (1999): 47–73.

———. "'Our Race Today [Is] the Only Hope for the World': An African Spaniard as Chieftain of the Struggle against 'Sugar Slavery' in Puerto Rico, 1926–1934." *Caribbean Studies* 35, no. 1 (2007): 107–40.

Scharf, Lois. *To Work and to Wed: Female Employment, Feminism, and the Great Depression.* Westport, CT: Greenwood, 1980.

Schell, Herbert S. *History of South Dakota.* Lincoln: University of Nebraska Press, 1975.

Schildgen, Robert. "How Race Mattered: Kagawa Toyohiko in the United States." *Journal of American East-Asian Relations* 5, no. 3 (1996): 227–53.

Schmitz, David F., and Vanessa Walker. "Jimmy Carter and the Foreign Policy of Human Rights: The Development of a Post–Cold War Foreign Policy." *Diplomatic History* 28, no. 1 (2004): 113–43.

Scholz, Sally. *Political Solidarity.* University Park: Pennsylvania State University Press, 2008.

Schuler, Harold H. "Patriotic Pageantry: Presidential Visits to South Dakota." *South Dakota History* 30, no. 4 (Winter 2000): 339–90.

Seijo Bruno, Miñi. *La insurrección nacionalista en Puerto Rico, 1950.* San Juan, PR: Editorial Edil, 1997.

Shaffer, Robert. "Women and International Relations: Pearl S. Buck's Critique of the Cold War." *Journal of Women's History* 11, no. 3 (Autumn 1999): 151–75.

Sherwood, Marika. "India at the Founding of the United Nations." *International Studies* 33, no. 4 (1996): 407–28.

Sikes, Arthur M. *Richard Sikes and His Descendants: The First Seven Generations.* Suffield, CT: Sikes/Sykes Families Association, 2000.

Singh, Emmanuel. *Jesus the Sadguru and His Discipleship.* Delhi: Indian Society for Promoting Christian Knowledge, 2010.

Slate, Nico. *Colored Cosmopolitanism: The Shared Struggle for Freedom in the United States and India.* Cambridge, MA: Harvard University Press, 2012.

Sneider, Allison. *Suffragists in an Imperial Age: US Expansion and the Woman Question, 1870–1929.* New York: Oxford University Press, 2008.

Solomon, Barbara Miller. *In the Company of Educated Women*. New Haven, CT: Yale University Press, 1986.

Soto Fontánez, S. *Misión a la puerta: Una historia del trabajo Bautista Hispano en Nueva York*. Santo Domingo: Editora Educativa Dominicana, 1982.

Starr, Meg. "'Hit Them Harder': Leadership, Solidarity, and the Puerto Rican Independence Movement." In *The Hidden 1970s: Histories of Radicalism*, edited by Dan Berger, 135–54. New Brunswick, NJ: Rutgers University Press, 2010.

Stevens-Arroyo, Anthony M. "The Catholic Worldview in the Political Philosophy of Pedro Albizu Campos: The Death Knoll of Puerto Rican Insularity." *U.S. Catholic Historian* 20, no. 4 (2002): 53–73. www.jstor.org/stable/25154830.

Stoler, Ann Laura. "Tense and Tender Ties: The Politics of Comparison in North American History and (Post) Colonial Studies." *Journal of American History* 88, no. 3 (December 2001): 829–65.

Thomas, Lorrin. *Puerto Rican Citizen: History and Political Identity in Twentieth-Century New York City*. Chicago: University of Chicago Press, 2010.

Thomas, Lorrin, and Aldo A. Lauria Santiago. *Rethinking the Struggle for Puerto Rican Rights*. New York: Routledge, 2019.

Thompson, Harry F., ed. *A New South Dakota History*. Sioux Falls, SD: Center for Western Studies / Augustana College, 2005.

Torres, Benjamín, ed. *Pedro Albizu Campos: Obras escogidas, 1936–1954*, vol. 3. San Juan: Editorial Jelofe, 2022.

———. "Símbolo de la América irredenta." *Suplemento de Claridad*, September 17, 1972.

Tovar, Federico Ribes. *Albizu Campos: El revolucionario*. New York: Plus Ultra, 1975.

Trías Monge, José. *Puerto Rico: The Trials of the Oldest Colony in the World*. New Haven, CT: Yale University Press, 1997.

Truman, Harry S. "Statement by the President upon Signing Bill Approving the Constitution of the Commonwealth of Puerto Rico." July 5, 1952. *Public Papers of the Presidents of the United States, Harry S. Truman, 1945–1953*. Washington, DC: US Government Printing Office, 1966. www.trumanlibrary .gov/library/public-papers/198/statement-president-upon-signing-bill -approving-constitution-commonwealth.

Tyrrell, Ian. "American Exceptionalism in an Age of International History." *American Historical Review* 96, no. 4 (1991): 1031–55.

Vega, Bernardo. *Memoirs of Bernardo Vega: A Contribution to the History of the Puerto Rican Community in New York*. Edited by César Andreu Iglesias. New York: Monthly Review Press, 1984.

Velázques, Norberto Barreto. *Rexford G. Tugwell: El ultimo de los tutores*. San Juan, PR: Ediciones Huracán, 2004.

Von Eschen, Penny M. *Race against Empire: Black Americans and Anticolonialism, 1937–1957*. Ithaca, NY: Cornell University Press, 1997.

Wagenheim, Kal, and Olga Jiménez de Wagenheim, eds. *The Puerto Ricans: A Documentary History*. New York: Praeger, 1973.

Walker, Samuel. *In Defense of American Liberties: A History of the ACLU.* New York: Oxford University Press, 1990.

Weigand, Kate. *Red Feminism: American Communism and the Making of Women's Liberation.* Baltimore: Johns Hopkins University Press, 2001.

Weinberg, Marjorie. *The Real Rosebud: The Triumph of a Lakota Woman.* Lincoln: University of Nebraska Press, 2004.

Welsome, Eileen. *The Plutonium Files: America's Secret Medical Experiments in the Cold War.* New York: Delta, 1999.

Whalen, Carmen Teresa. "Colonialism, Citizenship, and the Making of the Puerto Rican Diaspora." In *The Puerto Rican Diaspora: Historical Perspectives,* edited by Carmen Teresa Whalen and Víctor Vázquez-Hernández, 1–42. Philadelphia: Temple University Press, 2005.

Winks, Robin W. "The American Struggle with 'Imperialism': How Words Frighten." In *The American Identity: Fusion and Fragmentation,* edited by Rob Kroes, 143–77. Amsterdam: Amerika Instituut, Universiteit van Amsterdam, 1980.

Wittner, Lawrence S. *Rebels against War: The American Peace Movement, 1941–1960.* New York: Columbia University Press, 1969.

Wolfe, Patrick. "Settler Colonialism and the Elimination of the Native." *Journal of Genocide Research* 8, no. 4 (2006): 387–409. https://doi.org/10.1080/14623520 601056240.

Yellow Robe, Chauncey. "The Menace of the Wild West Show." *Quarterly Journal of the Society of American Indians* 2, no. 3 (1914): 224–25.

———. "My Boyhood Days." *American Indian Magazine* 4, no. 1 (January–March 1916): 50–53.

Index

Note: Page numbers in *italics* indicate illustrative matter.

kristagraha, 34–35
Kunstler, William, 183

Lakota people, 18–20, 22–24, 27–29
Latin America, 64, 66, 162
Lebrón, Lolita (Dolores), 147–48, 158,
  161, 165, 174, 184, 186–87. *See also*
  "The Five"
letter writing, 186
Levy, Herbert, 132–33
Liberal Party of Puerto Rico,
  68–69
Little Big Horn, Battle of, 19–20, 22
Little Big Horn River, 19–20
"Little Smith Act." *See* Insular Law
  No. 53 (Gag Law)
López Vázquez, Eduardo, 109, 126
Lynn, Conrad: Albizu Campos release,
  160, 168, *169*; ALPRI membership,
  152; Reynolds and, 113, 123–24, 127,
  131–33, 158; United Nations lobbying,
  156

"Manifesto to the Puerto Rican People"
  (Muñoz Marín), 88–89
Marcantonio, Vito, 55–56, 61, 190,
  210n21
marriage, 81. *See also* gender and
  politics
masculinity, 46, 217n73. *See also* gender
  and politics
Matos Paoli, Francisco, 199, *199, 200*
Mejías Flores, José, 109, 127
Meneses de Albizu Campos, Laura, 43,
  106, 108, 162, 164, *171*, 178, 188–89,
  198
Methodism, 6, 17, 21, 24, 25, 30, 34. *See
  also* Christianity
methodology in solidarity activism,
  79–82, 104–5
Mielke, Thelma: Albizu Campos and,
  50, 161; ALPRI membership, 56–57,
  121; APRI membership, 152; CJPR
  and, 162–63; as Nationalist Party's
  UN observer, 65, 154, 155, 188,

236n23; personal life of, 81; protest at
  Casa Blanca, *168*; reputation of, 163;
  RRDC leadership, 122
migration, 37, 39, 178, 201
military draft, 31, 42, 46, 127, 129, 151
Miller, Ruth, 152, 161, 163, 168–69, *170*
MIRA (Movimiento Independentista
  Revolucionario Armado), 177
Modak, Ramkrishna Shahu, 63
Moreno, Yolanda, 57, 152, *169*
Movimiento Independentista Revolu-
  cionario Armado (MIRA), 177
Movimiento Pro-Independencia (MPI),
  175, 178, 182, 189
Moya Vélez, Antonio, 109
MPI (Movimiento Pro-Independencia),
  175, 178, 182, 189
Muñoz Marín, Luis: Albizu Campos and,
  96, 147–48, 160, 161, 168–70; attack
  on, at La Fortaleza, 116; background,
  68; Commonwealth of Puerto Rico,
  inauguration of, 5; Concepción de
  Gracia and, 72; critiques of, 84,
  88–90; governor election, 94–95; on
  independence, 87; Insular Law No. 53
  and, 101; "Manifesto to the Puerto
  Rican People" (author), 88–89;
  "People's Catechism," 69; Public Law
  600, 114; Reynolds and, 70–71, 77–78,
  131–32, 221n3; shift away from
  independence stance of, 70–71, 78,
  88–89, 110; Tydings Bill testimony,
  63, 69–70; Tydings-Piñero Bill, 71,
  72; University of Puerto Rico
  influence, 97–99; on voter registration, 119
Muñoz Rivera, Luis, 68, 77–78
Muste, A. J., 30, 31, 34–35, 122, 162–66,
  214n16

NAACP (National Association for the
  Advancement of Colored People), 35,
  54
National Guard of Puerto Rico, 44, 86,
  99–101, 116–18, *120*

University Crusade, 101, 102
University of Puerto Rico at Río Piedras (UPR): about, 96–97; American Civil Liberties Union and, 93, 102–4; closing of, 99; influence of Muñoz Marín on, 97–99; Partido Popular Democrático (Popular Democratic Party; PDD) at, 96–99; police attack at, 102; raising of Puerto Rican flag at, 99, *100*; Reynolds investigation, 93–95, 104–5, 226n46; student strike at, 99, 101, 102; student suppression at, 96–101; University Crusade, 101, 102
US Alien Registration Act of 1940 (Smith Act), 101, 132, 165–66
US Ambassador to the United Nations, 159
US Committee to Free the Five Puerto Rican Nationalists (USCFF), 174–75, 184–86
US Congress, 59, 161–63, 191–92
US Congress joint resolution (1979), 191–92
US democracy, 21–22, 40–42, 87, 115, 150. *See also* democracy
US invasion of Puerto Rico (1898), 5, 37, 77, 86, 156–57
US Military, 96; Navy, 196–97
US Senate Committee on Territories and Insular Affairs, 59
US State Department, 151–52
US Supreme Court, 3, 132–133, 166
Utuado, Puerto Rico, 116

Vázquez, Blanca, 197
Vieques, Puerto Rico, 96, 196–97
Vieques Support Network (VSN), 196–97

violence. *See* political violence; state violence
Viscal Garriga, Olga, 134–43
voter registration, 115, 119, 157
voting in Puerto Rico, 141–42, 157, 191, 192

wage inequities, 26–27
Waller, Annie, 35
Waller, Odell, 35
Walsh, Richard J., 54, 102, 121
"Why Puerto Rico Can Not Be Removed from Classification as a Non-Self-Governing Territory by the United States" (Reynolds), 156–57
Wiley, Jean, 50, 57, 152
Winship, Blanton, 86, 102
women in Nationalist Party, 134–43. *See also* gender and politics; *names of specific women; Nationalist Party of* Puerto Rico
women political prisoners, 114, 134, 137–41. *See also* embodied solidarity; prison conditions
women's leadership and political activism, 47, 56–59, 61, 65–66, 81, 121–22, 136–37, 162–66, 197–98. *See also* gender and politics; *names of specific women;* women in Nationalist Party
Workers Defense League (WDL), 35
World War II (WWII), 4–5, 34, 41–42, 46, 60, 156

Yellow Robe, Chauncey, 22–24
Young Lords Party (YLP), 175–76, 177–80, 182
youth political movements, 175, 177–79

9 781469 679921